F V

PROFILES OF
SOCIAL RESEARCH

PROFILES OF SOCIAL RESEARCH

The Scientific Study of Human Interactions

Morton Hunt

RUSSELL SAGE FOUNDATION   NEW YORK

The Russell Sage Foundation

The Russell Sage Foundation, one of the oldest of America's general purpose foundations, was established in 1907 by Mrs. Margaret Olivia Sage for "the improvement of social and living conditions in the United States." The Foundation seeks to fulfill this mandate by fostering the development and dissemination of knowledge about the political, social, and economic problems of America. It conducts research in the social sciences and public policy, and publishes books and pamphlets that derive from this research.

The Board of Trustees is responsible for oversight and the general policies of the Foundation, while administrative direction of the program and staff is vested in the President, assisted by the officers and staff. The President bears final responsibility for the decision to publish a manuscript as a Russell Sage Foundation book. In reaching a judgment on the competence, accuracy, and objectivity of each study, the President is advised by the staff and selected expert readers. The conclusions and interpretations in Russell Sage Foundation publications are those of the authors and not of the Foundation, its Trustees, or its staff. Publication by the Foundation, therefore, does not imply endorsement of the contents of the study.

Library of Congress Cataloging-in-Publication Data

Hunt, Morton M., 1920–
    Profiles of social research.

    Bibliography: p.
    Includes index.
    1. Social sciences—Research.   2. Social sciences—
Research—United States—Case studies. I. Title.
H62.H747   1985   300'.72   85-60759
ISBN 0-87154-393-1
ISBN 0-87154-394-X (pbk.)

The figures reproduced on pages 171 and 177 of chapter 4 appeared first in "Many Hands Make Light the Work" by Bibb Latané, Kipling Williams, and Stephen Harkins, in *Journal of Personality and Social Psychology*, 1979, v. 37, no. 6, copyright 1979 by the American Psychological Association, and are reprinted by permission of the publisher and authors.

10 9 8 7 6 5 4 3 2 1

to ROBERT K. MERTON

the giant from whose shoulders
so many view society

About the Author

Morton Hunt writes about the social and behavioral sciences. He attended Temple University and the University of Pennsylvania, worked briefly on the staffs of two magazines, and since 1949 has been a free-lance writer. He has written sixteen books and some 400 articles for the *New Yorker*, the *New York Times Magazine*, and other periodicals, and has won a number of prestigious science-writing awards.

Also by Morton Hunt

The Natural History of Love
Her Infinite Variety: The American Woman as Lover, Mate and Rival
Mental Hospital
The Talking Cure (*with Rena Corman and Louis R. Ormont*)
The World of the Formerly Married
The Affair: A Portrait of Extra-Marital Love in Contemporary America
The Mugging
Sexual Behavior in the 1970s
Prime Time: A Guide to the Pleasures and Opportunities of the New Middle
     Age (*with Bernice Hunt*)
The Divorce Experience (*with Bernice Hunt*)
The Universe Within: A New Science Explores the Human Mind

FOREWORD

In 1982 the Russell Sage Foundation, one of America's oldest general purpose foundations, celebrated its seventy-fifth anniversary. To commemorate this long commitment to the support and dissemination of social science research, we departed from our customary publishing procedures to commission several special volumes. These anniversary volumes were to be more personal and reflective than many of the books that emerge from Foundation-supported research, less constrained by the formal and rhetorical requirements of the scholarly monograph. As befits an anniversary celebration, the volumes would address issues that have been of traditional concern to the Foundation.

For decades, the Russell Sage Foundation has devoted a considerable share of its resources to strengthening the social sciences. In light of this concern with the process—and progress—of social scientific inquiry, we take special pleasure in publishing Morton Hunt's *Profiles of Social Research*, an Anniversary volume that offers lively accounts of noteworthy episodes in social research and cogent exposition of the social research enterprise itself.

Morton Hunt's book represents more than an anniversary for Russell Sage; it is also an adventure of sorts. This is the first time we have published a real introduction to social research, a lucid and informative portrait of an area of scientific investigation that has come increasingly to affect our lives. Few authors could be as qualified to prepare such an introduction as Morton Hunt, whose articles and books about the social and behavioral sciences have consistently achieved the balance of readability and accuracy we sought. In *Profiles of Social Research*, Hunt presents his case histories with characteristic skill, weaving narrative, context, and interpretation into a unique and engaging whole.

Profiles of Social Research explores methodologies as diverse as large surveys and small laboratory experiments, and research topics as intriguing as the impacts of segregation and the psychology of teamwork. A comprehensive and literate guide to its subject, this volume offers students and general readers an enhanced understanding of the scope and significance of those complex, often obscure endeavors we know as social research.

MARSHALL ROBINSON
President
Russell Sage Foundation

PREFACE

Although nearly all reasonably well-educated Americans know something about Spacelab, genetic engineering, artificial intelligence, and many other areas of current scientific investigation, very few have any idea what social research is. During these past three years, when I have mentioned to acquaintances and friends that I was writing a book about the subject, most of them have said, "Social research? What is it?" Yet social research influences our thinking and our daily lives in so many important ways that we owe it to ourselves to know something about it.

For one thing, federal, state, and city legislators and administrators frequently use the findings of social research to design and to implement the social programs that are reshaping our society. Similarly, the managers of the nation's businesses rely on social research when making many decisions that affect us as consumers. Thus, it is in our own interest to understand the uses—and the limitations—of social research; we have an obligation to hold and to express informed views about the decisions and policies that importantly influence our lives.

Most of us have heard of the mechanisms by which these data are generated without realizing that they are forms of social research or knowing enough about them to have valid opinions. These are only a few of the social-research mechanisms and products that are part of everyday life:

—Economic indicators such as GNP (gross national product), the unemployment rate, and the cost-of-living index are used by government agencies in operating major social programs, including social security and unemployment compensation.

—Social indicators such as the mortality rate and marriage and divorce rates enable Congress, the agencies, and business to anticipate the future needs of the society. The Consumer Confidence Index is a datum of primary importance for forecasting purchasing and prices.

—Survey research and marketing research are the primary sources of up-to-date information needed by government and business about everything from the state of the nation's health and family income to the public's preferences in consumer products and its attitudes on political issues.

—Standardized testing plays a major role in education, employment, and mental health; "normed" tests enable professionals to make optimal placements of students, employees, and patients. Testing is also a research tool that enables social researchers to trace human development over the life span.

Another reason that thoughtful people owe it to themselves to understand social research is that it offers the inquiring mind far better explanations than conventional wisdom can of a variety of matters of universal interest and importance: why we love or hate, cooperate or compete, submit or dominate, conform or rebel, strive or drift, give succor or do harm. In sum, how and why we interact as we do in every kind of social group from the couple to the nation—and why some of those groups endure and others disintegrate.

In the past, these were questions about which even the wisest men could offer only conjectures, but with the advent of social research it became possible to gather data about human behavior, look for patterns in them, construct hypotheses to account for those patterns, and then test these explanations by further observation: in other words, to study society by scientific methods, thereby understanding it better and becoming better able to deal intelligently with social problems.

It is not only social scientists who participate in this intellectual adventure; all of us do so to the degree that we think in terms of the findings and concepts of social research. As pervasive and influential as are the data of social research, its most significant impact on us may be the enlarging and refining of our thoughts about social matters. How could we think about contemporary society if we did not have in our mental armamentarium such concepts as *alienation, cost-benefit ratio, norm, peer group, power structure, quality of life, reference group, role conflict, socialization, status,* and *subculture,* to name but a few?

□

This book attempts to picture, for those with no special knowledge of the social sciences, something of what social research is; to let them see it being done; and to suggest some of the values it may have for their lives—but not without also showing, as per Cromwell's famous instruction to the portraitist John Lely, its "roughnesses, pimples, warts, and everything."

The portrait of social research herein consists of an introduction (an overview of its principal forms), followed by five case histories or eyewitness accounts of major social research projects. To do justice to the subject, I would have had to write not five but perhaps a score of such accounts, each dealing with a different kind of social research. But I bore in mind that most famous of comments about authorial long-windedness, the Duke of Gloucester's oafish response when Gibbon presented him with the third volume of *The Decline and Fall of the Roman Empire:* "What! Another damned, thick, square book! Always scribble, scribble, scribble! eh, Mr. Gibbon?" I have avoided producing a damned, thick, square book; I hope it is more than mere scribbling.

CONTENTS

PART II: FIVE CASE HISTORIES OF SOCIAL RESEARCH

*Chapter 2: The Dilemma in the Classroom. A
cross-sectional survey measures the effects of segregated
schooling.*

James Coleman asked to do a major survey of educational
   segregation; considers the problems of doing policy
   research; decides to proceed.

*Chapter 6: Twenty Thousand Volunteers. A massive
real-world experiment tests a bold proposal to combat
poverty by means of a guaranteed annual income.*

*I have sedulously endeavored not to laugh
at human actions, not to lament them,
nor to detest them,
but to understand them.*
—Spinoza, Tractatus Politicus, i, 4

PART I
Overview

THE WORLD OF SOCIAL RESEARCH

Something New Under the Sun

In a waiting room, two undergraduate men are filling out questionnaires. One of the two is a "stooge," playing a part in an experiment; the other is an innocent. In the next room, separated from them by a collapsible cloth curtain-wall, they hear the young woman who gave them the questionnaires opening and closing drawers, then climbing up on a chair apparently to get something. Suddenly there is a crash and a scream as the chair falls over; then the woman moans and cries. (Actually, the sounds are produced by a high-fidelity tape recorder.) The innocent, about to rush to her aid, looks at the other student, who glances up quizzically, shrugs, and returns to his work. The first student hesitates and then turns back to the questionnaire, but he seems deeply troubled by his failure to help the woman in the next room.[1]

Every day for over a week, 1,800 men and women in cities, towns, and rural areas from Maine to Hawaii call at homes of every kind from sharecroppers' shanties to beachfront mansions—some 66,000 in all—and politely but unabashedly ask a number of questions usually considered no business of strangers. They want to know such things as who in the home is employed, what they do, how much they earn, and what kinds of benefits they receive from government programs. But nearly everyone answers their questions freely and even gladly, for the callers are interviewers from the Bureau of the Census who are collecting data for *Current Population Survey*, the government's chief source of up-to-date figures on employment, unemployment, and the financial conditions of households throughout the nation.[2]

The mental hospital staff considers Mr. X schizophrenic, though he has been lucid and has made no trouble since being admitted. A well-dressed and well-spoken man of middle age, he came in complaining of hearing voices. "They're unclear," he told the admitting psychiatrist, "but as far as I can tell, they were saying 'empty,' 'hollow,' and 'thud.' " He says nothing more about the voices after admission, but the doctors believe him still to be mentally ill and the nursing staff every day notes one consistent peculiar activity in his chart: "Patient engages in writing behavior." Several of his fellow patients see him differently. As one of them says to Mr. X, "You're not crazy. You're a journalist or a professor. You're checking up on the hospital." The patients are right and the staff is wrong. Mr. X, a psychologist, is one of eight sane people working on a research project; they have had themselves admitted to mental hospitals in order to observe the social relationships of staff and patients as participants in the milieu, not as visitors or known observers.[3]

ONE OF THE MOST significant ways in which we human beings differ from other creatures is that we study our own social behavior scientifically, an activity that we did not begin until a century ago. And only within the past two generations have social scientists developed most of the methods that enable them to empirically investigate matters that formerly they could only make educated guesses about. Among these techniques: subjecting unknowing volunteers to ambiguous social situations (such as hearing the cries of a person in distress) in order to discover what conditions foster various kinds of response; gathering data from a scientific sample of the nation's people (as in the Census Bureau's monthly *Current Population Survey*) in order to swiftly and reliably ascertain certain conditions throughout the nation; and acting as "participant observers" in special social situations (such as a mental hospital ward) in order to gain an insider's view of the prevailing social relationships and their effects.

Philosophers, of course, had long sought to understand the nature of society and social phenomena but, having no tradition of empirical research, relied on deductive reasoning based on common knowledge, ancient beliefs, and fantasies about the past. Their social theories, in consequence, though sometimes insightful, were largely plausible myths, like prescientific explanations of illness or the weather and other natural events. The "social contract" theory, for instance, as put forth by the seventeenth-century philosopher Thomas Hobbes, held that society exists because individuals are willing to give up certain rights in return for the protection of an absolute sovereign; while this may have seemed to fit the realities of Hobbes's time, it was as fanciful and inaccurate as the medical theory of his time that sickness is due to an imbalance among the four "humors"—blood, black bile, yellow bile, and phlegm.

By the late nineteenth century, the social sciences emerged from social philosophy and other disciplines in something like their present form—in essence, based on empirical data that are systematically scrutinized for regularities, which are then tentatively explained by hypotheses that must be either verified or falsified by further observation and by experiment. Thus, the foundation of the social sciences— sociology, anthropology, economics, political science, and social psychology*—is social research.

Even though these disciplines are relatively young and most of their research techniques younger still, it is curious that so few people have any idea what is meant by social research. No image of the social researcher at work has entered the common fund of visual and conceptual clichés. "Research chemist" calls up a vision of a white-coated scientist, in front of a battery of flasks and retorts, adding drops of some mysterious reagent to a fuming mixture. "Paleontologist" suggests a dusty, sunburned scholar delicately brushing earth away from some half-buried fossil jawbone. Such clichés, though simplistic, do illustrate activities characteristic of each discipline. But there is no comparable image of the typical social researcher at work.

Yet how could there be? The social sciences are, for the most part, differing disciplines; each, moreover, assumes varied guises in academia, in industry, and in government; and, most important, they use a wide variety of dissimilar research methods.

But while there is no archetype of social research, the components

---

* Some authorities include geography, mathematical statistics, and history, but this book considers only the core social-science disciplines.

of the category are as significantly related, despite their diversity, as the various vanished species of the genus *homo* are to each other and to modern humankind. Here, then, is a sampling of specimens of the varied species within the genus *social research* that may offer a first impressionistic answer to the question, "What is it?"

We start by looking at a number of forms of social research that formerly dominated the field; today, while still used—and still the methods of choice for the investigation of certain subjects—they account for only a small part of total social research effort. Later in the chapter, and in the five major case studies making up chapters 2 through 6, we will examine the species of social inquiry that are the mainstays of the field today.

Direct Observation

OVERT PARTICIPANT OBSERVATION

On a winter afternoon in 1962, in the Downtown Cafe, a dingy bar in a slum area of Washington, D.C., a number of poorly dressed black men were drinking beer, talking, and joking. Some stared at and others ignored a man whose white, Jewish, scholarly features were strikingly out of place there but who was sitting and chatting amiably with a black companion. Another man, suspicious, came over and bluntly asked the latter who the white man was. "This here's Ellix," the black man said. "We had a long talk the other day. He's my friend and he's okay, man, he's okay. At first I thought he was a cop, but he's no cop. He's okay."

Elliot Liebow—nicknamed "Ellix" by the men who hung out at the Downtown Cafe and the nearby New Deal Carry-Out shop—was an anthropologist working for the Child Rearing Study, a project of the Health and Welfare Council of the National Capital. For nearly three years, council researchers had conducted family interviews to gather data on child-rearing in the black inner city, but now the project director, Dr. Hylan Lewis, wanted "field material" about low-income urban males and their part in family life and child-rearing. "Go out there and make like an anthropologist," he told Liebow. But, Liebow asked, what was he to look for? "Everything is grist for our mill," said Lewis. "The scientific method is doing one's darndest with his brains, no holds barred."

Liebow thereupon spent more than a year "hanging around," much of every day and many evenings, with the men of what he came to call "Tally's Corner." Tally was the closest black friend he made; the corner was the vicinity of the Carry-Out shop—the center of communal life for the men who lived in the area. Liebow, who had grown up in a predominantly black neighborhood, knew enough to play it straight: He told Tally and anyone else who asked that he was working on a study of family life in the city, he made no attempt to conceal his education, and, though he adopted some local words and expressions, he never tried to sound like the men of Tally's Corner.

Beginning with a chance conversation with Tally, Liebow slowly became known to these men and accepted by them as part of the local scene. He ate, drank, talked, and joked with them; like them, played the pinball machines and the numbers; visited their apartments and lounged around with them; went to a huge dance with them but, in order not to arouse any hostility, avoided any involvement with black women; and watched them shoot crap and play cards but stayed out of the games because, as he explained, in his job he couldn't take the chance of getting into a fight.

The resulting study, published under the title *Tally's Corner*, had little to say about child-rearing but much about the street-corner society of poor black men. Or, at least, one such society; Liebow refrained from claiming he had discovered principles that applied elsewhere, though his vivid and richly detailed account of life on Tally's Corner, like every penetrating case history, strongly suggests the operation of social principles that one can reasonably suppose operate in similar groups elsewhere.

Liebow's chief finding concerned the importance of street-corner society to poverty-level urban black men. "Losers" in the social struggle and all but rootless, they had adapted to their failure and survived it by forming a network of pseudo-friendships—largely superficial and based on false accounts of themselves—that gave them a sense of belonging while permitting them to hide their failures from each other. Thus, life at Tally's Corner was not chaotic and alienated, as slum society had been commonly supposed to be, but highly organized around a small pseudo-intimate network—in social-science terms, a "primary group"—of a special nature.[4]

Tally's Corner is a celebrated example of the form of social research known as field work or field studies, in particular that kind based on "participant observation" by a known observer—the gathering of data by a researcher who takes part in the daily life of the people being studied and whose identity and goals the observed are aware of.

In the past, most accounts of remote cultures were written by conquistadores, explorers, missionaries, and others who remained aloof from the "natives." Social scientists, however, realized that they needed to get closer to their material and to minimize the distorting influence of their own upbringing on their perceptions. Seventy years ago, the Polish-British anthropologist Bronislaw Malinowski became the first to describe the use of participant observation toward this end when, in order to study the Trobriand Islanders, a primitive Melanesian people, he lived among them for several years and ate with them, watched them at work and play, gossiped with them and interviewed them about their sexual lives (he spoke three Melanesian languages plus pidgin), attended their festivals, and adopted many of their customs. "I am completely under the spell of the tropics," he wrote in a private diary, "as well as under the spell of this life and my work."[5]

As a result, he saw the Trobrianders so clearly and understood them so well despite the vast cultural distance between him and them that his method became the standard for anthropological investigations of tribes and peoples outside Western civilization. Following Malinowski's lead, innumerable anthropologists have used this ethnographic approach and struggled with the difficult sounds and linguistic intricacies of tongues totally unlike those of the Indo-European family, bravely drunk bizarre liquids and swallowed repellent foods, and endured noisy straw pallets, stinging insects, boredom, loneliness, the lack of plumbing, and a variety of physical ills, all in order to experience alien cultures from within.

At about the time Malinowski began his stay among the Melanesians, Robert E. Park and other members of the "Chicago school" of sociology began using similar methods in America to explore the exotic societies of the ghetto, hotel life, the hobo world, "taxi dance" halls, and the "gold coast."[6] Since then, the ethnographic method has been used many hundreds of times by sociologists and others to study such other subcultures in our society as those of the police, automobile salesmen, immigrants, and faith healers.

Still others have used participant observation to study the ways of groups close to their own experience (the sociologist Howard S. Becker, for instance, who had been a professional pianist, later wrote about the sociology of the world of jazz musicians) and the patterns of life in particular American communities. The classic of the latter genre is Robert and Helen Lynd's *Middletown*, a study of a typical midwestern town (Muncie, Indiana) in 1924, which involved participant observation along with such other methods as surveys and interviews.

What makes these studies social research rather than mere reportage is the special two-part cognitive process the researchers engage in.

One part consists of their consciously attempting to identify with those they are observing and to empathize with their experiences, ideas, and values in order to share their social reality. Ethnographers, it has been said, use themselves as their research instrument; they seek to understand the people they are studying by trying to feel as they do. Max Weber, a major figure in early sociology, considered this kind of understanding-through-empathy (or *Verstehen*, as he called it) essential to a scientific explanation of behavior, and many of today's social scientists, especially those of a phenomenological bent, agree. They maintain that the reality of social behavior consists not of events, as in the natural sciences, but of the subjective *meanings* those events have for a people. Thus, in many societies an eligible bachelor who bargains hard for dowry with his fiancée's father is admired for doing so, while in most of present-day America the same behavior would be considered contemptible. In some lands the savaging or even murder of an unfaithful wife is seen as an act of honor; in our country such acts are viewed as deranged or sociopathic.

In the other part of the cognitive process (which may take place concurrently with the first, or at quiet times away from the observed scene), researchers stand apart and consider their observations in the light of existing data from comparable studies and of accepted social-science concepts and theories. While participating in the activities of a deeply religious group, they may empathize with its members' belief that adherence to the group's strict rules about diet, dress, and ritual signifies pious obedience to God's wishes, but shifting to the scientific framework, researchers may see the raison d'être of those rules as binding the people together and preserving their identity as a group.

Such analysis, relating the new observations to existing data and theory, seeks to explain them in causal terms, or at least to cautiously state that given certain conditions it is likely that such-and-such behavior will ensue (which is really much the same thing). As Weber himself said, "[Verstehen] is the interpretive understanding of social action *in order thereby to arrive at a causal explanation of its course* and effects."[7]

Participant observation has its limitations and hazards. Many researchers who have tried it have testified to how hard it is not to get drawn in too far and "go native." James Mannon, a young sociologist who recently spent a year and a half accompanying ambulance emergency teams working out of a city hospital, was at first made physically ill by the blood, shattered bodies, agonies, and deaths that he witnessed; gradually, however, he learned to view them in the same way the team members did—depersonalizing the patients and regarding them as "cases" or "objects" to be dealt with in a trained, dispassionate, technical fashion. Having achieved this stance, he was dismayed to find himself, like the team members, hoping for a "big run"—a particularly serious emergency—and feared that he was becoming "a sociological ghoul, taking some sort of professional delight in someone else's medical horror."[8]

An even more serious problem in any research project based on participant observation concerns the generalizability of its findings. How likely is it that the principles deduced from observing one ambulance team or one street-corner society apply to any other? They may, if the other is very much like the observed one, yet no two human groups are subject to an identical set of influences.

Social psychologist Donald Campbell, a noted methodologist, says that this difficulty can be overcome through cross-cultural comparison (which, unfortunately, places a great extra burden on the researcher). This use of cross-cultural comparison relies on what Campbell calls "the heterogeneity of irrelevancies"; that is, in a set of similar instances from different cultures, irrelevant factors will differ from one to another, with the result that those factors that do co-occur in all cases are likely to do so for some real reason—some causal, functional, or structural relationship to each other.[9]

An example given by Robert LeVine, professor of human development at Harvard: Jews in medieval Europe, Hindus in East Africa, Lebanese in West Africa, and Chinese in Southeast Asia were or are all considered cunning and greedy by the indigenous peoples. Why? Not because of their skin color, religion, language or national origin, since these vary among the four cases. But, says LeVine, what all four do have in common is that they are "alien trading communities of urban sophistication in largely rural societies"; these omnipresent features probably account for the formation of the similar stereotypes.[10]

Possibly the most serious problem in participant observation is the fact that known observers are inevitably a contaminant of what they are studying. When people are being observed and know they are, they are quite likely to act somewhat differently from the way they would if they were not being observed or were but didn't know it. They may censor their words and actions; they may be self-conscious; they may try to make themselves look better—or worse—than they are.

The explorer Vilhjalmur Stefansson, who spent many years studying the Eskimos early in the century, learned only after several years of work that on many topics his hosts had politely told him not the truth but what they supposed he would like to hear.[11] The young Margaret Mead, when she was a novice anthropologist, got most of her information about Samoan premarital sex practices from teen-age girls, whose account of a paradiselike freedom from inhibition and guilt she took at face value. But other later studies told another story: Educated Samoans who read Mead's work told one researcher that Mead's informants must have told her lies to tease her, and anthropologist Derek Freeman, in a recent attack on Mead's Samoan work, says that "deliberately duping someone" was a pastime the Samoans enjoyed because it gave them "respite from the severities of their authoritarian society."[12]*

One way to avoid being misled is known as "triangulation": The researcher uses more than one observer and more than one method

---

* In her subsequent ethnographic studies, Mead was better equipped and more sophisticated; the possible flaws in the Samoan work do not constitute an impeachment of her career.

(observation plus, say, the use of questionnaires, plus official statistics). If these varied approaches confirm each other, one can have a reasonable degree of confidence in the results. But of course it greatly increases the cost and the labor of the project.

COVERT PARTICIPANT OBSERVATION

Researchers therefore sometimes resort to a related method that is both simpler and yet more difficult: covert participant observation, in which investigators infiltrate a group by concealing their true identity and "passing" as bona fide members. Of course, this is often impossible; Liebow could not have used it at Tally's Corner. But in other cases, it is both possible and the only practicable way to observe behavior that the members of a group would not knowingly display to an outsider. There is, however, intense controversy about the propriety of covert participant observation since it involves deliberate deception of those being observed; ethics committees of the several disciplines look askance at it and many institutional review boards will not okay proposals involving it.

On the evening of November 23, 1954, nine people seated in a circle in the living room of a midwestern city were about to hold a séance in which they hoped to receive important information from the "Guardians" on the planet "Clarion." Mrs. Marian Keech (not her real name), the group's leader, a slight, fiftyish woman, had begun receiving messages from Clarion nearly a year earlier during trances in which she did automatic writing, and three months prior to the meeting she had been told that on December 21 a great flood would cover the northern hemisphere. This evening's little group—there were also a number of other believers who had been unable to attend—was expecting orders as to how to prepare for the flood and information about how they would be saved.

When the tenth and final member, a young businessman, arrived, Mrs. Keech took him aside and told him that the group was expecting orders; then she added, "We want you to lead us tonight." He seemed disconcerted, and protested that he could not officiate because he was not "ready." Mrs. Keech disagreed; she firmly said that he *was* ready and added, "We all have to face our great responsibilities and take them."

Reluctantly, he yielded, but in the living room, with all eyes on him, he stalled, saying, "Let us meditate" and bending his head. He waited, hoping something would happen, and neither said nor did anything more as twenty minutes passed in agonizing silence. The reason for the officiant's inaction was that he was neither a businessman nor a believer but a social psychologist, Henry W. Riecken, one of a team of three researchers from the University of Minnesota (Leon Festinger, the senior member, and Stanley Schachter were the others) who, with five student assistants, were covertly studying Mrs. Keech's millennial group to see how its members would react when the promised flood failed to materialize.

(According to Festinger's celebrated theory of cognitive dissonance, believers would be unable to endure the conflict between their belief and its failure to come true. Some might resolve the conflict by giving up their belief, but others, who had been deeply committed—a few had even quit their jobs—might find ways to "explain" the failure and end up believing even more deeply than before.)

That night, Riecken was extricated from his predicament by Bertha Blatsky (another pseudonym), a woman in her 40s who, seated on the couch with her head thrown back, began to pant, moan, and gasp, "I got the words, I got the words," followed by, "This is Sananda, Sananda speaks." (Sananda was the key spokesman of the Guardians.) Mrs. Keech eagerly turned from the supposed businessman who had failed her to Bertha, and throughout the evening and night she and the others hung on her words. Disappointingly, however, these consisted of greetings and spiritual messages for each member but no specific orders.

At later meetings orders did arrive (via Mrs. Keech) telling members to stand by at a precise time for spaceships that would come to convey them to safety. When the spaceships failed to appear at several such rendezvous and when the flood did not occur, the members of the cult behaved as predicted by Festinger's theory. Mrs. Keech received word that, thanks to the light and the goodness created by the group of believers, God had decided to call off the cataclysm and spare the world. Some of the cult members reacted with disillusionment and broke away, but those who had been most deeply committed emerged more strongly convinced than ever.

The field-work phase of the project lasted seven weeks; during that period, researchers visited groups of cult members or took part in their meetings twenty-nine times in one city and thirty-one times in another, making notes on the site (in the bathroom or while stepping outside for a breath of fresh air) or dictating details to a tape machine as soon as they got away. They were also able, as ostensible believers, to obtain copies of many of Mrs. Keech's most important messages and tapes of semi-public meetings.

Festinger, Riecken, and Schachter, in their written account of the research, candidly admitted that "the procedures used in conducting this study departed from the orthodoxy of social science in a number of respects." But after naming their lapses from grace, they concluded, "We were able, however, to collect enough information to tell a coherent story and, fortunately, the effects of disconfirmation [of the prophecy] were striking enough to provide for firm conclusions." Their report, *When Prophecy Fails*, was hailed in reviews in both the *American Journal of Sociology* and the *American Sociological Review* as difficult research well done; it remains to this time a classic example of covert participant observation.[13] It also was the center of controversy for some time, being sharply criticized by those who regarded its methodology as an unethical invasion of privacy.

Like Festinger and his colleagues, a number of other researchers have used covert methods when they had good reason to think that, if their purposes were known, they would be either refused access to the group or accepted but "sold a bill of goods."

One researcher, who wanted to study the behavior of corporation managers, learned that others who had openly tried to observe and investigate the subject had been steered and manipulated by managers into seeing only what they wanted seen. He therefore said that he was interested in studying "personnel problems," and with this disguise was more or less freely able to witness authentic and unedited managerial behavior.[14]

The vignette about Mr. X at the beginning of this chapter is based on the published account of a noteworthy study of mental hospitals that employed covert observation. David L. Rosenhan, a psychologist and professor of law at Stanford University, and seven research assistants got themselves admitted to twelve mental hospitals on the east and west coasts by presenting themselves to the admissions offices and claiming that they heard voices. As patients, they were able to observe staff interactions with patients in a way they could not have, had their identity been known. The study yielded a disturbing finding: Even though the pseudo-patients ceased all abnormal behavior immediately upon being admitted, the diagnosis of schizophrenia caused staff members, for all their diagnostic expertise, to continue to see their behavior as schizophrenic and to interact with them accordingly—most notably, avoiding them as much as possible.[15]

Others have used covert methods where the group they wanted to study imposed rules of secrecy on its members. One research team posed as alcoholics in order to gain admittance to an Alcoholics Anonymous group, since the organization's requirement that nothing said at its meetings be disclosed to outsiders would have barred them from attending and kept them from exploring how AA functioned and why it was unable to attract a larger number of alcoholics than it did.[16]

Covert participant observation, though it enables researchers to investigate some groups that would otherwise be inaccessible to study, is demanding and tricky. Presenting a false self and keeping it intact is difficult and stressful for most people: At any moment, they may "blow their cover" by some inappropriate remark or slip of the tongue, incorrect use of an "in" word, momentary failure to recognize a joke—or effort to make a joke that turns out to be a giveaway.

Researchers may even simply have the bad luck to be spotted by someone who knows them. Jack Douglas, a sociologist who was doing a participant observation study of a notorious nude beach in California, spoke to two young women there one day without revealing his identity; after chatting with them for some time about their attitude toward the beach, he casually asked, for research purposes, "You're college students, aren't you?" One of them said, "Oh, yes," and added, "We're even sociology students." Then, as they walked away, she turned back and said, "We even took your intro class last quarter."

Douglas was abashed; he realized that he, not they, had been the "research dupe."[17]

Another hazard of covert observation is that the chance of going native is greater than in overt observation, since the more thoroughly one adopts the false role, the harder it is to maintain one's objectivity. According to the popular literature of espionage, double agents sometimes lose track of which side they really believe in; whether or not this is actually true of spies, it does occasionally happen to social researchers. One team that successfully infiltrated a religious cult, for instance, became actual converts and eventually wrote their report from that viewpoint.[18]

Perhaps the most serious of all problems of covert participant observation is the ethical conflict it engenders in researchers. They cannot hide from themselves the fact that they are deceiving others and will, in a sense, "betray" them by revealing their secrets. Some covert researchers have been bothered enough by this conflict to withdraw from their projects. But at least one who was deeply troubled was lucky in his choice of those he had been deceiving. He had joined the Church of Satan in San Francisco, feigning conversion and belief, and for several years had taken part in its secret rituals, but eventually felt so conflicted about his deception that he told the truth to the cult's leader and asked his permission to write a report of what he had learned. The leader not only gave him permission but expressed approval of what had been done to him and his group since, in his view, deception was an appropriately satanic act.[19]

But Lewis A. Coser, Edward Shils, and a number of other social scientists have characterized undercover participant observation as a breach of professional ethics. Sociologist Fred Davis has said even more harshly that those who use covert methods to get people to "give away" truths about themselves "violate . . . the collective conscience of the community" and have about them "a stench of disreputability."[20]

Covert researchers reply that their work should be judged on a cost-benefit basis; that is, not only by means but by ends. Little or no harm is done to the observed, they say, since most researchers, for reasons of both decency and self-interest, carefully conceal the identities of their subjects. If so, they argue, and if valuable knowledge not available in any other way is obtained, the deception of covertness is fully justified.

NONPARTICIPANT OBSERVATION

There is yet another method of observation that avoids all these problems, though at the cost of seeing only what is on the surface: This is known as nonparticipant observation. It is often used to study behavior in public places such as sidewalks, restaurants, and supermarkets, and in semi-public ones such as reception rooms, club premises, and parties in homes. In these and other situations where the researcher's interacting with the people being observed would disrupt their normal patterns of behavior, he or she may choose to be a passive onlooker, much like the ethologist lurking in the bushes to watch the courtship dance of the African crane.

Erving Goffman, a sociologist, used nonparticipant observation to excellent effect to study what he called the "dramaturgy" of social life—such aspects of behavior as the rules and rituals governing our interactions with strangers in public places (for instance, the keeping of "proper" distances under various conditions), and the ways we create the different impressions of the Real Us that we present to particular people. Goffman's most important way of studying such behavior was to be "the unobserved observer," as he called it, a part he was temperamentally well suited for and played superbly.

Unfortunately, having been a private and rather secretive person, Goffman left no descriptions of himself doing his field work. But from internal evidence in his writings it is easy enough to imagine how it must have gone. For although he weaves a tapestry of details in which he cites many studies by others, Goffman frequently describes some pattern of behavior without naming any source; in these instances, it can only be that he himself observed what he portrays. Here, for instance, is a passage in which he discusses one aspect of territoriality in public:

Personal space [is] the space surrounding an individual, anywhere within which an entering other causes the individual to feel encroached upon, leading him to show displeasure and sometimes to withdraw. A contour, not a sphere, is involved, the spatial demands directly in front of the face being larger than at the back. . . . This is nicely illustrated in Eastern seaboard parlor cars designed with a wide, longitudinal aisle and single seats at intervals on either side, the seats arranged to swivel. When there is crowding, travelers maximize their "comfort" by turning their seats to exactly that direction that will allow the eyes, when oriented in the direction of the trunk, to gaze upon the least amount of passenger flesh. [21]

Goffman cites no source for these observations; it seems obvious that he himself unobtrusively studied the positions of passengers, probably while riding trains from Philadelphia (where he lived) to New York or Washington, a run on which parlor cars were always available. And while anyone in those cars *could* have seen the same thing, only someone with Goffman's capacity to notice patterns of microbehavior and brilliantly surmise their social purpose *would* have noticed them and recognized their kinship to other patterns of spacing we use to maintain our sense of self in public places.

Consider this passage, in which Goffman is talking about "withs," his term for parties of two or more people who are perceived by others as being together in contrast to people who in the same situation are seen as "singles":

When one member of a two-person with leaves his partner temporarily to telephone, or to go to the bathroom, or to talk to someone across the room, this may leave the latter looking like a single. But this appearance is correctable; every overture can be answered with a "I'm with someone," and body stance can underscore one's holding oneself in abeyance. Thus, as we might expect, persons alone who do not want to be seen as a single may give silent and spoken evidence of waiting for an imminent arrival. [22]

One can easily visualize Goffman in restaurants and hotel lobbies, or at sociological meetings, unobtrusively observing this behavior and jotting notes to be added to the proper file of minutiae and later used in an insightful essay on human behavior in public places.

Many other researchers have used the same method either by itself or in conjunction with participant observation. A few noteworthy instances:

- Anthropologist Edward T. Hall investigated how people vary the distances they maintain from each other in conversation according to their relationship and the nature of the setting. He did so partly through interviews but largely through looking and listening, wherever he went. [23]

- Sociologist Herbert Gans lived in a Boston slum for many months in order to study it; some of the time he interacted with the local people but mostly he sought "to abstain from participation so as not to affect the phenomenon being studied—or, at least, to affect it no more than is absolutely unavoidable. Much of my participation was of this type, when I was using the area's facilities, attending meetings, or watching the goings-on at area stores and taverns."[24]

- Martin Weinberg and Colin Williams of the Institute for Sex Research at Indiana University studied the unusual interactions of homosexual males in gay baths by paying the admission fee, wandering around the premises towel-clad like the others, and watching the traffic of solicitation and sexual activity without taking part in it. (This passive watching went unnoticed, since it is one of the common patterns of behavior in gay baths.) They found that the patrons maintained emotional and personal detachment from each other despite their orgiastic activity— indeed, did so precisely in order to be able to engage in it. The patrons would hardly have carried out their sexual activities in the customary fashion had they known that two straight male scientists were studying them in order to write an article for a professional journal on "the social organization of impersonal sex."[25]

A number of other social scientists have used unobtrusive observation to study not sexuality but sex differences (gender differences) in behavior, particularly conversation. As long ago as 1922, one enterprising researcher walked up New York's Broadway every evening making note of whatever scraps of conversation he could overhear. The method was primitive, but among the intriguing findings it yielded was that only 8 percent of male-male conversations concerned females while 44 percent of female-female conversations concerned males.[26] In view of the dramatic changes in the female and male roles in the past generation, it would be interesting to have this study replicated today.

Indeed the differences between male and female conversational behavior still do interest researchers. A recent study, unobtrusively tape-recording male-female conversations in coffee shops, drugstores, and other public places on a university campus, and in private homes, found that in cross-sex conversations, at least among undergraduates on that California campus, men were responsible for 96 percent of all interruptions. Even in a laboratory setting, in conversations between opposite-sex strangers men did 75 percent of the interrupting.[27]

Other researchers have eavesdropped on conversations in hotel and concert-hall lobbies, in department stores, and even in dormitory rooms (where one team, willing to endure discomfort in the name of science, hid under beds while students were having little parties). In "conversation analysis," an important area of interest in contemporary ethnomethodology, much of the raw material consists of audiotaped or videotaped conversations whose participants were unaware that they were being recorded.

William H. Whyte has employed quite a different form of nonparticipant observation as the basis of his charming studies of how people in the city use plazas, steps, sidewalks, and other small public urban spaces. He mounts time-lapse cameras in inconspicuous vantage points and photographs the human traffic in such locales at regular intervals. Among his interesting findings:[28]

- People often say that what they want is peace, quiet, and some space to themselves but they don't act that way; when they stop to talk on the street or even in a plaza, they remain in the middle of the pedestrian flow, and when they sit down to relax on plaza steps or ledges, they plunk themselves down in the mainstream, not out of it.

- Similarly, when tables in a plaza are bunched together, compressing people into meeting each other, they love it; they crowd in, strike up conversations, and act sociable. If a plaza offers no opportunity for crowding together, people are much less likely to come to it. Good hostesses know this, but many city planners do not. In Whyte's words, "What attracts people most, it would appear, is other people."

- With few exceptions, sunken plazas are dead spaces; people avoid them because, once there, "People look at you. You don't look at them."

- Like birds sitting on a telephone wire, people space themselves out along ledges or benches in a public place; Whyte's graphs of plaza-sitting derived from his photographs show an astonishing degree of uniformity and precision in such distancing.

Indirect Observation

It is possible to learn a great deal about the social behavior of a group of people without living among them, interviewing them, or even watching them from a distance. A number of research methods rely entirely on physical or written evidence of human social behavior, or on data already gathered by others. These methods are sometimes used to avoid any contamination due to the presence of the observer, but more often because they are the only feasible ones (as in cases where the people being studied are dead, or scattered around the world), or because they are highly economical (as in the reanalysis of existing data gathered by others).

PHYSICAL EVIDENCE

One method of indirect observation relies on the interpretation of physical traces of human social activity.

Every devotee of whodunit literature knows that a good investigator can learn a great deal about the character and social behavior of a murder victim or suspect by studying the shape of his toothpaste tube, the pattern of wear on his living room rug, or the debris in his cuffs. It is not far from such detection to those forms of social research that rely on physical evidence. A well-known monograph on methods of indirect observation by Eugene J. Webb, Donald T. Campbell, Richard D. Schwartz, and Lee Sechrest gives these examples, among others:

The floor tiles around the hatching-chick exhibit at Chicago's Museum of Science and Industry must be replaced every six weeks. Tiles in other parts of the museum need not be replaced for years. The selective erosion of tiles, indexed by the replacement rate, is a measure of the relative popularity of exhibits.

Library withdrawals were used to demonstrate the effect of the introduction of television into a community. Fiction titles dropped, nonfiction titles were unaffected.

[Frederick] Mosteller . . . [studied] the degree to which different sections of the *International Encyclopedia of the Social Sciences** were read. He measured the wear and tear on separate sections by noting dirty edges of pages as markers, and observed the frequency of dirt smudges, finger markings, and underlining.[29]

The examples may seem frivolous; one could, after all, simply count the people looking at the chick exhibit. But the authors were making the point that there are excellent indirect ways to get sound social information—and sometimes they may be the best way. Counting the people looking at all the exhibits in a museum would be time-consuming and costly, and doing an on-the-spot survey might elicit not the truth but answers that people imagine will do them credit (such as saying that they most liked some highly intellectual exhibit, rather than the chick-hatching one). Wear and tear on the tiles and pages that give evidence either of use or of virginal status tell no lies.

In other cases, physical evidence may be the only kind available. Many an ancient or vanished primitive people left no written or pictorial records of their social life, but archaeologists can reconstruct at least some of it from the remains of tools, fragments of containers, the foundations of houses, and the like. Relics of these kinds can reveal whether women or children were segregated or shared quarters with men, whether the people were bellicose or peaceful, how large their communities were, whether they had any moneylike medium of exchange, and much more.

Kitchen middens (accumulations of garbage and trash) can tell a good deal about what kinds of foods a people ate centuries or even millennia ago, indicating whether they were hunters, gatherers, or agriculturalists, whether or not they were cannibals, whether they traded for food from outside their domain, whether they cooked their food and therefore presumably dined together, and so on.

The study of refuse plays a part, albeit a small one, even in social research on contemporary life. Webb et al. tell of one researcher who wanted to know how much hard liquor was being drunk in a town that was officially "dry" and so had no records of liquor sales. He could have conducted a survey, but people might have been evasive. Instead, he chose the unappetizing but solidly factual method of counting the

---

*A minor correction: David L. Sills, editor of IESS, says that Mosteller actually examined its predecessor, the *Encyclopaedia of the Social Sciences*.

empty bottles in the trash from a sample of the town's homes, from which he was able to estimate total liquor use in the community.

Making a specialty of this approach, anthropologist William Rathje of the University of Arizona has for ten years directed studies in what he calls "archaeology of us"—the Garbage Project, funded by the Department of Agriculture, the National Science Foundation, and the Environmental Protection Administration. In Tucson, Milwaukee, Marin County, and Mexico City, students working with Rathje and other social scientists have collected and sorted through large-scale samples of household refuse, primarily gathering data about the waste of food and the discarding of recyclable or environmentally hazardous materials. "If important facts about the nature of life in ancient societies can be gleaned from old garbage," Rathje writes, "then fresh garbage can tell us useful things about modern society." Among the project's findings:[30]

- People apparently eat much less red meat and meat fat than they say they do: Garbage Project workers interviewed people whose garbage they were studying and found important discrepancies between their verbal reports and the physical evidence. This could be an important corrective factor in studies linking fat intake and cancer.
- Higher-income people claim to recycle more of their newspapers than do lower-income people, but garbage analysis shows no difference between them. (One implication might be that more higher-income people feel they ought to recycle the papers, and accordingly deceive themselves or the interviewers.)
- People living near a new liquor store in Los Angeles said they drank no more after it opened than before, but garbage analysis showed a sharp increase in their use of beer, wine, and hard liquor.
- The volume of nonbiodegradable refuse from a colonial household in Massachusetts that was occupied for half a century made eight small piles on a large laboratory table; nonbiodegradable refuse from a typical Tucson household over a five-year period would fill and overflow the room.

As Rathje tartly comments, "Our garbage speaks in an eloquent material vocabulary." Or to borrow from Hamlet: Garbage, though it have no tongue, will speak with most miraculous organ.

WRITTEN MATERIALS

Another form of indirect observation of human social behavior is the use of written materials, especially those portraying social behavior in the past.

The obvious sources are descriptions of social life in bygone times written by those who lived in them. But diaries, plays, novels, poems, sermons, and other writings that depict the society the writers themselves lived in do so from the perspective of those who are a part of it rather than from the perspective of social science. (When social researchers study the society they themselves live in, their training and methodology enable them, more or less, to view it with objectivity and detachment.)

Social researchers therefore treat such sources as raw material which must be analyzed in the light of social science concepts. Just as important, it must be verified or corrected by other kinds of data. A researcher interested in middle-class Victorian marriage may get an idyllic picture of it from sources like Coventry Patmore's long poem *The Angel in the House* but will qualify this with such objective data of the time as the incidences of prostitution and desertion and the lowly status of woman in nineteenth-century law.

Social researchers look for hard data of this sort in the same kinds of written historical materials often used by historians and generally referred to as "archival sources"—government records of tax collections and births and deaths, medical reports, church records of fines for wrongdoing or public confessions of sins, correspondence, contracts, ledgers, business documents, compilations of laws, newspapers and other sources of current events, and the like. Even library records, showing the frequency with which particular books have been used, are a vast statistical base that records an important and illuminating aspect of behavior.

This form of social research is very much like historical research, but its goal is somewhat different. Historians tend to view each event as unique and to describe its circumstances from that viewpoint; social researchers regard each event as an instance of principles that may apply elsewhere. The Goliards were defrocked monks and priests of medieval France and Germany who lived as beggars and itinerant students, and who celebrated drinking and wenching in scandalous parodies of sacred poetry; a historian might examine the conditions that engendered their behavior at that time and place, but a social researcher might use the same material to test a hypothesis about deviance that would explain not only the Goliards but other deserters from strict institutions who cheerfully mocked, rather than savagely attacked, what they had abandoned.

Some examples of social research using archival sources:

- In Marxian doctrine, the economic structure of society shapes everything else in it, including people's ideas and beliefs. Early in this century Weber hypothesized that, quite the other way around, people's ideas and beliefs could shape their society's economy. He took as a case in point the economic effects of the ideas of John Calvin. The key doctrine of that sixteenth-century theologian's system was that, from birth, everyone is predestined either for salvation or damnation, the mark of assured salvation being material success here on earth. Calvin's followers accordingly sought to exhibit the signs of having been chosen for salvation by working hard and reinvesting, rather than spending, their money. Calvinism thus fostered the development of capitalism— as per Weber's hypothesis.[31]
- The distinguished sociologist Robert K. Merton early in his career built upon Weber's insight to study the relationship of Puritanism to scientific discovery. Poring over letters, biographies, diaries, speeches, and other sources documenting the attitudes of seventeenth-century English scientists, he found that what they said about the why and wherefore of scientific work had a "point-to-point correlation with the Puritan teachings on the same subject." In particular, they felt that the best way to venerate God was through the diligent scientific study of the world he created. As the physicist Robert Boyle wrote, the "attentive Inspection" of God's creations would glorify him far more than reliance on the "confus'd and lazy Idea we commonly have of His Power and Wisdom." Puritanism, Merton concluded, thus tended to promote scientific thinking and research.[32]
- In a landmark research study, W. I. Thomas and Florian Znaniecki investigated the social adjustment of Polish peasants coming to this country early in the century. The researchers leaned heavily on such archival materials as court and social agency records, but they also made notable use of a more personal form of written

evidence: They gathered a large number of letters exchanged between the immigrants and people in Poland and from these documents obtained some of their keenest insights into how living in America changed the immigrants' attitudes, family lives, and intimate relationships. [33]

- The sociologist Kai T. Erikson wanted to test the Durkheimian hypothesis that deviance is useful to certain institutions in that it highlights what is permissible and impermissible, and thereby reaffirms the identity of the group. Taking Puritan New England of the seventeenth century as his case, Erikson drew primarily on court records but also on such materials as sermons and diaries. These sources revealed that the leaders of the Massachusetts colony needed to clearly define the boundaries of acceptable belief and of Puritan society itself, and that this led them to launch witch hunts and to condemn any failure to identify totally with Puritanism. [34]

When researchers rely largely on such historical testimony, they judge for themselves how much significance to ascribe to the ideas or actions recorded in their sources. But they also sometimes use a more methodical and objective procedure known as "content analysis" for evaluating written historical materials, or, in fact, any kind of recorded communication, past or present. Content analysis is a set of techniques for counting the number of times various kinds of words, phrases, ideas, or images occur within a particular body of communication and classifying them in related categories. Its purpose is to replace intuitive judgment of the importance of content with quantitative measurement.

G. Ray Funkhouser, a communications researcher, wanted to know what matters had most concerned the public during the 1960s. Using the *Reader's Guide to Periodical Literature* as his primary data base, he tallied the numbers of articles on various topics that appeared in the three leading American newsmagazines during the decade. (He could have examined all 1,716 issues and classified and counted the articles himself but chose, in the interests of efficiency, to accept the coding already done by the *Reader's Guide* staff.)

His list contained no surprises; it closely matched Gallup Poll survey findings as to what people considered "the most important problem facing America" in that period. But it yielded something of value: an index of the relative importance of the fourteen leading problems—at least as assessed by news editors—in the form of the total numbers of articles dealing with each. The Vietnam war (the number 1 problem) was represented by 861 articles, crime (number 5) by only 203, and sexual morals (number 11), surprisingly, by a mere 62.[35]

Most content analyses are far more complicated and subtle than this. Often, researchers must make numerous fine distinctions among related terms or expressions and decide how much weight to assign to each. One content analyst, trying to measure the relative importance assigned by political theorists to various influences on international relations, scored .2 points for each time they used expressions like "may be due to," .3 for "depends in part on," .4 for "tends to," .5 for "strongly affects," .6 for "will determine," and .7 for "is directly related to."[36]

The units counted in content analysis may be words, phrases, sentences, or "themes" (major ideas or units of thought, whether expressed in a few words or a chapter). James A. Banks used thematic analysis to examine how blacks and race relations were treated in elementary-level American history textbooks. After developing eleven thematic categories, Banks and four assistants combed through thirty-six textbooks for passages falling into any of the categories. Two examples: Material implying or claiming that blacks could withstand the hot southern climate much better than whites was classified as "Explained Discrimination"; statements such as "Slaves were poorly fed" were classified as "Deprivation." The relative frequency with which material fitted into these and the other categories would indicate the degree to which each textbook discussed racism, justified or condemned it, or avoided the issues.

Banks concluded, among other things, that by and large the authors of elementary history textbooks did not neglect racial conflict or stress harmonious race relations, as sometimes alleged. But they rarely took a moral stand when discussing racial prejudice and discrimination (for the most part, they neither explained it nor condemned it), and, in Banks's opinion, they devoted too little attention to racial violence and conflict to give children a realistic understanding of race relations in present-day America.[37]

Content analysis can also deal with pictorial materials, examining such matters as the extent to which periodicals use flattering pictures of candidates they favor and vice versa, how often advertisements portray females seated lower than males and looking up at them, and how frequently ruggedly masculine men are the subjects of tobacco advertisements. There may even be a social-science dissertation to be written on what tomb sculptures reveal about medieval marriage: In Chichester Cathedral in Sussex, England, the effigies of Richard Fitzalan, Earl of Arundel, and his wife, Countess Eleanor, are holding hands, which suggests that not all nobles of that time held the unromantic view of married love portrayed in the chief medieval account of aristocratic love and adultery, the *Tractatus de Amore* of Andreas Capellanus.

EXISTING DATA

By far the most common form of social research relying on indirect observation is the analysis of data that already exist and, usually, were gathered by others. Many of the most important discoveries of the social sciences have been made by "secondary analysis," as this is called. (In a sense, the use of historical materials, of which we have just been speaking, is secondary analysis, but the term commonly refers to the use of statistical techniques to discover significant relationships in existing compiled data bases rather than raw records.)

A famous example is the study of suicide made in the 1890s by the French sociologist Émile Durkheim. In an effort to find out what conditions promoted or restrained suicidal behavior, he examined official suicide statistics gathered in previous decades in several countries. One extant theory linked suicide to climate—the rate was higher in hot weather—but Durkheim found the rates to be far lower in the warmer southern countries than in the colder northern ones. Since the seasonal data and the geographical data contradicted each other, Durkheim had to look further and more deeply.

Casting about for an explanation, he next hypothesized that religion might be a major factor, since the northern countries were chiefly Protestant and the southern ones Catholic. When he looked at the data by religion, it turned out that the predominantly Catholic countries had 50 suicides per million population; the predominantly Protestant ones had 190. One explanation might be that suicide was a mortal sin to Catholics but not to Protestants, but this suggestion was negated by the data on Jews, who did not deem suicide a sin but whose rate was the lowest of all.

Seeking other clues, Durkheim noted that single people were most likely to commit suicide and married people with children the least likely to do so; that soldiers were more suicide-prone than civilians; and that suicide rates rose during periods of economic upheaval.

He finally saw a common denominator and proposed an overarching theory: *Anomie*—a sense of social disintegration—increases suicide, whereas belonging to a strong social network counters it. This would explain all the findings: Protestantism stresses individualism, while Catholicism and Judaism stress tradition and integration in the life of the religious community; the single man and the soldier both lack the sense of belonging and integration that the family man has; and economic upheaval causes people to feel adrift and disconnected.[38]

Between Durkheim's time and the present, there has been an immense expansion of compiled data bases on virtually every topic within or related to the social sciences. In the United States these include the Decennial Census of the United States and many special surveys made by the U.S. Bureau of the Census, surveys and studies made by or for the National Center for Health Statistics, and many hundreds of other sets of findings made by university and independent social-science research centers and by commercial public opinion and market research organizations. Worldwide, according to a 1974 directory, there were some 1,500 social-science data bases; today, according to an informal estimate made by the directory's publisher, there are at least 3,000.[39]

Many of these, including the major data bases produced by or for government agencies, have been computerized; researchers can obtain the data on tapes they can either buy or access by dialing on-line data bases via computer-telephone networks. In addition, George Murdock's 1967 "Ethnographic Atlas" compiles data gathered by anthropologists and ethnographers on 800 societies (mostly small and nonliterate) around the world, and the Human Relations Area Files, another compilation available in most major universities, does so in more detail for 300 societies.[40]

Social scientists sometimes do secondary analysis of data gathered by others in an effort to correct or improve on the primary analysis of those data, but more often they reuse existing data for purposes different from those of the researchers who gathered them. The scope of secondary research and its discoveries extends to virtually every area within the social sciences and defies summary, but here are a few illustrative examples:

- In the late 1950s and early 1960s, Gabriel Almond and Sidney Verba conducted surveys of political participation in five countries as the basis of a study of forms of democracy. Some years afterward, Earl Babbie, then a graduate student at the University of California at Berkeley, was able to put their data to quite a different use. As he explains:

  [Charles] Glock had suggested that people who saw, and felt capable of achieving, secular solutions to social problems would seek those means. Those who did not seek secular solutions would turn to the church. I wanted to test that notion, though I didn't have the resources necessary to conduct a large-scale survey. The Almond-Verba data, however, contained information about both religious and political activities— and about people's perceptions of political solutions to problems. As a result, I was able to examine whether people who did not see political solutions were more religiously involved than those who did. [He found, as he expected to, that religious and political activity were essentially alternatives; those who did one didn't, by and large, do the other.][41]

- In the post-World War II period, many large cities began to run into financial problems. A debate raged as to whether this was the result of the growth of the suburban population, which used the city but paid taxes elsewhere, or of increases in the number of central-city poor who needed social services, or both. In 1970 John D. Kasarda sought the answer in two unrelated categories of Bureau of the Census data: Censuses of Business and Compendia of City Government Finances. He found that the growth of the suburban population was indeed correlated with increasing central-city costs. But both might have grown coincidentally; to find out whether the first had caused the second, or whether instead the growth of the urban poor was responsible, Kasarda used a statistical technique known as "path analysis." This broke down the correlation into its component parts and showed to what extent suburban growth was linked with the growth of each category of trade in the city, and how each kind of trade was directly related to the need for police, fire, highway, and other services. Thus, he could trace the connection between suburban growth and city costs. His conclusion:

> The suburban population in general, and the commuting population, in particular, exerts strong effects on police, fire, highway, sanitation, recreation, and general administrative functions performed in the central cities . . . [and] substantially raises the costs of municipal services. While suburban residents do partially reimburse central cities . . . through employment and sales taxes, it is not likely that these "user charges" generate sufficient revenue to cover the additional costs.[42]

- For the Joint Economic Committee of the U.S. Congress, M. Harvey Brenner and his colleagues at Johns Hopkins University investigated the effects of recessions on national health and social well-being. Using data of several kinds from 1950 through 1980, they compared the unemployment rate, the business-failure rate, and per capita income with such health indicators as mortality from various diseases, the rate of first admissions to mental hospitals, and the crime rate. A substantial set of correlations appeared: A rise of 10 percent in the unemployment rate, for example, was associated with a 1.7 percent increase in deaths from cardiovascular and renal disease, a 4.2 percent increase in the population of mental hospitals, and a 4 percent increase in the number of arrests.[43]

- Many social scientists, relying on generalizations derived from the Murdock "Ethnographic Atlas" and the Human Relations Area Files, have held that human social structure is based on a division of roles related to biological differences. According to this view, in nearly all small societies men had the "instrumental" roles (they brought home food, fought the enemy, and in general were responsible for societal survival), while women were assigned the "expressive" roles (they reared children, provided comfort, and in general were the socioemotional specialists).

Recently, however, psychologists William Crano and Joel Aronoff wondered whether these generalizations might be based on too simplistic a tallying of roles, since women did play some part in societal survival and men some part in child-rearing. Using Murdock's estimates as to how dependent each society was for survival on each of five activities—hunting, fishing, food-gathering, animal husbandry, and agriculture—Crano and Aronoff multi-plied these figures by the extent to which each activity was per-formed by women. The results, added up, indicated that women contributed substantially to the survival of many societies:

> In fully 45 percent of the societies investigated, women's subsistence contributions accounted for more than 40 percent of the foodstuffs of their respective groups. . . . It is obvious that, in terms of sheer mag-nitude, the role of women in task-oriented activities long has been underestimated.

A somewhat similar reanalysis of child care revealed that while mothers were usually the principal caretakers, fathers' total con-tribution was more considerable and widespread than it was usu-ally thought to be. In summary:

> [Our] results provide no support for the proposition that males generally assumed the role of instrumental leader or that females uniformly adopted the socioemotional specialist role—though they undoubtedly assumed the task of nursing. . . . The universal role allocation rules, so plausible at first glance, now appear unfounded. [44]

As these examples show, statistical analysis is not just an adjunct to research but is itself a major form of research. This is true not only of secondary analysis but of the primary analysis performed by researchers on data they themselves have gathered. For data tell nothing about social behavior until the researcher sorts or arranges them in a way that shows the relationships among different variables.

Divorce statistics, for instance, can be subdivided according to whether the divorcing couples were or were not childless. This reveals a correlation—namely, that childless couples are more apt to break up than couples with children. But does this mean that the presence of children strengthens marriage or that it inhibits divorce? The analyst, looking for explanations, tries rearranging the data in other ways, such as according to how long the marriage lasted—and finds that the divorce rate is highest in the first years of marriage, when many cou-ples are still childless. Perhaps, then, the correlation means only that gross incompatibility causes both divorce and childlessness by breaking up many marriages very early. [45]

Yet to make sure there is no more to the correlation than that, the analyst would need to see whether children exert any effect one way or the other in later phases of marriage. He would have to turn to data on people divorcing after ten or fifteen years of marriage; if he still found that parents were less likely to divorce than nonparents, he could feel fairly sure there was some real connection between them. Yet this still wouldn't tell how many couples are made closer by the presence of children, how many stay together, though unhappy, for their sake, and how many have a good marriage and therefore have children *and* stay together. To answer this question, the analyst would have to look for other correlations in the data base, such as the relationship between parenthood and various measures of marital happiness, and, if he found such evidence one way or the other, hypothesize the mechanisms that might account for it. But if the data base did not include statistics on such matters, he would have to seek them in other data bases that were compatible with the one he is using. (To date, no researcher has reached any definitive finding on this matter.)

Statistical analysis is thus an intellectual adventure and a contest with one's self (to find the hidden messages); for all its forbidding jargon, it is a part of what has been called "the game of science."[46] Some of the ways of playing that game statistically will be illustrated in the following chapters of this book. The two most often used are these:

- Analysis of variance. The cases are divided into groups according to one variable (white or nonwhite, for instance); then the analyst compares the groups in terms of a second variable such as average income. If there is a difference, the analyst then tests its importance by looking at the variance in each group—how wide a scattering of incomes there is within it—and compares this with the normal scattering one would statistically expect. This shows how much of the difference between the two groups is due to normal variation and how much is related to the first variable— race—and thus enables the analyst to determine whether the difference in income between the groups is accidental or "statistically significant."

- Regression analysis. The analyst uses algebraic methods to "hold constant" all the factors involved in some social phenomenon except one, in order to see how much of the net result that one accounts for. If the analyst is studying, say, the results of different styles of parenting, he or she has to take into account many other influences on how children turn out, such as how much education the parents had, the kind of schools the children attended, the families' church affiliation, the local mores, the number of children in the family, and each child's place in the birth order. By mathematically holding constant or balancing out all factors but one at a time—as if comparing cases identical in every respect except that one—the analyst can measure the part it played in the end result.

These examples give only the merest hint of what such analyses are like, and none at all of the range of procedures available for special purposes. A recent guide to the analysis of social-science data lists nearly 150 statistical tools and techniques and directs the user of the guide to work through a 28-page "decision tree," or sequence of questions and answers, in order to determine the appropriate technique for the problem at hand.[47]

Because many advanced statistical procedures require vast numbers of calculations, they became feasible—and in fact were developed—only with the advent of inexpensive high-speed computers. Such computers have transformed much of social-science research: In 1946, roughly half of all research articles in the two leading sociological journals did not rely in any way on mathematical analysis, but by 1976 this was true of only 12 percent.[48]

Advanced statistical techniques coupled to computer power have also made possible a recondite form of social research known as "simulation." This involves the construction of an "econometric model"—a set of equations representing the interplay of a host of forces at work in the economy, such as the prices of various kinds of goods, employment data, and the inputs and outputs of specific sectors of the economy. Such a model may consist of dozens to hundreds of equations that must be solved simultaneously (one model consists of more than 2,000 equations), representing the interrelationship of hundreds or even thousands of facets of the economy. Econometricians go through this herculean procedure in the effort to predict the future of the economy and the effects of policies being considered; when the right data and assumptions are entered, the computations simulate what would happen in real life if those conditions existed. (Other social researchers use the same technique to forecast other phenomena, such as migration and immigration, population growth, and changing demands for education and other services.)

The distinguished economist Wassily Leontief and his associates recently used this method to project what would happen to the demand for human labor as computer-based automation reaches into the service and manufacturing sectors of the economy. Using three different assumptions—(1) that no further new technology would be introduced after 1980; (2) that there would be a moderate amount of further modernization; and (3) that there would be major further modernization—the study predicted different amounts of decline in clerical employment and increase in professional and technical jobs, but, in general, showed a steady level of employment in manufacturing.[49]

A far cry, that, from living as a patient on a mental hospital ward in order to observe its social structure and relationships; no wonder one cannot represent social research by a single image. Yet even the many forms we have seen thus far by no means represent the whole spectrum of social research; in fact, while those we have looked at are important for all the reasons noted, we have not yet come to the two categories that make up the bulk of present-day social research. It is to these that chapters 2 through 6 of this book are devoted, but by way of seeing the spectrum whole, let us look at them briefly here.

Surveys

THEIR CREDIBILITY

The methods we have looked at thus far were the chief sources of data in social research several decades ago and are still important today, especially in social psychology and anthropology. But in recent years these disciplines have made increasing use of survey data, and in sociology and economics the survey has become far and away the primary source of research data.

It is also the one form of social research the public is widely aware of. The media constantly report the results of surveys and opinion polls on every imaginable subject, and virtually every magazine article, TV documentary, and popular nonfiction book on any topic of current interest is strewn with survey data. Typically, the cover story in the April 9, 1984, issue of *Time*, dealing with the waning of the sexual revolution, cited figures from surveys by *Cosmopolitan*, *Playboy*, the National Center for Health Statistics, *Psychology Today*, Yankelovich, Skelly & White (a leading public opinion research firm), the National Opinion Research Center of the University of Chicago, and half a dozen others.

Unfortunately, many people are not able to judge which surveys are worth believing and which are not. When *Psychology Today* reports on the "more than 1,000" replies it received in response to a questionnaire in its pages,[50] unwary readers—many of whom know that national opinion poll samples are sometimes no larger than that—may accept the results without question, at least as relating to the kind of people who read that magazine. But in professional public opinion polls, the sample is scientifically selected by the researchers and is representative of the population being surveyed, while in the *Psychology Today* survey the replies received come only from those people who were motivated to fill out and return the questionnaire. Such a self-selected sample may give a badly distorted picture of the magazine's readership, let alone of the population at large. For a sample made up entirely of those who volunteer to reply is apt to be disproportionately composed of those who feel strongly one way or the other about the subject, especially if the survey concerns touchy or controversial matters such as religion, drugs, or sex.

Even when researchers select the sample themselves and phone or call on every person on their list, unless 60 percent or more are willing to answer their questions the results may not be trustworthy, since those who didn't answer may differ considerably in unknown ways from those who did. Yet even a very modest survey—a couple hundred students on one campus—can be quite trustworthy if the sample is truly representative and the percentage of refusals low. (Random selection, even by so crude a method as taking every tenth or fiftieth or hundredth name in the student directory, is one way to obtain a genuinely representative miniature of the population being studied.)

However accurate, our little campus survey tells us only what the students on that campus, or other very similar ones, are feeling or doing. The findings may not apply to students in general, much less young people not in college, older people, or the population at large. Yet such surveys are often accepted by the public as having far-reaching implications, and researchers themselves, though they dutifully warn against generalizing from their conclusions, are prone to imply that there are profound and widely applicable truths in them. But within the social-science community and the government, the survey research projects that have intellectual impact are those using large, carefully selected samples that represent, with reasonable accuracy, the entire population or some specified segment of it such as people in the labor market, homeowners, or persons receiving disability benefits.

(The criteria of sound and faulty survey methods and the importance of survey data to modern society will be discussed in detail in chapter 3.)

CROSS-SECTIONALS

The most common kind of survey is the one-time cross-sectional. Such a survey, like a still from a movie, is a frozen frame of reality showing what existed at one moment in time. Since it does not show motion or change, it cannot directly reveal how things came to be as they are or what consequences are likely to follow. But it can do so indirectly in the form of correlations among the sets of numbers it contains. If a survey finds that smokers are, on the average, less healthy than nonsmokers and that the heaviest smokers are the least healthy, statisticians say that this correlation may mean there is a cause-and-effect relationship between the two factors.

Such a correlation, however, doesn't prove which is the cause and which is the effect; in many cases the researcher can't tell. If taller children eat more, eating may make for tallness—but it is also possible that inherited tallness is the cause of larger appetite. In the case of smoking, however, experience and common sense help one to judge: It is most unlikely that ill health causes smoking and thus probable that smoking causes ill health. Still, the correlation is only presumptive evidence, since some other overlooked factor might be the real cause of both smoking and ill health; perhaps, for instance, job stress leads many people to smoke—and also harms their health. Clinching proof

of causality requires a far more complex research design than that of
the one-time cross-sectional.

A typical cross-sectional survey that many people are familiar with is
the New York *Times* Poll.[51]

From time to time, the newspaper's editors decide to conduct a
national survey on some subject such as patriotism, education, or
women's issues. (In election years, the *Times* also joins forces with
CBS News to do political polling.) Specialists on the *Times* first prepare a computer-generated sample of telephone exchanges from a
complete nationwide list; the chance each exchange has of being
picked is proportionate to the population it serves. Within each chosen
exchange, the computer then generates numbers randomly, and the
list is pruned to eliminate business phones. This yields a sample that
represents the national population, or at least that vast majority who
have home telephones.

Such a sample can be rather small and still yield reasonably accurate
measurements of the national pulse: In a *Times* poll of 1,500 respondents, there is a 95 percent chance that the percentage who answered
any question one way or another is within 3 percentage points of what
interviewers would have found if they had been able to ask everyone in
the nation.

After the preparation of the sample and other preliminary steps, the
actual polling begins in a large room at the *Times*'s building on West
43rd Street; there, sixty interviewers, tucked into cubicles like bee
grubs in a honeycomb, dial numbers from the prepared list. As the
calls are answered, the interviewers introduce themselves and state
their purpose; only a small percentage of those they reach refuse to
answer. But unanswered calls and refusals to reply might bias the
sample in some unknown way (they may represent a minority with a
special viewpoint); numbers that did not answer are later dialed again
at least four more times, and people who did answer but refused to
reply to the questions are called back by more experienced interviewers
who usually are able to convert at least half of them to respondents.

The process of interviewing takes four to five days, after which
technicians transfer the answers to the computer. Several statisticians
then examine the raw totals and "weight" the data, adjusting the
sample to make it an accurate miniature of the country's population. If

the interviewers happen to have reached a larger percentage of women than Census data show to be the national percentage, the analysts arithmetically rebalance the number of answers by men and by women to match the national ratio. They go through the same process for age, education, and income.

The computer then prints out weighted tables, showing the percentages of answers to every question broken down in ways likely to show significant correlations, such as how men and women answered, how the answers of the college-educated compare with those of the non-college-educated, and so on. One or two reporters confer with the statisticians to obtain interpretations of these correlations and then prepare the article giving the findings. Weighting the data, finding significant correlations among the subtotals, drawing conclusions from these data, and writing the news story usually takes no more than twenty-four hours.

(In more elaborate cross-sectional surveys by research organizations, the planning, preparation, data-gathering, and analysis can take months or years. Chapter 2 tells the story of a complex and historically important survey of this type.)

LONGITUDINALS

When researchers need to study social changes or ongoing social processes, they choose any of several "longitudinal" designs, that is, surveys that measure a particular phenomenon or group of phenomena over a period of time.

One such design asks the same set of questions, at intervals, of samples drawn from the same population by the same method; even though the individuals are not the same, the samples are equally representative of the group being polled. Two or more cross-sectionals taken at different times constitute a "trend study" that shows changes such as growth or decline in the percentage approving the President's handling of his office, the increase or decrease in the percentage of people who are currently sick, and countless similar matters.

A typical trend study, conducted for many years by the Institute for Social Research at the University of Michigan, measures the degree of trust Americans place in various institutions. A 1982 sampling showed that one third of all Americans said they trusted the federal government all or most of the time, as compared with 1980, when only one quarter expressed such trust. But in 1964, the figure had been three quarters; the 1980–82 upturn thus represented only a small repair of a long-term erosion of public confidence in the federal government.[52] (A related but not identical query in a New York *Times*/CBS News Poll in November 1984 found that the rise was continuing and had reached 40 percent at that time.[53])

Not only do trend studies show movement, they can also come much closer than single cross-sectionals to pinpointing cause-and-effect relationships. If a cross-sectional survey shows widespread fear of crime in a given city; if police patrolling is then stepped up; and if a second wave of the survey taken after the increase in patrolling began shows a drop in the fear of crime, the data are fairly good evidence that, other things being equal, the increase in patrolling reduced fear.

But trend studies have certain defects, the most serious being that they indicate only *net* change; much more may have taken place than the figures reveal. A series of cross-sectionals might show no change in the percentages of voters preferring one candidate or the other, yet there may have been shifts of considerable importance in each direction that canceled each other out; to know what is really happening to public opinion, the researcher needs better information than the trend study offers.

One solution is a more difficult form of longitudinal survey relying on a "panel"—a sample of people who are resurveyed at intervals. Such a survey of voter preferences would show not just what percentages favored each candidate each time but what kinds of voters had shifted from one to the other.

The panel study, moreover, because it is a running record of each individual's life, can come closer than trend studies to identifying causes of change. A trend study, being made of cross-sectionals, might show no change in the proportions of liberals and conservatives over a period of years; a panel study, looking at the same people each time, might find that people shift toward conservatism as they grow older, or perhaps that those who prosper financially do so, or both.

Longitudinal panel studies do, however, have grave disadvantages, among them the high cost and considerable effort involved in keeping track of people over a period of time, the tendency of panel members to get bored or weary of being questioned, and many others. One way to minimize these problems is to use a panel for a couple of years or a limited number of interviews and then replace it with a similarly chosen panel.

(Chapter 3 deals with a large-scale short-term panel survey and discusses survey methodology in general. Chapter 5 describes a small-scale panel study that followed panelists for a generation, and discusses long-term panel studies in general.)

Experiments

INHERENT PROBLEMS

The last in this array of specimens, the experiment, is the research method most favored in those natural sciences in which it can be used; it is the major form of inquiry in such disciplines as chemistry and physics, but not, of course, in such others as astronomy and geology.

In simplest terms, an experiment in any science is a known situation into which the researcher introduces one change at a time to see what happens. The chemist adds a reagent to a mixture; the physicist increases the speed of colliding particles; the biologist removes a particular component from the feed given to the laboratory mice.

In social research, experiments cannot be so neatly managed. Both ethics and law restrain researchers from secretly performing experiments on society or imposing experimental conditions on people against their will. Even when people agree to have some experimental influence introduced into their lives, researchers cannot prevent unforeseen events or social changes from taking place that affect the outcome and muddy the results.

Finally, when human beings are aware that they are part of an experiment, they are apt to act differently from the way they otherwise would. This was the unexpected and perhaps most important finding of a famous early social-research experiment. In the late 1920s, at the Hawthorne (Chicago) plant of the Western Electric Company, researchers told a small group of women doing wiring in the Relay Assembly Room that they would be the subjects of experiments on the improvement of working conditions. The researchers then increased the lighting in several stages, introduced monetary incentives, and made other changes, one by one. Gratifyingly, every improvement in working conditions increased productivity, but when the researchers sought to verify their conclusions by reversing the changes—for instance, by dimming the lights—productivity increased again.

Clearly, some other force was at work. The researchers speculated that the group had developed new norms and that its members felt obliged to live up to them. But fuller analysis led other researchers to conclude that the major but unintended influence had been the women's response to the interest taken in them by the research team; no matter what change was introduced, being the center of attention spurred the women on. This became known as the "Hawthorne effect," and ever since, researchers conducting experiments have gone to some trouble to avoid or counteract it.[54]*

Despite these inherent problems, four different types of experiment have proven valuable in social research.

THE NATURAL EXPERIMENT

One type is the "natural experiment," an event such as a disaster or historical occurrence (the passage of a law, the outbreak of war) that is followed by certain changes in social behavior. Researchers comparing the behavior of people before the event with that after it attribute changes to that event. But they do so tentatively, and for good reason. First, they had no control over other new influences that came into being during the same period and may have played a part. Again, because most natural experiments are unanticipated, researchers are unable to assemble a comparison group of people beforehand who will

---

*Recently, some consideration has been given to an alternate explanation of the Hawthorne effect that we need not go into here.[55]

not be affected by the event; yet only by means of such a group can they see whether the changes would have come about even without the influence of the event in question. Natural experiments therefore do not provide definitive proof of cause-and-effect relationships, but are chiefly a source of hypotheses and insights that need further proof.

(Sometimes, however, researchers can find a setting like the one affected by the disaster or historical occurrence but where that influence has not been present; this is a "natural control," and if it does not exhibit the same consequences as in the first setting, the researchers' conclusions about the effect of the natural experiment are strengthened.)

At 8 A.M. on February 26, 1972, at Buffalo Creek, West Virginia, a coal-mining area of Appalachia, a huge dam made of mine waste gave way after several rainy days. An entire lake—132 million gallons of water—plus the mud of the dam itself went surging down the narrow, 17-mile-long valley, sweeping people, cars, and whole settlements away; 125 people died, 4,000 were made homeless, and the extremely close community life in the string of 16 villages in the flood's path was shattered.

A year after the disaster, Kai T. Erikson began a detailed study of the aftermath of the Buffalo Creek disaster. He visited the area a number of times, interviewed many of its residents at length, and read somewhere between 30,000 and 40,000 pages of legal depositions and transcripts gathered by lawyers for the flood victims and by other researchers. From these sources he formed a picture of life along Buffalo Creek before the flood, and another of life one to two years afterward.

Research on a number of similar disasters had shown that there is usually a good deal of personal and community recovery within a year or so, but at Buffalo Creek, a year and more after the flood, Erikson found little restoration of community life and a surprising degree of unabated depression, anxiety, and lethargy. Typical of what he heard again and again were statements like these:

I don't want to get out, see no people. Why? I don't know. I'm just a different person. I just don't want to associate with no people. It bothers me.

*

Sometimes when you go to sleep and start to relax, the nightmares start. The water comes down again; you lay there and can't move, screaming for

help. I believe that everyone concerned would have been better off if everyone
had been killed . . . then you wouldn't have to be sorry that your friend was
killed and you were not.

*

Well, I have lost all my friends. The people I was raised up and lived with,
they're scattered. I don't know where they're at. . . . Down here, there ain't
but a few people I know, and you don't feel secure around people you don't
know.

One of the crucial influences acting on the flood victims, Erikson
came to think, was that the government agencies that lent assistance
after the disaster housed the homeless in trailer camps without regard
to what communities they had lived in before the disaster. Thus, not
only had their lives been shattered, but they had lost the sense of
"communality"—of sharing their lives with an intimate network of
long-time trusted neighbors and friends—that had been so important
to them before. As Erikson says:

Most of the traumatic symptoms experienced by the Buffalo Creek survivors
are a reaction to the loss of communality as well as a reaction to the disaster
itself. . . . The fear and apathy and demoralization one encounters along the
length of the hollow are derived from the shock of being ripped out of a
meaningful community setting as well as the shock of meeting that cruel
black water.

This has important implications for the rest of us, Erikson feels, not
only because of the possibility of nuclear war—which, in addition to
all else, would destroy the social networks of its survivors—but because
of the many ways in which modern society is robbing us of communality:

What happened on Buffalo Creek, then, can serve as a reminder that the
preservation (or restoration) of communal forms of life must become a lasting
concern, not only for those charged with healing the wounds of acute disaster
but for those charged with planning a truly human future. [56]

THE QUASI-EXPERIMENT

As fertile a source of hypotheses as natural experiments are, they fall
far short of the ideal of the controlled experiment. Somewhat closer to

it is the "quasi-experiment," a species of research in which the social scientist compares the behavior of a group of people who have experienced a particular condition with that of a control group of similar people who have not. If the two groups are alike in every other way, any difference between them is attributable to that condition.

In many cases researchers do not have complete control over the formation of the two groups and therefore cannot be sure they balance each other perfectly. Some unknown factor may be more common in one group than the other and could be partly or even wholly the cause of the difference between them—hence the term "quasi-experiment."

This is the weakness of quasi-experiments. Whenever researchers have to assemble a control group after the fact, they match it to the experimental group on the basis of the factors they are aware of—income, education, age, and the like. But human beings are very complicated and there may be subtle and hidden differences between the groups that the researchers do not sense. In assembling an ex post facto control group to compare with volunteers for a job training experiment, a researcher might match them in all obviously important ways, yet not inquire whether the volunteers were by nature more optimistic than the controls, although such a difference could play a significant part in the outcome.

The best way to eliminate, or at least minimize, all such unknown differences between an experimental and a control group is to gather a sample and randomly assign individuals from it to both groups before the experiment starts; this tends to even out the many inscrutable factors that might make the groups different. But researchers may have no chance to do so, for lawmakers often launch a program that affects a certain number of people and only later order studies to find out what it is accomplishing. Nonetheless, quasi-experimental research based on painstaking evaluation of the experimental and control groups produces findings in which one can have a fair amount of confidence.

THE TRUE EXPERIMENT

The research method that, in theory, can yield highly trustworthy conclusions about the causes of various kinds of social behavior is the true experiment. There are two quite dissimilar kinds: The first, small-scale, artificial, and wholly controlled by the researcher, is usually called a "laboratory experiment" although sometimes it takes place outside laboratory walls; the second, generally large-scale, naturalistic, and taking place in a real-life setting, is called a "social experiment."

Laboratory experiments are conducted chiefly by social psychologists and are the dominant form of research in their discipline. In such experiments, researchers create a miniature social situation in the laboratory and observe volunteers in that setting. They divide the volunteers into two groups, experimentals and controls, and add some particular stimulus or condition—the "treatment," as it is called—to the setting of the experimentals but not of the controls. Since the only difference between the groups is the treatment, it must be the cause of any difference in the behavior of the two groups. Researchers avoid the Hawthorne effect and other distortions of the volunteers' behavior that might result from an awareness of what is going on by the use of distraction or of a cover story that masks the purposes of the experiment and the treatment being investigated.

Several years ago, Joel Cooper of Princeton University wanted to test the hypothesis that people who freely choose to engage in an effortful activity that they hope will change their behavior *do* change—chiefly because they don't want to feel they wasted their efforts. (This hypothesis is an offshoot of Festinger's theory of cognitive dissonance, which we saw at work in the case of the prophecy that failed.) Cooper thought this mental mechanism might explain why various forms of psychotherapy all seem to have some effect: What works may be not the particular techniques so much as the fact that in every case patients spend time, money, and effort hoping to bring about a change in themselves.

He recruited volunteers through an ad in a campus newspaper offering $2 for one hour of participation in a procedure designed to help them act assertively. Of the 100 male volunteers who showed up—too few females responded to be included in the experiment—Cooper chose the 50 who scored least assertive in a paper-and-pencil test. These volunteers were then seen one at a time: Half were told that the procedure was effortful and possibly embarrassing and asked if they chose to go ahead with it; the other half were given an explanation which made no mention of effort or embarrassment and offered no opportunity to choose to continue or not.

The members of each group were then split again. Half got forty minutes of intensive behavior therapy; the other half were made to exercise vigorously for the same period of time (the pretext being that this would "increase activity at emotional and neural levels"). Then each volunteer was thanked and told that the receptionist would pay him $2.

When the volunteer stopped by at the reception desk, however, the receptionist—who was, in fact, an accomplice of Cooper's—gave him only $1. If he took it quietly and left, he was scored zero on aggressiveness; if he looked quizzically at the dollar, shuffled his feet, or tried in some other nonverbal way to signal that it was insufficient, he was scored 1; if he verbally questioned the size of the payment, 2; if he persisted but finally took the dollar and left, 3; and if he said he was going to find the experimenter then and there to complain, 4.

The results: Volunteers who had had the chance to choose whether or not to expend effort on assertiveness training stood up for their rights, no matter which form of treatment they had received. Those who had had behavioral therapy averaged 3.4 on the assertiveness score, while those who had performed hard physical exercise did nearly as well, averaging 3.2. But those who had not had the chance to choose whether or not to go ahead were considerably less assertive, scoring only 2.1 if they had received behavior therapy and 1.9 if they had exercised. [57]

(A fuller discussion of laboratory experiments in social behavior and an account of a noteworthy series of experiments on teamwork are presented in chapter 4.)

In contrast to laboratory experiments, social experiments are among the largest, most expensive, and most prolonged of social research projects. Some have involved thousands of volunteers, cost many millions of dollars, and lasted several years; a few have far exceeded these dimensions.

Social experiments also differ from laboratory experiments in that they are applied, rather than basic, research, being funded chiefly by federal agencies interested not in gaining profound understanding of social behavior but in measuring the effects of some proposed government intervention in social processes. Yet such experiments do yield new basic knowledge, for their data are subjected to countless secondary analyses by researchers interested in theoretical issues.

Typical social experiments have given jobs or cash to groups of drug addicts and convicted thieves to see whether either form of help would enable them to go straight; paid cash subsidies to poor people in substandard housing to see how the money would affect the general level of housing and quality of life in that segment of society; and offered thousands of volunteers different kinds of health insurance programs (including totally free care) to see what demands they would make of the medical system under each plan and what effects each would have on their health.[58]

Projects of this kind are true experiments rather than quasi-experiments for two main reasons. First, they use samples that are reasonably representative of that part of the population that would be affected by the proposed program or law. Second, these samples are divided into experimental and control groups by random assignment before the experimental treatment begins. Since the two groups thus created are genuinely comparable, any differences between them once the treatment begins are almost certain to have been caused by it.

This is not to say there are no difficulties in interpreting the results. Indeed, because such experiments involve human beings living in society, they involve innumerable problems and ambiguities. For one, people in control groups may learn of the benefits those in the experimental groups are getting, and, as a result, resentfully drop out or react in some other unforeseen way. Again, unpredictable changes in society itself may so alter the social environment that the results are hard to interpret: A guaranteed annual income experiment in New Jersey was set up as an attractive alternative to the existing welfare system, but soon after it got under way, New Jersey passed a much more generous welfare law that all but undercut the appeal to the poor of the experimental program.

(The story of one major social experiment is narrated in chapter 6, along with discussion of the scientific and political difficulties of conducting research of this type.)

And now, having walked through this museum and glanced briefly at these varied specimens of the genus *social research*, let us look more closely at its dominant species.

PART II
Five Case Histories of
Social Research

THE DILEMMA IN THE CLASSROOM

A Cross-sectional Survey Measures the Effects of Segregated Schooling

Unwelcome Opportunity

It is hardly every day that a young social scientist with relatively few years of experience receives an unexpected phone call asking him to head a $1.5 million study that could have a major impact on American society. It is even rarer for such a person to politely refuse an offer of this kind because the study, ordered by Congress to help carry out a recently enacted law of major social importance, would take him away from more basic or, as it is sometimes called, "pure" research.

Both those improbable things happened one winter morning in 1965. James S. Coleman, full professor and chairman of the sociology department at Johns Hopkins University in Baltimore—although only 39, his rugged features and prematurely bald head made him look suitably mature—answered the phone in his office and with no advance warning was tendered an extraordinary opportunity.

His caller, a well-known statistician named Alexander Mood, had recently left the Rand Corporation to become assistant commissioner for educational statistics in the Office of Education, at that time a part of the Department of Health, Education, and Welfare. Mood said that, as Coleman was surely aware, the Civil Rights Act of 1964 required the Office of Education to carry out a survey showing "the lack of availability of equal educational opportunity for individuals by reason of race, color, religion, or national origin" in public schools throughout the nation. Coleman, as the author of *The Adolescent Society* and *Introduction to Mathematical Sociology*, knew a good deal not only about education but also about large-scale survey methodology, and Mood was inviting him to direct the huge undertaking.

Taken aback by the offer—he'd been a sociologist less than nine years—and needing time to think, Coleman stalled by asking Mood details about the size, scope, and timing of the job. What he heard was disconcerting: Not only would the survey be massive and complex, but there was little time in which to carry it out. Half a year had been wasted in planning a small-scale study to be carried out by Office of Education staffers; now, however, Commissioner Francis Keppel had decided that only a full-scale professional survey conducted by outside professionals would do. But the Act required that the results of the survey be submitted to Congress and the President by July 2, 1966, only a year and a half away. Still, money would be available—the budget would be about a million and a half dollars—for hiring all sorts of specialized help.

Nonetheless, Coleman wasn't at all sure it could be done in respectable scientific fashion in that little time. And in addition to his disinclination to spend time away from basic research, he was concerned that the survey might be intended less to provide objective data than to aid the Justice Department in prosecuting schools the survey identified as failing to obey the law.

"Above all," Coleman recently recalled, "I was reluctant to accept because it would mean stepping out of my role as a sociologist—as I then saw it. At that time, sociologists didn't do government-sponsored applied research. We did make proposals to the National Institute of Mental Health and the National Science Foundation, trying to get government funds for research we wanted to do, but somehow we never did research that was initiated by the government.* So after talking to Mood for some time, I said I regretted that I couldn't undertake the job—I think I pleaded other commitments—and offered to help him find someone else."

Coleman's regret was sincere. He sensed his own ambivalence: He wanted the job as much as he feared it.

It attracted me because it represented a new phase in social science, one in which social research would be taken seriously by policy-makers. We'd been concerning ourselves with scholarly and academic kinds of problems, but because society is the object of sociology, it seemed to me that it was time the discipline began to have something to say that was practical and useful for society's functioning. We could provide a window for policy-makers through which to see things they couldn't clearly see without it. The more I thought about it, the more I became entranced with the idea of doing this survey, particularly because it dealt with an area where the impact on policy was so important.

As it happened, I never did find anybody else who was willing to take on the job, so I finally called Alex Mood and said I'd thought it over and if I could have a co-director to handle the part of the survey dealing with institutions of higher education, I'd do it after all.

(Mood agreed, and Coleman got Professor Ernest Campbell of Vanderbilt University to accept the assignment.) That decision changed Coleman's life—and the lives of millions of Americans.

Behind his decision, as is probably true of most scientists' selections of what to investigate, there were motives deeper-seated than the intellectual ones he spoke of. Born in a small town in Indiana, he spent a number of boyhood summers at an uncle's farm in Kentucky, where he gained a disturbing sense of the schizoid relations between whites and blacks in the rural South—intimacy and interdependence in their work, segregation and gross inequality in their social lives and living conditions. As an adult, Coleman became a liberal on racial issues

---

*That, at least, was how many academic sociologists then felt, although in fact a number of others had already performed applied research of various kinds for the government, such as the studies of the social psychology of the American soldier during World War II made by Samuel Stouffer and others, and much of the work done at Columbia University's Center for Applied Social Research in the 1950s by Paul Lazarsfeld, Robert K. Merton, and other leading figures in sociology.

and from time to time, in his capacity as a citizen rather than a social scientist, acted upon his beliefs. In the fall of 1963, for instance, during the era of demonstrations against racial segregation, Coleman, his wife, and their three young children joined a CORE protest at a segregated amusement park in Baltimore. The police were arresting demonstrators who entered the park, but Coleman and his family went in anyway—and were promptly hustled off in a police car to an armory, where they joined a crowd of blacks and whites arrested at the park for violating a trespassing law. "We were fingerprinted," Coleman recalls, "booked to be tried, and kept there until 2 or 3 A.M. It made us proud; we felt we had done the right thing." The charges were later dropped and the mass trial canceled when the trespass law was ruled invalid.

Until the chance to head the education survey came along, however, Coleman's work as a sociologist had in no way been aimed at eliminating segregation or, indeed, at making any changes in society or exerting any influence on government policies. He had done respectable studies of community conflict, adolescent life, and the social climate of American schools, all of which had been marked by the objective detachment and avoidance of value judgments that characterized good academic sociology. The aim of that kind of social science, as one of Coleman's most distinguished mentors at Columbia University, Robert K. Merton, used to tell his students, was to find out, "Is it really so? Why is it so?" Now, however, Coleman was about to undertake research that seemed inspired more by two very different and less disinterested questions, namely, "Is it right that it is so? What should we do about it?"

His motives were in fact far from that simple. Deeply opposed, in his personal life, to racial segregation, he was powerfully drawn to do research that would discover and document its effects; yet by training and temperament he could not let himself do a hasty research job superficially "proving" school segregation as pernicious as he thought. And in fact Coleman's approach to the school survey, as conscientious and impartial as that of his more basic research, would yield some findings that contradicted many of his own assumptions about the effects of segregated schooling and led him to conclusions too complex and qualified to please his government sponsors—but that nonetheless had major impact on federal policy, the nation's school systems, and the racial makeup of America's large cities.

The Goals of Social Research

Coleman's inner conflict about the primacy of basic research, and the urgent need for survey data that would help carry out the Civil Rights Act of 1964, were part of an old tradition.

In the "hard" sciences, researchers have long had two distinct and often disparate goals: understanding why things are as they are and learning how to solve practical problems—in popular terms, "basic" research versus "applied" research. Basic research, the lineal descendant of philosophy, has always been the more intellectually prestigious, but in pragmatic, success-oriented America, applied research has long been far better supported by business and, latterly, by the government.

Researchers in the social sciences, particularly sociology, have had the same conflict, with one or the other of the research goals dominating their thinking at various times. In this country, applied research was initially in the ascendant: Toward the end of the last century, most sociologists were interested chiefly in promoting "social control," by which they meant the democratic self-regulation of industrial society.[1] As stated in the lead article of the first issue of the *American Journal of Sociology* in 1895, the aim of the young science was to "increase our present intelligence about social utilities that there may be [greater] promotion of the general welfare,"[2] and much of the research published in that journal over the next two decades dealt with proposed solutions (such as the eight-hour work day) to specific problems of city life and industrial work. This species of sociology has often been called "social engineering."[3]

At the same time, a very different concept of sociology was being promulgated in Europe—one in which the goal of research was to discover laws or principles that accounted for social phenomena in order to understand them better. Practical applications of that understanding were a welcome by-product of the research but not its raison d'être. In the 1890s, for instance (as we saw in chapter 1), when Durkheim explored suicide he did not conduct little experiments on ways to reduce the tendency toward such behavior but analyzed data in search of a basic principle that would account for the confusing correlations of suicide with religion, region, the political and economic situation, and other social factors.

In America, after the turn of the century, a number of younger sociologists began trying to recast sociology in this mode. By the 1920s, they had largely succeeded: Academic sociology was dominant, social engineering was looked down upon as "politics," and William Ogburn, in his 1929 presidential address to the American Sociological Society, labeled "concern with practical problems" a major obstacle to the emergence of a "cumulative science of society."[4]

During the 1920s and 1930s, social research on relations between whites and Negroes* was, accordingly, primarily aimed at better understanding rather than social change. Typically, sociologist W. Lloyd Warner and several colleagues sought to make sense of the bewildering complexities of Negro-white relations in America in terms of the concept of a *color-caste system*: The caste aspect subordinated Negroes to whites, but each caste had a class system of its own by means of which status and power were distributed within it and between the castes.[5] Work of this sort made sense of much about race relations that had been obscure or confusing but did little to move the public or leaders of American society to reduce the inequities and injustices of the system.

In 1944, however, there appeared a major work of a very different sort. *An American Dilemma,* by the eminent Swedish social economist Gunnar Myrdal, was a vast, inclusive, and hugely detailed study of the Negro problem that drew upon nearly three dozen research papers specially commissioned by Myrdal plus a mass of existing empirical data and theoretical studies. Myrdal's thesis was that "the American Negro problem is a problem in the heart of the American. . . . It is there that the decisive struggle goes on."[6] Americans, he said, suffered from a conflict of values—their democratic moral precepts and ideals on the one hand, and their prejudices and selfish interests on the other. He saw this clash of attitudes, this moral dilemma, as a major source of social strain and disorder, and as America's greatest failure.

What made the work startlingly different from most race-relations research of the time was Myrdal's passionate plea that social research combine objective inquiry with a morally inspired search for remedies to social problems:

* I will use the terms "Negro" and "black" according to the usage of the times.

The rationalism and moralism which is the driving force behind social study, whether we admit it or not, is the faith that institutions can be improved and strengthened. . . . To find the practical formulas for this never-ending reconstruction of society is the supreme task of social science.[7]

Myrdal said that the aloof and academic sociology of William Graham Sumner, who had described race relations in terms of deep-seated folkways and mores that no law could change, was an apologia for the status quo. Totally disagreeing with Sumner's well-known assertion that "stateways cannot make folkways . . . legislation cannot make mores," Myrdal called on Americans to create the mechanisms by which stateways could, in fact, bring about such changes.[8] But his work had been commissioned by the Carnegie Corporation, not the government, and he did not presume to specify how such changes might be brought about by law or other governmental mechanisms. It was not, therefore, what later came to be called "policy research"— social research intended to produce specific government policies or aid in carrying them out.

Ten years went by before an arm of the government discovered a way to use the kinds of information provided by Myrdal and others. Then it was the courts, not the legislative or executive branches, that did so: In 1954 the Supreme Court handed down its historic decision in the case of *Brown* v. *Board of Education,* in which it found that the doctrine of "separate but equal" facilities, by means of which the South had been able to maintain racial segregation in the schools, deprived Negro children of their right to the equal protection guaranteed by the Fourteenth Amendment.

Schools in the South had been segregated ever since the post-Reconstruction era; Negro children went to dirt-poor schools, where the education they received fitted them only for lowly roles in society.[9] (In the North, segregation had disappeared after the Civil War.) Efforts to attain equality through integration were totally blocked in the South by the 1896 Supreme Court decision in *Plessy* v. *Ferguson,* a case concerning a Louisiana law requiring Negroes to ride in separate railroad cars; the Court had held, in *Plessy,* that such segregation did not deprive Negroes of their rights if the facilities were "separate but equal."

A number of social forces at work from the 1930s on brought re-
newed legal efforts to break down segregated education. Urbanization
and industrialization were luring many blacks from southern farms to
northern cities; New Deal labor and social welfare legislation was
setting the precedent for laws that would give Negroes something
closer to equal economic opportunity; World War II and the emergence of the Third World nations were changing Negro expectations
and raising Negro consciousness.[10] In this milieu, civil rights activists
brought new cases challenging school segregation—and for the first
time in American history, social research made the difference.

For it was just such research that enabled the Supreme Court to find
the "separate but equal" doctrine flawed and unconstitutional. In the
lower courts, lawyers for the Negro plaintiffs in *Brown* (and three other
cases considered at the same time by the Supreme Court) had called
over forty social scientists and professional educators as expert witnesses; in addition, the appellants' brief to the Supreme Court included an appendix by thirty-two social scientists. Reviewing this
material, the Court concluded that segregated education, even if
schools were equal in every way, created a sense of inferiority in the
Negro children; this harmed their motivation to learn and retarded
their intellectual development, thus depriving them of equal rights, a
finding that the Court said "is amply supported by modern authority."

Citing such authority in a footnote, the decision named six social-
science studies, primarily of an experimental nature, plus *An American Dilemma*. Leading the list and offering the most specific experimental evidence for the decision was a study made in 1950 by the
Negro psychologist Kenneth Clark.

Clark had asked 253 Negro children, aged 3 through 7, to choose
the "nice" doll, the "bad" doll, the doll they liked best, and so on,
from a group of four dolls identical except that two were white and had
blonde hair, two were brown and had black hair. Most of the Negro
children had rejected the brown dolls. (A subsequent study showed
that most white children liked and chose white dolls.) Clark concluded
that racial segregation caused Negro children, even at an early age, to
suffer from low self-esteem and hostility toward themselves.[11] Chief
Justice Warren applied such findings to the case in hand in decisive
and succinct words: "We conclude that in the field of public education

the doctrine of 'separate but equal' has no place. Separate educational facilities are inherently unequal."

But while *Brown* v. *Board of Education* said that laws requiring segregated schools must be struck down, it did not say how rapidly desegregation was to proceed, much less by what means (a matter on which the social scientists had little concrete information). A year later, therefore, in another unanimous decision, the Court ordered desegregation to proceed "with all deliberate speed."[12] It was an unfortunately vague phrase that left room for all sorts of foot-dragging. At first, scattered counties and a few large cities in border states began to desegregate their schools, but then southern resistance stiffened and desegregation came to a standstill. Ten years after *Brown*, only 1.2 percent of Negro public school students in the Deep South, and less than 10 percent in the entire South including border states, were attending schools with whites.[13]

By that time, the civil rights movement had gotten under way, and in March 1963, to highlight the failure of the courts in the South to carry out the intent of *Brown*, a quarter of a million persons—the most impressive protest meeting in American history—marched on Washington. In response, Congress passed the Civil Rights Act of 1964, the strongest such act since Reconstruction. The Act created mechanisms to combat a number of forms of racial discrimination; in the case of school segregation, it directed that federal funds be withheld from localities that intentionally maintained segregated schools.

To aid policy-makers in putting that directive into effect, Section 402 of the Act sought to establish the extent of such segregation by ordering the Office of Education to conduct a survey and report back within two years on the lack of availability of equal educational opportunities, by reason of race, color, religion, or national origin, in public schools and institutions of higher learning throughout the nation.

Such a survey would be research directed at a specific problem and intended to assist the federal government in carrying out its policies regarding that problem. It would be, in a word, policy research—not only applied but motivated by a view of the desired state of affairs—an undertaking very different from the basic and disinterested research that had long been, and to a large extent still was, the preferred model in social science.

"Hey, Look at This!"

A number of Coleman's fellow sociologists had told him that the education survey simply couldn't be done in the sixteen months available. When he took on the job, his view was that it *had* to be done in that time and so it *would* be. Although soft-spoken and seemingly easygoing, he is an uncommonly energetic and dogged laborer; one colleague calls him "an extremely industrious fellow," another a "voracious" worker. It is not unusual for Coleman, when caught up in some research task, to keep going at night long after his wife and children have gone to bed, stopping only when warned by the first hint of dawn that barely an hour or so is left for sleeping.

He himself ascribes this industriousness to his fascination with his subject. Having majored in chemistry in college, he worked for Eastman Kodak for two years but was troubled by the fact that he simply didn't think about his work after five o'clock. "I wanted to do something that would occupy me so intensely that I couldn't think of anything else," he says. Belatedly, it seemed to him that sociology might have been the right choice. Since he'd saved some money and his wife worked, he was able to quit his job and go to graduate school at Columbia University. "In a sense," he says, "my life began when I started at Columbia. From that day, I've been thinking about my work after five o'clock."

After agreeing to direct the education survey, Coleman's first order of business was planning. In part, this consisted of solo brainstorming: For weeks, at all hours of day and night, he scrawled semi-legible notes on sheets of lined yellow paper that accumulated in drifts on every surface in his office (he is not a tidy man). These jottings captured his thoughts about every aspect of the survey—topics to explore, questions to ask, statistical methods to use, ways to gather a reasonably representative sample of schools and students, and many other considerations.

More formally, he held many planning sessions at the Office of Education with Alexander Mood, various OE staffers (some two dozen of whom were assigned to his project), and teams of outside contractors, including sociologists, lawyers, statisticians, and educators. He shuttled constantly between his home in Baltimore, the OE in Washington, and the offices of advisers and contractors in several other cities. One of his more frequent ports of call was Princeton, where he met with researchers of Educational Testing Service, which he and Mood had selected as their principal contractor. ETS would send out, receive, and process the materials to be used, a staggering task: Well over 500,000 students would complete a battery of questionnaires and tests (verbally at the lower grades, with teachers recording the answers, and in writing at higher grades), and over 70,000 teachers and 1,000 principals would fill out lengthy questionnaires.[14]

Much of the planning, although complicated, was straightforward and presented no unusual problems. Deciding what information to gather was no great challenge to Coleman and the other social scientists on the project: It would, of course, include basic demographic data about the students such as race, family income, and their parents' educational background; a number of significant parameters about the schools they went to (money spent per student, size of classes, teachers' training, and the size of the library, among others); and, of course, the crucial issue—how well the students did in schools of varying levels of merit.

This last point, however, posed a knotty philosophic problem. Congress had ordered a survey to measure the extent of "inequality of educational opportunity" but had not defined the term. It could mean schools that had unequal resources; this is known as inequality of educational "input." But it could also mean schools that, despite apparent equality of resources, produced unequal levels of achievement; this is inequality of educational "output."

Some members of Congress had indicated that they thought input was the essential indicator, while others had favored using output. Coleman and his staff therefore decided to investigate both matters, but they considered output the more relevant: The critical issue was whether, even in comparable schools, black students benefited as much from their schooling as white students. If not, something about the input of those schools differed systematically for blacks and whites and represented a subtler and possibly more pervasive kind of inequality than that of obvious differences in school resources.

Aside from this problem, most of the preliminary work was routine. Devising questionnaires and choosing tests were old, well-known tasks with half a century of accumulated experience to draw on; moreover, ETS had a battery of proven test materials to choose from. Selecting schools and students who would make up a sample representative of the country was a complex but familiar task; social scientists and statisticians had been developing survey methodology for thirty years, particularly those aspects that had to do with sampling technique. Contacting those schools, though onerous, was only a matter of paperwork: In June and July the OE staff churned out thousands of letters to school officials and superintendents citing the Civil Rights Act of 1964 and asking their cooperation in having the tests and questionnaires completed and returned.

What was not routine, and deeply distressing to Coleman and his staff, was the refusal of many school officials and superintendents to cooperate. (They were emboldened to do so by the fact that Commissioner Keppel had not been authorized by Congress to penalize any school system that failed to participate, if asked.)

The highest rate of refusal was, of course, in the South, which was even then resisting the desegregation efforts of the Johnson Administration. Many southern cities and schools, and the entire state of Florida, flatly declined to play a part in the survey. More surprisingly, a number of nonsouthern school districts and entire large cities— including Los Angeles and Chicago—proved refractory. Some superintendents feared that comparisons would make their schools look bad; some district officials said that the information they were being asked for might be subpoenaed and used against them by civil rights groups; in San Francisco and certain other cities, school boards resisted on the specious ground that asking the students' race was objectionable and created tension where none existed; and in Cincinnati and some other cities, minority groups and libertarians strongly objected to such "intrusive" questions as, "Who is now acting as your father?"[15]

Coleman telephoned or visited a good many resistant school officials, trying both to reassure them and to point out how crucial it was that the survey be based on a sample undistorted by a high refusal rate. But he loathed doing so and recalls finding it "enormously difficult":

It's very hard to ask people to do something that's a lot of trouble, gives them no benefit whatever—and may work against them. It's the worst part of doing survey research. I'd go around pleading with superintendents and officials and they'd just sit there saying no, and I'd get knots in my stomach and be unable to sleep at night. I *hated* it.

Los Angeles was a real blow. I flew out there and talked to them but it was no good. The survey asked sensitive questions and was done with a fairly heavy hand, and they felt it was too intrusive, and wouldn't cooperate. Neither would a number of other cities at first, though some did come around. In the end, we managed to get participation ranging from not quite two-thirds in the non-metropolitan South and Southwest to over four-fifths in the non-metropolitan North and West. Overall, about 30 per cent of the schools selected didn't participate, leaving us with a somewhat biased sample.

But we used a number of standard techniques to reweight the sample so as to make it representative according to region and rural-urban location. For instance, in California, we drew extra schools from elsewhere in the state that were approximately the same in student composition and other factors as the missing L.A. schools. Because we were going to make statements about areas, not localities, the refusals weren't as damaging as they might have been. Still, it left open a question of possible bias in the sample, and our results wouldn't be totally representative of the nation's schools.

In late September 1965, teachers in 4,000 schools throughout the country administered the survey's tests and questionnaires to over 632,000 students (about 5 percent of the nation's public-school population) selected by the sampling procedure from the 1st, 3rd, 6th, 9th, and 12th grades. Within a short time, completed tests and questionnaires were arriving by the carload at the ETS offices in Princeton; there, staff workers fed them into optical scanners which read the answers and transferred the data to magnetic tapes for the computers. Compared with the computers of today, those of 1965 were huge, slow, and of limited capacity, so ETS—whose own machine was unable to handle so big a job—rented time on two others in New York belonging to IBM, and one in Paramus, New Jersey, belonging to ITT.

Throughout the winter and spring, Coleman and Albert Beaton, the head ETS researcher on the project, spent many interminable days in one computer room or another. Generally they would arrive at 7 or 8 A.M. to punch out control cards that told the computer what procedures to perform. Depending on whether or not there was a queue of other researchers, they might then have to wait as much as a couple of hours for their tapes to be installed and run. The actual run, once it began, took something like fifteen minutes, though it felt like hours as they fidgeted around waiting for the results to pour out.

When the printer began to clatter, they snatched what they could of the oracular stream of paper issuing from its mouth and hurried to a table in some corner, where they pored over the numbers as if studying a kind of Rosetta Stone for the key to mysteries. Then they started all over again with another and different run. Only grudgingly did they interrupt their work after many hours for such mundane needs as going to the toilet or gulping down a hamburger, and not until midnight or later did they head homeward bleary-eyed.

Those endless days were, nonetheless, memorable. Like an archaeological dig, they consisted of long hours of tedium transformed by occasional high moments of exciting discovery. Sometimes this would be simply proof of their hypotheses about the effect of segregation on Negro children's ability to learn. The data showed, for instance, that at the first-grade level in every region of the country, Negro children scored distinctly lower on the average than white children in verbal ability, the most broadly indicative test included in the survey. In terms of percentiles—an individual's or group's standing in relation to the whole population—Negro children were 30 points below whites. But schooling did nothing to narrow the gap; quite the contrary, in many regions Negro children slipped further behind white ones as they proceeded through school. The decline was the greatest in the totally segregated, nonurban South, where by 12th grade Negroes averaged 40 percentile points below whites. In contrast, there was hardly any slippage in city schools in the North, Midwest, or West.[16]

Far more exciting were those moments in the computer room when numbers crawling out of the printer contradicted widespread beliefs and expectations. Beaton, recently thinking back on that time, said, "The data would come up, and we'd pull off the paper and look at it, and Jim Coleman or someone else would point to something and cry out, 'Hey!—hey, look at this!' What a good feeling that was—working under such tremendous stress, doing something we all felt was so important, and finding things that made us shout, 'Eureka!' "

One of the findings that caused Coleman and others to make such an outcry directly refuted one of Coleman's confident predictions. Everyone who knew anything about public-school education was sure that segregated schools for Negro children were greatly inferior to those for whites and that the South made only a pretense of abiding by the separate-but-equal doctrine; Myrdal, in 1944, had amply documented this.[17] Liberal whites and Negro activists were opposed to school segregation not only on moral principle but on the ground that all-Negro schools, being impoverished, provided definitely inferior education. As Coleman himself, while waiting for the survey results to come in, said to a reporter for the *Southern Education Report*, "The study will show the difference in the quality of schools that the average Negro child and the average white child are exposed to. You know yourself that the difference is going to be striking."[18]

Time and again, however, the computer runs surprised him by showing that this simply was no longer so. True, in a few respects Negro schools in the South were less well equipped than white schools; outside the cities, for example, 76 percent of Negro elementary schools but 94 percent of white elementary schools had enough textbooks, and at the secondary level there were four library books per student in Negro schools against over six in white schools. But in most respects Negro schools in the South were not much different from the white ones. Far greater differences existed between city schools and noncity schools, or between schools in the South as a whole and those in other regions.[19]

This was sure to be a highly controversial finding, since it was the very opposite of what the proponents of the Civil Rights Act of 1964 expected the survey to show. Yet Coleman, far from being discomfited by the finding, was excited by it. Any discovery produced by social research that controverts received wisdom—even one that seems negative and undesirable—galvanizes him, he says, because it holds out the possibility of a clearer vision, a better understanding of reality. But of course an unexpected finding is only a conundrum until one satisfactorily explains it. As Coleman says,

I had expected to find large differences between the school resources available to white children and those available to black children in each part of the country. When the data showed that the differences were quite small, I was puzzled and intrigued. Then the question I had to ask myself was, "What could account for the difference in outcome? If the differences in the inputs provided by the schools aren't the answer, what is?" That seemed to me a most important question and one that might lead to a better understanding of the problem.

To look for that better answer, Coleman, a mathematical sociologist, used a statistical tool called "regression analysis," a way of mathematically isolating the effect of each factor when a mass of factors together produce a result.

The differences between Negro and white children's scores in the survey could be due to many things other than the minor variations in what the schools within each area had to offer. One such factor might be the family's economic level; another, the parents' education; another, the amount of reading material in the home; and still others, the number of siblings in the family, the child's view of his or her chances in life, the proportion of whites and blacks in the school, and so on. To find out how much any one such factor contributed to the end result, Coleman had to "hold constant" all the other important factors—that is, mathematically set them aside.

The ideal way to conduct a scientific experiment is by means of what the philosopher J. S. Mill called "the method of single difference." One sets up two test tubes, say, each containing equal amounts of identical material under identical conditions; then one adds a measured amount of a reagent to one of the two tubes. If a difference appears, it can only be due to that reagent.

In all of Coleman's mountains of data, however, there was nothing like such an experiment: Each child's experience was the result of a unique mixture of multiple influences over which the researchers exercised no control. But if each child's case was set down, with all the details, on a card, one could sort out the cards, picking out all those alike in some one characteristic such as number of siblings; this is called "holding constant" the number of siblings, or looking only at cases that are alike in that particular respect and so excluding any differences due to it.

Next, one could select from this pile those cards also alike in a second respect—children who not only had the same number of siblings but also came from families with the same income. Eventually, one might arrive at a small pile of cards which were the same in—that is, "held constant"—every one of dozens of factors except the one being studied at the moment, such as the proportions of white and black children in the school. At that point, the difference between children's school achievement would be due to that one remaining factor.

(Or would be if one could assume that because that factor and differences in school achievement were correlated—varied together, to some extent—one was the cause of the other. But since this was not an experiment over which the researcher had exercised total control, it might be that some other factor, unmeasured and not accounted for in the sorting process, was actually the cause of *both*. Or that still other unmeasured factors were the real reason Negro children in all-Negro schools did so poorly: Perhaps, for instance, their preschool social experiences in areas practicing segregation had stunted them, while in areas where schools were integrated Negro children had rather better preschool experiences. As we saw in chapter 1, human beings and social behavior are so complex that there are almost bound to be unmeasured factors that may play some part in the result; this is why regression analysis, despite its analytic power, is inferior to evidence obtained by means of controlled experiments.)

Card-sorting is not a practical method when dealing with large volumes of data or numerous factors; regression analysis achieves the same end mathematically by constructing equations in which the various factors to be held constant are entered one by one and numerically manipulated. From the raw data, Coleman and his coworkers separated out some 30 of the potentially most important factors and entered each one into the equation (every time they examined a different factor, it meant constructing a somewhat different equation), and then computed the effect due to the one factor not held constant.[20] The whole procedure would have been impossible, at least on the scale carried out in this survey, before the computer era.

Again, this took place in day-long sessions in computer rooms, with the computer being instructed to juggle its millions of pieces of information according to a particular regression equation. Now, even more than before, the sessions were punctuated by exclamations of the "Hey-look-at-this!" genre, for time and again the chattering printer churned out tables of numbers that cast grave doubt on favorite beliefs of the educational establishment and pointed to quite unsuspected reasons for the failure of Negro students to do as well in school as whites.

One such finding was that rather little of the gap between Negro and white school achievement was attributable to differences in school facilities; within any one school, there was a far wider range of achievement among the students than there was between the total student bodies of different schools. The researchers stared at each other incredulously. Was it possible that what every reasonable person knew wasn't really so? That better buildings, better libraries, a richer curriculum, more books, and better-paid teachers weren't the major factors in turning out higher-achieving students? Yet the data showed that while these factors did make a difference, they were far less powerful than certain others that had nothing to do with school facilities.

Of these, one of the most striking was the makeup of the student body: A student's fellow students had a greater effect on his or her school achievement than any other school factor. For one thing, the greater the proportion of white students in a school, the higher the achievement of all the children in that school—including the Negroes. The effect occurred in schools with poor resources and in those with good ones, so it wasn't the school's own input that made the difference but the input due to the student body.

This seemed to provide the first large-scale scientific evidence for the benefits of desegregation, but Coleman's microscopic analysis showed that the answer was not that simple. Most Negro students came from poor and educationally deprived families, while most white students came from better-off and better-educated families; thus, economic status, rather than race, was the most significant factor. As Coleman later wrote in the report of the survey:

The higher achievement of all racial and ethnic groups in schools with greater proportions of white students is largely, perhaps wholly, related to effects associated with the student body's educational background and aspirations. This means that the apparently beneficial effect of a student body with a high proportion of white students comes not from racial composition per se, but from the better educational background and higher educational aspirations that are, on the average, found among white students.[21]

Yet this emphasis on socioeconomic factors rather than race did not imply that racial integration was unimportant. On the contrary, while the intellectual skills and aspirations of Negro students were strongly dependent on the socioeconomic status of their fellow students, this in turn was strongly correlated with race. Thus, in effect it was desegregation that brought about the kind of mix that benefited Negro students, at least when the whites were in the majority.

By spring Coleman could no longer spare the time to travel to the computers and wait upon the deliberating machinery to yield answers to his questions. So much had yet to be done and so little time remained to do it in that he decided to go into seclusion, sequestering himself for more than a week in a motel room in Washington near the OE. There he studied printouts sent daily by Greyhound bus from New York and Paramus and brought to his door by OE messengers; these provided him with answers to questions that he phoned in several times a day to Beaton at ETS. As he recalls this period:

I sat in that room day after day, working around the clock and never seeing anyone but the people who brought me printouts or took my handwritten pages to the OE to be typed up or brought me food from the local send-out place. Every morning I'd call Al Beaton to tell him what I wanted run, and when the figures arrived later that day, I'd study them and see what the next questions were that I needed to ask. I was looking for missing links and finding them, one by one.

It was a very exciting period. I'd be trying to write up what I'd found and get things to come clear, and I'd get to a point where something didn't fit. I'd call for a different run and when the figures came, I'd carry the analysis further and eventually it would become clear. I'd feel a moment of exhilaration, and then I'd go on until, again, something else wouldn't come clear or there would be another missing link, and so on.

It was a kind of dialogue with myself, the computer being an extension of my pad and pencil. And while it was a very solitary process, the moments of discovery made it immensely exciting.

It is clear that Coleman looks back on his days in the motel room as one of the high points of his life.

After the analytic period came the writing up of the findings and the preparation of the report's many tables and charts, a job that would have taken a year or two had Coleman tried to do it by himself. But with less than three months left, it had to be an all-out collective effort. Mood wrote some of the most technical statistical material, aided by a consultant, John Tukey, while Coleman wrote a lengthy section on the factors related to student achievement—the highly controversial policy-related issues. A number of other people, working under his supervision, produced chapters dealing with the survey methods and marshaling huge amounts of data. Throughout, the findings were couched in technical language and the policy implications left largely unstated; this was, after all, a scientific report, not a political manifesto. For the benefit of the press and Congress, there was to be a summary chapter offering the major findings and conclusions in simplified form. This would probably be the only part of the report that ever became widely known; in consequence, a fierce, highly charged fight went on about it within the OE for many weeks.

One faction was led by two lawyers in the Department of Health, Education, and Welfare, David Seeley and Howard Nemerovsky, who had been part of the survey project from its beginning. Both were civil rights activists and deeply committed to federal efforts to achieve school desegregation. Coleman's results, which they heard about from Mood at staff meetings, seemed to them off the mark and dangerous to the goal of the survey. [22]

Seeley compaigned against the survey report as it was taking shape, vehemently declaring at one OE executive board meeting that it was likely to "bring great distress upon the Office of Education. . . . Segregation statistics are buried with a mass of other factors. . . . Negro and white differences should be stressed throughout. . . . The main conclusion of the report . . . instead of the most important messages outlined above, [seems to be] that school characteristics have very little to do with pupil achievement."[23]

As a result of efforts by Seeley, Nemerovsky, and others, the first draft of the summary, written by an outsider hired for the purpose, ignored most of Coleman's findings and concentrated on the effects of segregation on educational input, relying chiefly on a few small-scale studies begun by Seeley before the national survey got under way. Coleman and Mood read it and were outraged; Coleman called it a travesty of the facts. They protested strongly to the new Commissioner of Education, Harold Howe (who had replaced Keppel in December), and got the draft scrapped. Mood then wrote a summary himself, taking a scientific and statistical approach to the realities uncovered by the survey. The activists fought back until this version, too, was set aside. [24]

A third version, written by Helen Rowan, a long-time editor, was something of a compromise, but touched only lightly on Coleman's most controversial findings and gave most of its space to the extent of segregation and the poor achievement of Negro students. (Harvard political scientist—later Senator—Daniel P. Moynihan said, after closely studying the full report, that the summary "withheld from all but the cognoscenti any suggestion that major, and in effect, heretical findings had appeared."[25]) But Coleman and Mood settled for this third version of the summary; Coleman, in fact, later wrote that he was glad that the summary had become the focus of the struggle:

I . . . saw the concentration of political attention on the summary as a welcome diversion, reducing the possibility of political interference in the main body of the report. . . . No political attention at all was given to the main body of the report, and it passed unchanged by political review. . . . [Since section] 3.2 had important analytical conclusions, [I was] quite content that the controversy was not surrounding it.[26]

Commissioner Howe knew there was trouble afoot but was far too busy handling OE desegregation efforts to pay much attention to the controversy. His present recollections of that period:

I heard that there were things in Coleman's report that were different from what was expected and that there would be some problems connected with it. The federal government was moving, through Title I of the Elementary and Secondary Education Act, to improve the inputs to minority children—and here was Coleman seeming to question that strategy.

As for desegregating the schools, his findings clearly showed that low income imposes a learning handicap on kids—but how these findings would provide a basis for desegregation was muddy to me at the time, and still is. I tried to get a clear answer from Coleman, but there were some elements in his report that substantiated our government education programs and desegregation activity, and others that did not and even seemed to question some of them.

The report had to be submitted by July 2nd, according to the Act, and we needed every day, so we scheduled the release of the summary and a press conference for the last possible moment—the Friday before the July Fourth weekend. As a result, it was very lightly attended and the report got little publicity. We didn't plan it that way, but in fact I was delighted, because we didn't really understand the implications of it. Later on, a reporter said to me, "You seemed to be uncomfortable, and you never seem that way at other press conferences. Why were you?" I said, "I was uncomfortable because I didn't know what the hell I was talking about."

Coleman, after so many months of high-pressure work, exciting discoveries, politics-versus-science infighting, and strenuous efforts to meet the deadline, found the completion of the report an anticlimax and a letdown. He felt the import of the press conference had been that "the report contained little that was not already known and that there was nothing special to be made of the results."[27]

The immense tome, 737 large, two-column pages long, was entitled *Equality of Educational Opportunity* and bore Coleman's name as principal author and the names of six other people as coauthors, but almost from the start it was generally known as "the Coleman Report," and, being endlessly praised, attacked, cited, and rebutted, made Coleman's name something of a household word. But when the summary was first released, none of that was the case. The press conference came and went, and nothing happened. The book itself appeared a few weeks after the press conference, and still all was quiet on the front. Shortly thereafter Coleman left for London to spend a year on a Guggenheim Fellowship and tried, without much success, to put the whole thing out of mind; it seemed to him that if the objective scientific discoveries yielded by a piece of policy research didn't show what the makers of policy wanted it to, it was simply buried. The whole thing hardly seemed to have been worth the effort.

A Special Kind of Science

The findings of social research, especially when they have policy implications, are far more likely than those of the natural sciences to be ignored, disputed, or tendentiously interpreted. The obvious reason is that such knowledge often threatens the position of dominant groups and lends strength to those they dominate. But there is a subtler and perhaps more important reason: Social research yields knowledge that is necessarily less objective and more debatable than that of the natural sciences, for it deals not only with observable reality (actual events) but subjective reality (what those events mean to the people involved— and to observers of their behavior).

Divorce, for example, is an objective reality, but in some times and places it has been disgraceful and stigmatizing behavior and in others acceptable and even praiseworthy, while to outside observers, according to their philosophic outlook, it is a symptom of either breakdown or adaptation in the marriage system. School segregation, similarly, is objectively real, but what is more significant than separate buildings and resources, according to the Coleman data, is the inner experience it engenders in Negro students; the data revealing this, however, meant one thing to Coleman and quite another to the civil rights activists in HEW and OE.

Early in this century, Max Weber in Germany and William Graham Sumner in America argued against such subjectivity in sociological research: If sociology was to become a true science, comparable to such disciplines as physics and chemistry, it would have to be "value-free." Until then, much social research had been anything but that: Early social researchers, for instance, assuming monogamy to be the highest form of male-female relationship, described the sexual and marital customs of polygamous peoples in pejorative terms. Weber and Sumner said that sociologists should rigorously isolate their professional acts and mental processes from their own value systems and backgrounds; failure to do so would distort and invalidate their findings.[28] The same argument could be and later was applied to the other social sciences.

Ever since, many social researchers have subscribed to this doctrine, but some years ago a contrary view emerged: Social science could not and should not be value-free because the essence of social behavior is what it means to people. As the philosopher-sociologist Alfred Schutz pointed out:

There is an essential difference in the structure of the thought objects of mental constructs formed by the social sciences and those formed by the natural sciences. . . . The world of nature, as explored by the natural scientist, does not "mean" anything to the molecules, atoms, and electrons therein. The observational field of the social scientist, however, namely the social reality, has a specific meaning and relevance structure for the human beings living, acting, and thinking therein.[29]

A value-free social science is a science only of external happenings, not internal social realities; social researchers have to deal with the meaning of behavior to the people involved in it.[30] But to accept that people's interpretation as the correct one is to be in effect a convert to their belief system; the task of the social scientist is to interpret *both* the behavior and its indigenous meaning in the light of social-science concepts. Even those researchers who gather purely statistical data have to supply social-science meaning to them: As John M. Johnson writes in *Doing Field Research*, "Statistical measures of social existence are highly truncated accounts. They clearly do not speak for themselves . . . they require a perspective for their interpretation."[31]

Thus, in order to study a social phenomenon scientifically, researchers have to deal with meanings—not just the one it has for the people involved in it, but the one it has for social scientists themselves. Yet the abstract concepts of social science, as Peter Berger and Hansfried Kellner point out in *Sociology Reinterpreted*, are not "real" but are "artificially" devised for specific cognitive purposes.[32] "Bureaucracy," "conformity," and "correlation," for instance, are not actual entities but abstract notions that enable the social scientist to think analytically about the realities that do exist.

Still, Berger and Kellner argue, science—even social science—can transcend its own cultural biases and know reality in an objective fashion: The very concept of objectivity, though it is a cultural creation, liberates scientists from cultural bias, enabling them to monitor their own thinking in the same way that physicians may diagnose their own ailments.[33] But only within limits. If social scientists were routinely and naturally objective about their own thinking, why would they so often arrive at contradictory conclusions about the same phenomenon? How could there be such a thing as a conservative sociologist or, for that matter, a radical one? How could there be endless debates in the journals between those who report their research and others who reanalyze the data and arrive at different conclusions?

Even when social researchers are on guard against their own biases, at an unconscious level their values and personality traits may influence the kinds of questions they ask—and hence the kinds of answers they find. As a number of philosophers of science have pointed out, what one finds through research is in considerable part determined by the hypotheses by which one sets out to look for data.[34] Kenneth Clark, himself black and a civil rights activist—for whom the subject of segregation was simple and clear-cut—did a kind of research that yielded simple and clear-cut results. Coleman, white and liberal—but trained to see social phenomena in complex, multivariate, mathematical terms—did a kind of research that yielded complex and conflicting results.

Precisely because subjective meaning is involved in it, the knowledge obtained by social research does not, like that yielded by nuclear physics or astronomy, command acceptance by lay persons but often meets with their disdain, disbelief, or even organized hostility. Congressmen who would only rarely presume to dispute scientific reports on the nature of quarks or the age of the universe will freely attack social-science findings that challenge their beliefs or those of their constituents and will fight to cut off funds for the furtherance of such research.

At a 1982 conference on progress in the social sciences, Stanford University's Alex Inkeles argued that to a far greater extent than the natural sciences, the social sciences are severely constrained by the tendency of individuals and public authorities to respond to their findings in ideological terms. "Not only government and the public," he said, "but also the very members of the profession, war on certain ideas or lines of work purely on ideological grounds, while developing equally intense commitment to other ideologies."[35]

Yet sometimes social research is praised and used to promote social change in ways going far beyond anything anticipated or considered warranted by its author. Such turned out to be the case with the Coleman Report: Coleman's findings, though civil rights activists at HEW thought they failed to deal simply and unequivocally with the evils of segregation, were soon interpreted by desegregationists as doing just that and used effectively by them in a number of court cases.

None of this means that social science has no better claim to the truth than either traditional or radical beliefs concerning society or than common-sense wisdom. To the extent that one system of thought has greater explanatory and predictive power than another, it is a better representation of reality. Meteorology, imperfect as it may be, forecasts rain better than the *Farmer's Almanac* does; probability theory is a more reliable basis for shooting craps than hunches or lucky numbers; and social research, for all its inherent subjectivity, provides a sounder foundation for policy decisions than party loyalty or efforts to obtain divine guidance such as were made by Presidents Nixon and Carter.

Social research is still young and often deficient in rigor, but even when it is mature it will always be a special kind of science, lacking the detachment possible in the natural sciences. But those who scoff at or attack social-science knowledge that runs counter to their private opinions are the modern counterparts of those who, earlier, scorned or castigated the discoveries of Copernicus, Galileo, Vesalius, Darwin, and Freud, because they contradicted hallowed beliefs.

Finally, the knowledge yielded by social research may, for another reason, arouse the ire of some who have no political or scientific quarrel with it. People may feel threatened by social researchers who claim to know more about human nature and social behavior than they do, and who, they fear, may show them things they don't want to see. Senator Proxmire struck this very note when, attacking behavioral research on love, he said it might tell him something he would rather not know. He was voicing the same alarm Keats expressed, more eloquently, when he complained in *Lamia* that "philosophy" (by which he meant science)

> *will clip an Angel's wings,*
> *Conquer all mysteries by rule and line,*
> *Empty the haunted air, the gnoméd mine—*
> *Unweave a rainbow.*

Keats's fear of Newtonian physics was unwarranted; everyone understands, nowadays, how white light is refracted by droplets of water to form a spectrum of colors—and we seem to enjoy rainbows none the less for knowing.

"Not My Cup of Tea"

When Coleman took on the education survey because the idea of doing a major piece of policy research appealed to him, he expected to perform the research and leave the policy outcomes to others. As he later wrote, "The political digestion [of research results] . . . is not a task of the researcher, but of the whole political process. The research informs that process, but does no more."[36] It did not cross his mind that he himself would be drawn into the arena of public affairs to promote and justify the policy implications of his findings and that in doing so he would adopt the roles of public speaker, polemicist, witness at congressional hearings, and celebrity in the news.

If one were making a documentary TV show of Coleman's life as a social researcher, these sallies into alien territory and their rewards and penalties might be rendered by a series of still shots or brief film clips (some played by actors, perhaps, and mildly fictionalized, though true in the larger sense) such as these:

• Raw winter day in London; seen through window, Coleman, huddled by an electric heater and appropriately sweatered and sniffling, is reading a letter, his expression grim as he learns that his report has sunk from sight. The Office of Education's deliberately low-keyed press conference in July pleased OE staffers by producing only a small crop of bland news stories, followed by silence; the director of public information later noted, with a sense of achievement, "The report has created no public relations problems." Commissioner Howe did meet in October with a small group of scholars to get their advice as to what to do about the report, but they disagreed about the implications of its findings, and since then Howe and the OE have paid no attention to the Coleman Report.[37]

• Same setting; Coleman pounds his desk in frustration as he reads another letter telling him that the lawmakers, too, are ignoring his work. Congress, preparing to extend the Elementary and Secondary Education Act, has paid no attention to the implication of his findings that costly special school programs and compensatory education for underprivileged minority children may be unfruitful; none of the staff members of the House and Senate committees concerned with education have even read the report—perhaps because, aware of its implications, they want nothing to do with it.[38]

• Shots of magazine presses running, and of magazines on newsstands and coffee tables; camera closes in on articles about the Coleman Report in the *Saturday Evening Post, Saturday Review*, the *New Republic, Science, Fortune*, and various newspapers. Although Congress and the OE have had nothing to say about the Coleman Report, the public is hearing of it through the media—which interpret it as anything from a conservative attack on special educational programs for the underprivileged to a radical argument for an all-out assault on the social inequities, such as segregated housing and job discrimination, responsible for poor school achievement.

• A conference table at the Harvard Faculty Club in summer 1967; Coleman is addressing an elite seminar to which, this evening, some two dozen faculty members and doctoral candidates have come. It has been meeting weekly since last fall, when it was founded by Moynihan and social psychologist Thomas Pettigrew (who had been on Coleman's advisory committee). Both men felt that the Coleman Report was an extraordinarily important work, and that its data should be reanalyzed (carefully sifted through by sophisticated statistical methods for further valuable conclusions), and its policy implications set forth by social scientists rather than left to the vagaries of politics.[39] Coleman is deeply gratified that a number of reanalyses already made by seminar members have confirmed his conclusions, though somewhat modifying or expanding them. It is evident that word of his report is spreading throughout the intellectual community via articles, reports, and books generated at this table.

• A series of shots of Coleman looking incredulous, then dismayed, then furious, as he reads an article in *Journal of Human Resources* in 1968 (or a later one in *American Sociological Review*, or still others elsewhere) ripping his report to shreds on methodological grounds.[40]

Cut to scene of Coleman scribbling furiously in pencil on a lined yellow pad late at night. The critical article—by economists—faulted his way of doing regression analysis and claimed that a more refined method would have shown school factors to be important in student achievement. Coleman, normally a mild-mannered man, counterattacks furiously: The real problem, he writes, is that his findings undercut the economists' pet preconception—that schools are to be viewed in terms of "production," like factories, where output can be increased by added investment. We hear Coleman's voice reading his concluding riposte: "Bowles and Levin apparently do not like the way the results came out and would like to compensate for the statistical damage to their a priori preferences by tortuous reasoning. . . . In no case have they shown positive evidence to support their beliefs."[41]

(Many statisticians, however, see some merit in what Coleman's critics had to say. Regression equations are constructed on the basis of a number of necessary assumptions about how the variables interact; it is possible to disagree with those that Coleman made and to arrive at somewhat different conclusions about the relative impact of the variables.)

• Coleman in the witness chair in a Washington, D.C., courtroom; he is testifying in a civil rights case involving the schools. After hearing what he has to say about the educational benefit to a low-income black child of attending a school where most students are middle-class whites, Judge J. Skelly Wright orders the school board to integrate its facilities—to the degree possible in a system already 90 percent black—and to provide busing to take children from over-crowded black schools to less crowded, mainly white ones.[42] . . . Shots of courtrooms in Norfolk, Berkeley, Denver, and elsewhere in succeeding years; expert witnesses cite the Coleman Report's findings again and again in suits brought by the NAACP and others after Nixon's election makes the courts seem a likelier mechanism of school desegregation, both in the South and North, than the administration or Congress.[43]

• Quick shots of Coleman advising school boards and school superintendents who, along with the general public, are now beginning to call him "the father of busing." Although his report never mentioned that subject, Coleman himself is now publicly saying that busing (and other techniques) should be used to end both the dual school system of the South and the unofficial school segregation that exists in parts of the North due to segregated housing patterns.

(Busing was not actually fathered by Coleman, though his findings and statements helped it catch on. The major impetus, however, came from Supreme Court decisions in 1968 and 1969, ordering an immediate end to official southern segregation in view of the fact that the South had been finding ways to delay obeying the *Brown* decision ever since 1954.[44] Still another decision, in 1971, found that assigning children to schools by race to achieve integration—and busing them to the assigned schools—was constitutionally permissible.[45])

• Coleman, waiting outside the Oval Office of the White House with Moynihan; the latter is now, in 1970, a key adviser to President Nixon on urban affairs and has told him about the Coleman Report and its valuable findings. Two weeks ago, Nixon delivered a major education message, citing the "Equal Educational Opportunity Survey of 1966" (the Coleman Report) to justify a conservative policy on spending for schools and a more liberal one on desegregation, though he said nothing about how to carry out the recent Supreme Court decisions requiring immediate compliance with *Brown*. Coleman spoke out in response: In a front-page interview in the New York *Times* by staff writer Jack Rosenthal, headlined "School Expert Calls Integration Vital Aid," he praised Nixon for knowing and speaking of the report's findings on the educational benefits of integration, but criticized him for saying nothing about how to make it work. Within days, Moynihan phoned Coleman and asked him to come talk to the President.

Cut to a shot of Coleman talking to Nixon; the conference lasts several hours. Nixon's desegregation message of the following week restates the message of the Coleman report about the educational benefits of mixing the underprivileged with the privileged. Nixon proposes lending the government's strength and aid to enforce integration—but only in the South, to break up the dual school system maintained by local laws.[46] Coleman speaks out again: In a letter to the *Times*, he applauds and opposes Nixon's proposals in equal measure and urges him to extend federal support of integration plans to northern schools as well.

•   Coleman is seen calling regularly at the executive offices of the White House; despite his candor, he has been invited by presidential aide Leonard Garment to be a consultant to the new Cabinet Committee on Desegregation. He confers with Garment, Moynihan, and with Labor Secretary George P. Shultz and various other Cabinet members, helping them devise a bill that will not only enforce integration through the courts but give substantial economic support to those school districts facing a difficult task in complying with the Supreme Court's tight deadline.[47]

Cut to various shots of Coleman testifying about the proposed legislation at hearings of House and Senate committees concerned with education. Democrats, suspicious of the bill—and of Coleman— question him sharply, viewing him as an advocate of a Republican bill rather than as an impartial social scientist. He appears so often at such hearings this spring that we now see an inside page of the New York *Times*, where he is the subject of the "Man in the News" feature; the subhead labels him "BUSY ADVOCATE OF GAINS FOR NE-GROES."

(In the end, a bill emerges—the Emergency School Aid Act of 1970—earmarking $1.5 billion to aid schools that are undergoing court-ordered desegregation, chiefly in the South, and to assist voluntary plans to increase integration in the North. Coleman says it provides a carrot as well as a stick to get the South's cooperation. Moynihan more tartly—though approvingly—calls it a "bribe"; it was he who conceived of the bribe, which does, in fact, bring about rapid desegregation in the South.)[48]

· Closing shot: Coleman at his desk at Johns Hopkins, roughing out an article titled, "Clustering in N Dimensions by Use of a System of Forces," for the *Journal of Mathematical Sociology*. It is summer, 1970; he is no longer in the news, no longer an authority hearkened to by presidential advisers, Cabinet members, Representatives, Senators, and the President. An acquaintance drops by to chat and asks him, "Don't you miss it? The sense of power and all that?" Coleman smiles faintly and answers: "I didn't really like that role; I wasn't comfortable in it. It *was* gratifying to be able to play a part in giving my findings a practical outcome, but I'm a social scientist, not a politician. I like it when my *ideas* have power, but not when *I* do. I recognize that ideas often become effective only through that sort of personal involvement, but it's really not my cup of tea." He points to his penciled notes for the new article and says, *"This* is."

The Social Researcher as Social Leader

No one ever had a more exalted vision of the role of the social scientist than Auguste Comte, the founder of sociology. Nearly a century and a half ago, when he first advanced the notion of a science of society, Comte maintained that it could be as exact and objective a science as physics and that its practitioners would be the unchallenged leaders of society. For in a world in which science replaced religion as the source of truth, social scientists would be the new priesthood—people with special access to truth about social relationships, whose privileged knowledge would confer on them unquestioned authority and power.[49]

Nowadays, people who teach the social sciences treat this prediction as a curiosity and a personal quirk; Comte, after all, did have a mental breakdown in 1826 when he was 28, remained rather peculiar ever after, and got much more so as he grew older. But while modern social scientists make light of the early linkage of their profession to the priesthood, something of that flavor has clung to it down to this day. As recently as 1964, over a quarter of the members of the American Sociological Association, replying to a questionnaire survey sent out by Alvin W. Gouldner and Timothy Sprehe, said that at one time or another they had considered becoming clergymen.[50] Charles E. Lindblom and David K. Cohen of Yale's Institution for Social and Policy Studies maintain that social researchers often act as if their approach to social problems were the only rational and knowledge-based one and, with manifest bias and audacity, deprecate or ignore all alternative approaches to those problems.[51]

In contrast, other social researchers go to great pains to avoid any hint of practical problem-solving or public advocacy of policies based on their findings; it may be that they are deliberately trying to dissociate themselves from the role of Wise One/Leader and to identify themselves with that of Disinterested Searcher for Knowledge. In a secular society, these two roles—Comte notwithstanding—are somewhat contradictory; as Jerome E. Singer and David C. Glass point out in talking about applied social psychology, the advocate must seem positive and certain that he or she possesses the truth, while the investigator is a skeptic, always aware that there may be an alternative explanation.[52]

Berger and Kellner, similarly, say that advocacy and science call for different mental frames of reference; the sociologist cannot be a moral guide because when he acts as the latter he is not acting in his capacity as a sociologist.[53] The same applies to other social scientists: Consider the case of Kenneth Clark, whose own psychological research was so important in the *Brown* decision but who dismissed some of the awkward findings of the Coleman Report and other subsequent studies on moral, but distinctly unscientific, grounds: "Courts and political bodies," he said, "should decide questions of school spending and integration not on the basis of uncertain research findings, but on the basis of the constitutional and equity rights of human beings."[54]

The disparity between the roles of investigator and advocate makes for a curious paradox: A social researcher may understand a social problem better than anyone else, but if he publicly advocates policies based on that special knowledge, he has to be prepared for attacks by both the public and the academic community on his scientific reputation. Thus, from the right comes the disparagement not just of the political arguments of activist radical sociologists but of their research, while from the left comes the equivalent denigration of the studies of social scientists who have publicly spoken out for conservative causes. And from both sides come attacks on the scientific competence and integrity of an advocate of liberal policies such as Coleman, whose sociological objectivity and methodological skills were increasingly called in question by both laymen and scientists of varying shades of political opinion once he began to take the stump on behalf of policies derived from his survey findings.

Curiously, it seems to be chiefly *social* scientists who, in taking public positions on social matters, endanger their scientific reputations. No one belittles Noam Chomsky's psycholinguistic research because he is a political maverick; no one finds fault with William Shockley's physics because of his publicly stated views about the inferior intelligence of blacks. But social scientists, when they speak out for some value-based social policy, are thought to reveal that they are biased or slovenly in the practice of their profession.

There is, of course, a grain of common sense in this: When research and advocacy are in the same area, it is only fair to wonder whether the scientist has the cognitive discipline to be totally dispassionate while doing research on a matter about which, outside that role, he or she is thoroughly involved. It is neither common nor easy to be so. "All too often in sociology," Alex Inkeles has acerbically remarked, "simple moral conviction is seriously offered as a test of objective validity [and] presumed goodness is confused with truth."[55]

Yet the disciplined mind, Berger and Kellner argue, can shift from one "relevance structure" to another; the social scientist, even if drawn to a particular area of research by his or her personal values, can "bracket" those values while doing social science, consciously playing the part of the scientist rather than the advocate until the work is done, and only then shifting to the other role. That sort of bracketing of mental processes is routinely performed by many people every day— by opponents at chess or tennis who are foes while playing and friends afterward; by trial lawyers who are bitterly hostile to each other in court but cordial in the hallway outside; by husbands and wives who function as companions in front of the children, bracketing the perception of each other as sexual partners until an appropriate time.

If only because social scientists have the same rights as other citizens, they should be free to advocate social policies they believe in without having their professional integrity and competence challenged. But their fellow professionals and the public have a right to question whether, when social scientists publicly campaign in favor of social change, they are speaking as scientists or as citizens with a personal value system. Unfortunately, because their field of expertise concerns the very matters on which they are taking a public stand, criticism of their public position tends by a kind of osmosis to infiltrate and contaminate their scientific reputation. Comte's vision of a ruling social-science elite is the very reverse of the ways things work in a democracy: Social scientists, paradoxically, meet more resistance and run greater professional risks when they publicly advocate social change than do citizen activists or legislators with no scientific knowledge of society.

Asking Unpopular Questions

In the fall of 1974, William Gorham, president of the Urban Institute, a Washington-based foundation, asked Coleman to write a chapter on the state of urban education for a book the institute was preparing. Coleman readily accepted. He was well acquainted with the subject; besides, he had agreed to deliver a major address at the spring meeting of the American Educational Research Association and could use part of the chapter for that purpose. He began the work without any suspicion that he was about to stumble on a surprising discovery, or that making it known would embroil him in an intense professional and public controversy.

Coleman, who had moved to the University of Chicago, had been highly productive, out of the public eye, for the past four years; as if making up for lost time, he had written some forty articles, critiques, and chapters of books on a variety of sociological subjects. While little of this recent work dealt with desegregation, he remained interested in the subject, but had become increasingly concerned about the way it was proceeding outside the South.

The deliberately created dual school systems of the South had been rapidly replaced by integrated schools during 1970 and 1971 as a result of the Supreme Court's decisions and the money incentive offered to desegregating school systems by the Emergency School Act of 1970. Elsewhere, however, since school segregation was an unintended by-product of residential patterns, school officials were not under pressure from the high court or Congress to desegregate their systems. Civil rights advocates were therefore increasingly resorting to the courts—where commonly they cited Coleman Report data—and winning decisions that ordered school officials to mix children of different races in the schools even though this often necessitated busing many of them far from their homes.

These court-ordered measures were sometimes proving self-defeating; in a number of localities, busing was creating far more hostility and disruption than had been anticipated.[56] Evidence was mounting, moreover, that desegregation brought about in this way often failed to yield educational gains for black children: A number of recent studies, including one by Nancy St. John, a sociologist deeply committed to integration, had found that sometimes it had positive effects on black children, sometimes had none—and sometimes had negative ones.[57] The Coleman Report had made clear that what helped was a socioeconomic mix, not just a racial one, but the usual court-ordered formula ordered integration based on race alone; sometimes this achieved a socioeconomic mix and worked; sometimes it did not and failed.

Coleman himself had second thoughts about all this. "I began to think," he says, looking back, "that my 1966 report was being used to support programs that had negative consequences. School desegregation outside the South should have been carried out through the executive and legislative branches, not the courts—where it was aimed largely at symbolic success. The busing movement, as it had developed, was often counterproductive."

Coleman planned to cover four topics in the chapter, not by means of original research but by the reanalysis of existing data—the kind of rethinking and reworking of the figures in search of hidden relationships that the members of the Harvard seminar had done with his own 1966 survey results. During the fall and winter, he gathered material and wrote the chapter as promised, but was so intrigued by questions that reanalysis raised about one topic—segregation—that he kept reworking those data for many months.

Good raw material existed on the subject: From 1967 on, HEW's Office of Civil Rights had been collecting statistics on the racial distribution of students in the nation's schools. It was easy enough to see from the figures for the years 1967 to 1973 that segregation had been decreasing throughout the nation. But when Coleman broke down the figures in various ways, it became clear that the trend was not uniform; segregation had declined sharply in small to medium school districts (those in small cities, towns, and suburban areas) but rather little in the largest school districts (those in the centers of the largest cities).

He could have left it at that, but the goal of reanalysis is to find truths that lie below the surface. It is a somewhat arcane process, involving the use of a variety of statistical manipulations of the data for good and rational reasons, but also often for irrational ones—guesses, hunches, and unclear urges to simply *try* things. Reanalysis is thus akin to the kind of cognitive exploration familiar to inventors and discoverers and best described by the vernacular expression "messing around."

Coleman found himself wondering, for instance, how much additional exposure black children had to white classmates as a result of the decrease in segregation. To find out, he constructed an equation to extract that information from the data and discovered a paradox: While the percentages of largely white or largely black schools in most of the largest central cities had been decreasing—giving way to schools of mixed race—in over a third of these cities desegregation had not increased the average black child's contact with white schoolmates. In fact, in a quarter of these cities, there was a *decrease* in such exposure.[58]

At this point, Coleman began to feel something like the excitement an astronomer experiences when spotting a previously unreported nova. He wanted to present these findings at the upcoming AERA meeting, only weeks away. To enable himself to work with total concentration, he went by himself, in early spring, to the farm he owned in West Virginia; there, away from all distractions (there wasn't even a phone), he sat at the kitchen table with lined yellow pad, pencil, and pocket calculator, looking for an explanation of the paradox.

A curious relationship began to show up: As desegregation proceeded within central-city districts, a new kind of segregation was replacing it. Although busing and school assignment plans were making for less racial disparity among central-city schools, the proportion of blacks throughout such districts was rising, while the school districts outside the big cities were remaining highly white-segregated; thus, the racial disparity between central-city and suburban districts was increasing. [59] The crucial point—the question he had to ask, unpleasant as it was—was whether there was any connection between these factors: Could it be that the desegregation plans being put into effect in the large cities were actually *causing* some part of the decrease in white students?

"When I controlled for certain variables and punched in the data," Coleman recalls,

I found a very strong effect—an increase in desegregation was linked with a sharp decrease in the proportion of whites in the district. It was unmistakable. I knew I was on the track of something. I hadn't been looking for it at the outset—at that time, no right-thinking person would question the value of school desegregation. But the data were leading me to ask questions I suspected most social scientists would rather not ask, and to look for an answer— "white flight"—that they would rather not find.

Many conservatives, in opposing forcible desegregation in the cities, had said that it would cause many city-dwelling whites to move to the suburbs. Coleman now seemed to have some evidence of that—an ironic and bitter finding for one who had had such good reason to believe in integration. And who still did, even though it now appeared that when integration was brought about by official planning, it often produced resegregation on a larger basis, at least in large cities. Myrdal had hoped that Americans would soon resolve their internal dilemma, but apparently at the same time that they were telling pollsters they favored school integration, they were moving out of the central city if their children were forced to go to schools with large numbers of blacks.

To test his white-flight hypothesis, Coleman now performed a lengthy series of regression analyses involving a number of variables that were related to the shrinkage of the white student population: the size of the city, the number of children in the district, the proportion of blacks already in the schools, the degree of segregation, the region of the country, and so on. By holding constant different sets of these variables, he was able to calculate the "expected" loss of white students in any major city for the years 1968 to 1973, based on the movements of blacks into, and whites out of, large cities that had been going on for some years.

He then scrutinized the figures for each city to see whether in a year in which segregation dropped sharply (indicating official or court-ordered activity), there was an *additional* loss of whites above that expected.[60] In many cases, there was; indeed, he considered the results of his analysis, though still preliminary, so striking that he wrote down these conclusions in the draft of his AERA address:

It appears that the impact of desegregation, in these large cities, on whites' moving out of the central city is great. The governmental actions, reducing segregation within districts, provokes rather strong individual actions which partly offset that effect. . . . Insofar as one intended consequence of integration is an increase in achievement of black children, the intent is largely defeated.[61]

On April 2, Coleman delivered his address to a large AERA audience. It was an unorthodox and unwise thing to do: His findings were only preliminary, and it is considered professionally proper in the sciences to present such findings to one's peers first to get their critical appraisal, use it to improve and strengthen the work, and only then go public with the results. Coleman, having tasted the excitement of celebrity, seems to have yielded to a desire to make news—and paid dearly for doing so.

At first, however, his address drew little public attention. Then, a brief story about it in the Washington *Post* belatedly came to the attention of other reporters, one of whom, from the *National Ob-*

server, later interviewed him and wrote a piece, appearing on June 7, headlined, "A Scholar Who Inspired It Says . . . Busing Backfired."

The article ignited a controversy that blazed for a year and a half. It would probably have flared up in any case when the Urban Institute published a revised and more detailed version of the study by Coleman and two institute associates. But what made the controversy hotter than it need have been was Coleman's premature announcement of his findings—which, under fire from his critics, he considerably revised and strengthened in the published version, though by then the damage had been done. The Urban Institute document, titled "Trends in School Segregation, 1968–1973," listed three coauthors, but it was immediately and widely called "the second Coleman Report" or "Coleman II," and Coleman has been held directly accountable for it.

A complete record of the controversy would fill a book; a few scattered items will serve here to suggest the public and professional reactions to the second Coleman Report:

- In June 1975, two press conferences were held in New York to rebut Coleman's findings and the implications he had drawn from them. One featured statements by NAACP leaders Roy Wilkins and Nathaniel Jones, and by various white social scientists including, to Coleman's regret, Thomas Pettigrew, who with Daniel Moynihan had organized the Harvard seminar. At the other conference, called by a group of liberal social scientists, Kenneth Clark charged that Coleman was "part of an extremely sophisticated attempt . . . to evade the effects of the 1954 Brown decision."[62]
- An interview in the New York *Times* of July 11 by education writer Robert Reinhold found Coleman at fault on a number of technical points and made much of his apparent defection from the civil rights movement.
- The Detroit *Free Press* on August 19 ran a major article under the headline, "Sociologist's Busing Switch Based on Questionable Data." In it, education writer William Grant called Coleman's methods flawed and accused him of going far beyond his actual research findings to make "far-reaching statements about school integration and the courts."
- August 15: A symposium on desegregation and white flight, funded by the National Institute of Education, was held at the Brookings

Institution. Coleman was invited and attended, but was one against many: All of the numerous papers presented were rebuttals of his work.[63]

- Attacks on Coleman's data and his methodology appeared in *Educational Researcher, Phi Delta Kappan, Political Science Quarterly,* and, later, the *Harvard Educational Review.* The last of these, 53 pages long—almost unheard of for a critique—was by Pettigrew and a colleague; it found Coleman's new report riddled with "serious methodological and conceptual problems" and was intensely critical of Coleman himself for his "political opposition" to busing and his frequent public statements on behalf of his findings and his conclusions.[64]

- Over a period of some months Coleman testified in court and before House and Senate committees and subcommittees and presented his results before university symposia, the Massachusetts legislature, and professional groups. Senator Joseph Biden of Delaware, freely paraphrasing the gist of these appearances, fanned the flames higher: He was quoted in *TV News* and the *Congressional Record* as saying, "Professor Coleman, an educator, first suggested the possible benefits of busing in a 1966 report. Now in 1975 Coleman says, 'Guess what? I was wrong. Busing doesn't accomplish its goal.' "[65]

- In December 1975, the president of the American Sociological Association, Alfred McClung Lee, began a campaign to have the ASA's Committee on Professional Ethics and the ASA Council consider taking action against Coleman for what Lee regarded as unethical behavior—his revisions of his desegregation analysis and his public advocacy of his conclusions. As Lee wrote in a memo to all concerned, "It is my considered judgment that Professor Coleman deliberately used his public status and prestige as one of the most publicized American social scientists to mislead the American public into believing that his personal biases were supported by impeccable evidence." Letters, discussions, accusations, regrets flew back and forth among members of the ASA, and between Coleman, Lee, and their various supporters and opponents. After many months of activity, the Ethics Committee and the Council voted against considering the charges against Coleman; instead, the Council chose to hold a special plenary session on the busing controversy at its fall 1976 meeting in New York, with Coleman as a principal presenter. By then, a number of research reports were beginning to confirm

Coleman's unpopular findings; all the same, behind him on the wall when he spoke were posters plastered there by a group of activist students linking Coleman's name with swastikas. Ignoring them, he gave a careful formal presentation that was received with normal academic good manners by the large audience and the discussants on the panel.

With that, the furor began to subside. In perspective, the intensity of the debate cannot be accounted for by scientific disagreement. Coleman's critics disagreed with his choice of large cities, his regression equations, and the like, and some of these criticisms are widely held to have merit, but social researchers often disagree with their colleagues about such matters without attempting to destroy their reputation as researchers. Coleman, however, had violated the unwritten professional code by announcing his findings at a public forum before offering them to his colleagues for their study and criticism. Even that might not have drawn such fire if he had not been challenging a view popular among social scientists and expressive of some of their most deeply held values. They saw him as—and he was—an advocate, not only an investigator; the issue easily became confused, and it was easy for them not only to find his social views wrong-headed but his work as a researcher suspect.

In the years since then, however, the second Coleman Report, though flawed in some details, has been substantially confirmed by later studies of the effects of desegregation plans in large cities. Like many another piece of social research, it is an imperfect but significant contribution to the understanding of a complex social phenomenon.[66]

Coleman himself is unrepentant. Recently offering an apologia for the events connected with the second Coleman Report, he said,

It was disconcerting and upsetting to me. I was particularly distressed when Tom Pettigrew impugned my research capabilities and my values, and when Lee tried to have me censured by the ASA. I felt isolated from the sociological community. My friends were thinking, "My God, something's gone wrong with Coleman; he's gone off the deep end."

It's true that I'm guilty of not always going over results as much as I might, but I did rework my analysis for many months until it was truly robust. But that didn't help; most people involved in school desegregation were there because they wanted to aid the process, so when I came along with my results, they saw me as a turncoat.

But I *did* have those results, and I *had* to present them. There was real scientific worth to questioning policies that had been current, even if it seemed to go against what every right-minded person believed.

It was not that Coleman had turned against integration; to the present day he has continued to speak out in favor of cross-district integration on a voluntary basis, with special incentives to parents of both races and various economic classes to make it work. Rather, he had once again obeyed the emperor-has-no-clothes impulse to ask unpopular questions and acted upon his belief in the value of making unpopular findings known.

Unforeseeable Outcomes

The drama of the second Coleman Report lay in its having been written by Coleman himself. Had it been by any other social scientist, it would have been only one more proof that the well-thought-out behavior of human beings—including social scientists—often produces unintended results, a phenomenon nicely termed by Robert K. Merton some years ago "the unanticipated consequences of purposive social action."[67]

The paradoxical outcome of human intentions is, of course, a recurrent theme in history. The Roman emperors gave the proletariat bread and circuses to maintain social tranquillity, not anticipating that the gift would eventually enfeeble their people and lead to domestic instability. The empire-builders of the seventeenth and eighteenth centuries educated some of the natives they dominated, not suspecting that later the educated class would head the revolts that dismantled their empires. We Americans, in recent years, built a great interstate road system to improve travel among our cities, only to have it undermine those cities by enabling the middle class to live outside them.

But one might expect social scientists, understanding social processes better than most people, to see ahead more clearly than others, especially where the effects of their own work are concerned. They themselves do sometimes imagine that they have superior vision: Berger and Kellner, for instance, claim that "sociology gives one a constant awareness of the force of consequences, including and especially the force of (probable) unintended consequences. . . . Sociology, however tentatively, understands and can predict this ironical relation between motives and consequences."[68]

Perhaps so, where other people's behavior is concerned, but it cannot mean that sociologists understand and can predict the unintended consequences of their own behavior; how could results be "unintended" that they knew would happen? Besides, there is abundant evidence that social research often disturbs the phenomena it is dealing with and so partly invalidates its own findings. Panel surveys are a case in point: When the same people are interviewed about the same subject at regular intervals to observe changes in their health, income, or other matters, they tend to give somewhat different answers the second and subsequent times—even when objective records show that things have not changed—either because they know what to expect, or have thought the matter over, or have been changed in some other way by having been interviewed.[69] Social scientists may be more aware than other people that their own work is likely to have unintended results, but all they can predict is that whatever purposive social action they take will somewhat alter the forces they had reckoned with and to some degree deflect their aim.

The optimist might hope that as knowledge replaces ignorance, the unintended consequences of social research and social programs will be minimized, if not eliminated. But there will always be a new supply of unintended consequences—the product of increasing knowledge itself, for new knowledge, by extending human action, allows human beings to go beyond what they have seen and experienced until they stumble into areas in which they are again ignorant. Social scientists, though they may be particularly competent at predicting the outcomes of many social processes, therefore cannot fully foresee the consequences of their own research. Some recent instances:

- Latent behavior, invisible and beyond reckoning, may manifest itself only when social research produces a program that alters the social milieu. Gordon Allport, an eminent social psychologist, offered evidence in 1953 that increased close contact between whites and blacks diminishes white prejudice and benefits blacks psychologically; "contact theory," as this was called, was the premise of much of the reasoning in the *Brown v. Board of Education* decision and the Civil Rights Act of 1964. Yet as integration policies were put into effect, the milieu changed from the one Allport based his predictions on. Blacks, becoming prideful and defiant, ceased to see integration as their goal and began instead to aim at equal rights within a separatist framework. In many schools and colleges, blacks and whites went to the same classes but there was no reduction of prejudice or of mutual antipathy. The contact theory, once a valid predictor of behavior, was so no longer.[70]

- If the goals of a social program are not those of the people it is aimed at, they will find unanticipated ways to circumvent it; the end result may even be the opposite of the intended and predicted one. White flight from the major cities, resegregating the schools, was just such a paradoxical consequence of policies meant to decrease school segregation.

- Once the results of social research are made known, the researcher loses control of them; they become weapons in political debate, used or misused by various factions to serve their own purposes, often in ways the social scientist had neither expected nor wanted. Moynihan's 1965 study, *The Negro Family*, attributed the faulty development of many Negro children to the often broken and malfunctioning Negro family; the intent of the study, as liberals perceived, was to call for social programs meant to help those children. Black militants, however, labeled it a racist effort to blame blacks for their own failures and to absolve the white community of its responsibility; their hostility may have served the ends of black pride but undercut the study's usefulness.[71]

- Sometimes social research offers preliminary predictions about a program based on laboratory or special samples but is unable to study the actual phenomenon, since it will not exist until the program creates it. Yet the very fact that a phenomenon is generated by a program may make it different from the specimens that had been studied. As we will see in chapter 6, when poverty-level people in Seattle and Denver were experimentally given guaranteed annual incomes, most of them continued to work nearly as much as before. But methodologists Robert Ferber and Werner Z. Hirsch warn that local conditions may not prevail when a program goes national.[72] The Seattle and Denver effects might have been due in part to the American work ethic; if such a program were adopted nationally, the prevailing attitude toward work might conceivably change, with more of the poor being willing to take the money and quit working.

Every such unintended consequence, however, becomes a new datum to be understood; as Karl Popper has said, our ignorance grows along with our knowledge.[73] The comment may seem pessimistic; Lindblom and Cohen take it that way when, citing it, they add, "We suggest that the usual effect of PSI [professional social inquiry] is to raise new issues, stimulate new debate, and multiply the complexities of the social problem at hand."[74]

However, one can take Popper's remark to be profoundly encouraging: It is only when scientists know clearly what they don't know that they can intelligently explore the unknown. If so, then the unintended consequences of social research and policy will continually lead researchers to a fuller understanding of what caused them; they will not fail to foresee those consequences again. Yet no doubt they will press on beyond the boundaries of their knowledge, producing new unforeseen consequences—which, in turn, they will seek to analyze and understand.

Leitmotif

Coleman's life as a social researcher since the dying down of the controversy over his white-flight report has changed little; he still continues to be pulled in opposite directions.

On the one hand, he has invested much effort in academic sociology, producing over forty papers in the past half dozen years, among them theoretical efforts such as "A Theory of Revolt Within an Authority Structure" and methodological studies such as "Problems of Conceptualization and Measurement in Studying Policy Impacts."

On the other hand, he has continued to do applied research in education that has embroiled him in acrimonious debate. A few years ago he and two collaborators (Thomas Hoffer and Sally Kilgore, both of the University of Chicago) completed a study for the National Center for Educational Statistics that created a furor in educational circles, with Coleman, as principal author, getting most of the blame and praise. The NCES had conducted a survey of nearly 59,000 students in over 1,000 high schools and wanted the data analyzed. Coleman and his collaborators did so, producing a report called *Public and Private Schools* (later published by Basic Books as *High School Achievement: Public, Catholic, and Other Private Schools Compared*) in which were several inflammatory findings. One was that students in Catholic and other private schools score higher in achievement tests than students in public schools, in part because of differences in their backgrounds but in part because the private schools emphasize higher standards, discipline, homework, regular attendance, and the like. Another was that while there are far lower proportions of blacks in private schools than in public schools, segregation in the sense of schools that are chiefly white or black is less common than in the public schools.[75]

The debate among educators and sociologists was so heated, and many of them were so alarmed by what they took to be an attack on public education, that the *Harvard Educational Review* gave 64 pages of its November 1981 issue to seven critiques of the report and a response by Coleman and his colleagues; *Sociology of Education* did likewise with all 119 pages of its April/July 1982 issue. Predictably, most of the critiques attacked the study's methodology and reanalyzed its data, coming to different conclusions. Some even dismissed it as being not a work of research but a "policy argument"—a partisan effort to promote the use of vouchers or tuition tax credits for families that send their children to private schools.

Coleman replied like the boxer he used to be in college (as his flattened nose attests), counterpunching most fiercely when badly hit. After rebutting the points made in one critique, he characterized it as filled with "hyperbole, misstatements, and errors," and summed up, "Altogether, it is an excursion which careens from one mishap to another." For good measure, he delivered a roundhouse to the authors' motives: "The principal question is why so much affect rests on so little substance."[76]

In addition, he has continued to publicly advocate certain alternatives to court-ordered busing that he thinks would better serve the goals of desegregation. These include the establishment of "magnet schools" (schools offering special incentives to draw white children to largely black areas, and vice versa); parental choice of schools without regard to zoning; and busing—only for those who want it—across district lines to offset city-suburb segregation. Many civil rights leaders regard these proposals not as better methods of integration but as thinly disguised racism; Kenneth Clark has charged in the New York *Times* that those who urge such measures are actually foes of desegregation, who "directly contribute to the educational retardation of black children."[77]

Yet if one sees Coleman in his office or hears him speak at a professional seminar, the other side of him is very much in evidence. If asked about this latest controversy, he may sigh and speak wearily of the "motivated blindness" of his critics, but when the conversation shifts to what he is now working on—an ambitious theoretical effort that he has long dreamed of making and now is actually writing—his face lights up and he talks with a pride that he does not bother to hide.

This, not the education studies, is what I hope I'll be remembered for. The thing that has interested me intellectually most of all for twenty years is the question, "How can you develop a social theory if you start with the behavior of the rational person? How are the motivations and decisions of individuals transformed into mass social phenomena such as norms, social structures, or political decisions?" I'm working on a theory of "social action" in which I'm attempting to begin with individual premises but end with macrosocial implications.

What he has undertaken is a task comparable to working out a theory unifying the four forces of physics, for its aim is an explanation linking social forces as different from each other as that which binds the parts of a proton together is from that which holds billions of stars in swirling galaxies. If Coleman were to succeed, his wish would surely come true: He would be remembered for such an accomplishment long after his policy studies have become mere footnotes in history books.

3

SAMPLING SOCIAL REALITY

A Complex New Survey Measures the Impact of the Government's Social Programs on the American Family

"The Most Exciting Thing Going on in Social Science in the 1980s"

On Monday, October 3, 1983, in 175 localities all over America, 240 part-time survey interviewers, most of them middle-aged women, picked up heavy stacks of papers and set forth in their cars to start seeking out some 25,000 homes and asking personal questions of the strangers who lived in them.

Of itself, this was hardly unusual; in our research-oriented era many hundreds of local and national surveys and opinion polls are always under way in America. The government alone had 228 of them in progress on a typical recent day, and at least four times that many others were being conducted by or for academic and business groups.[1]

The one getting under way that Monday, however, the Survey of

Income and Program Participation (SIPP) conducted by the U.S. Bureau of the Census, was special. It would employ a new research instrument—a complicated questionnaire and a number of advanced procedures for extracting sense from the answers—that had been seven years in the making. It had been designed to elicit certain kinds of information vital to many large-scale government operations but which Americans are notoriously reluctant to talk about (especially to government representatives), namely, how much money they make, how much they have in savings and other assets, and how much they get from entitlement and welfare programs in cash, or in noncash benefits such as food stamps.

Over \$300 billion—a third of the national budget—was being disbursed each year in these programs, but no one in or out of government had any accurate idea which segments of the population were getting how much cash or other assistance, how many people received overlapping benefits, how many in need of particular benefits were not getting them, or what the impact of proposed changes in governing rules would be. For although each government program maintained figures about its own recipients, there was no way to assemble these separate tabulations into a composite social-economic portrait.

SIPP had been created expressly to provide answers to these questions. And much more: Since it would keep track for two and a half years of each individual, family, and household in the sample, it would provide the first longitudinal account of how changes in income and/or program benefits affect family formation and stability—one of the most important social issues of our time.

Not surprisingly, the small coterie of survey researchers who labored to create SIPP were and are enthusiasts; Charles Lininger, for one, an economist who directed developmental work on SIPP at HEW for three years, calls it "the most exciting thing going on in social science in the 1980s." But many onlookers in the social sciences are equally excited about SIPP's potential as a research resource for the study of contemporary social problems and of the effects of programs meant to remedy them. Joseph Duncan of Dun and Bradstreet, formerly top statistician in the Office of Management and Budget, has termed SIPP the most significant statistical survey in four decades, and economist Guy Orcutt of Yale University thinks its data will be the most important available in the 1980s for research on American families and individuals.[2]

Pilots, before they take off to fly cross-country, assemble the data they will need en route: a set of headings and flying times for each leg of the trip, predictions of the weather ahead, the radio frequencies to be monitored or contacted along the way, and so on. Congress, in contrast, often enacts a major new program and orders it aloft, only belatedly realizing that it did so without having gathered any flight information.

Such was the case with many of the Great Society programs created in the mid-1960s during the Johnson Administration to benefit poor, ailing, aged, unemployed, and undertrained adults, and children in families with inadequate income. As economist Martin H. David of the University of Wisconsin, a consultant to SIPP, says, "It wasn't until we had a proliferation of assistance programs that we realized we didn't know how many eligible people were out there, how many were simultaneously getting assistance from various programs, or how many weren't getting what we meant them to." Nor was there any technology that could provide those data. As Orcutt observed a few years ago, "Until the 1960s, the tools of analysis for assessing the potential costs and effects of welfare programs, and most other social programs, consisted of a few scraps of data, the back of an envelope, a sharp pencil, and an imaginative or foolhardy analyst."[3]

During the late 1960s and early 1970s the idea of a survey that could get at these complex questions was occurring simultaneously to a number of economists, demographers, program directors, and planners, some of them in HEW, which housed many of the new programs, others in the Bureau of the Census, which was being hounded for better information, and still others in the Office of Management and Budget (OMB), which keeps an eye on how well program money is being spent.

As Roger Herriot, a lanky man with a homespun, country-boy manner who was then in the Income Branch of the Census Bureau's Population Division and now heads that division, recalls, "We'd be sitting at lunch and we'd say, 'Goddammit, they're after us again for data on monthly income and who's getting multiple program benefits. How *can* we get a handle on that? Can we pull monthly figures out of

CPS* annual income data? Can we get program benefit data by expanding CPS? Or do we, maybe, need a wholly new income survey of some kind?' "

Joseph Duncan remembers comparable discussions at OMB: In particular, he recalls economist Bette Mahoney, a consultant to that body, arguing that the new social programs were giving millions of people noncash benefits—food, housing, and health care—that substantially altered the quality of life and the meaning of poverty but went unreported in CPS or elsewhere. An interagency committee set up by OMB produced a report suggesting that a new income survey survey was needed, but like many such committee reports it was read, filed, and forgotten.

What actually led to the development of the new survey, say many people who took part in it, were a number of unofficial and often impassioned conversations, chiefly among staff members of ASPE, the Office of the Assistant Secretary for Planning and Evaluation, at HEW. (Mrs. Mahoney had gone to work there in 1974 and begun actively advocating such a survey.) According to these participants, SIPP was collectively begotten in the hallways, lunchrooms, and lavatories of HEW, Census, and OMB somewhat as follows:

"We just *have* to collect much more comprehensive and specific income data than CPS provides."

"And more often than once a year. People forget the details over the course of a year, especially people who work irregularly or part-time."

"And we *must* try to measure noncash income. We don't know who's getting it or how it's affecting their lives."

*

"A person or a family can get benefits from three or four programs without our having any way of knowing about it."

"Or about people who deserve benefits but aren't getting them for some reason."

"The only answer is to ask everyone in a national sample to name all the programs they're getting anything from, and how much."

*

"A lot of low-income people have bad periods during the year when they need help, but these just don't show up in the annual CPS figures."

---

*CPS, or Current Population Survey, is a monthly sample survey of 66,000 households covering many topics; once a year, in its Annual Demographic Supplement, it includes a group of questions about income.

"We could add a few questions asking what their income was month by month and if they were ever out of work."

"But a lot of them don't keep records. They won't know. We need a new survey, taken every few months."

"That would take years to develop, and millions of dollars. We'd never get the money."

"But we might. They're begging for the data."

*

"We should look for short-term changes by repeating the survey every few months."

"Yes, but it shouldn't be a series of cross-sectionals. It ought to be a true longitudinal, using a panel. If we really want to see how changes in income and program benefits affect people, we should follow the same people over a period of years."

*

"Who should develop the new survey—Census?"

"No way. They're too stodgy, too inflexible. We'd be better off to do it ourselves in HEW—we've got good research people and we can afford to hire others."

"Okay, so we develop it—but then who takes it out into the field? Wouldn't Census be the obvious answer?"

"They're good at that, but they like to do things their own way. We might do better to contract it out."

So it went, during 1973 and 1974. Eventually the discussions assumed the mantle of respectability and took place within scheduled committee meetings at ASPE. But to transform the committee's plans into a reality required a good deal of diplomatic skirmishing and salesmanship. The outgoing and ebullient Mrs. Mahoney was ideal for that job.

"You don't just send the idea up to the Secretary of HEW," she says about the necessary maneuvering. "It might interfere with the research efforts of other HEW agencies by preempting research funds. They'd benefit from the new data but they just *might* not like having their own programs interfered with. So you have to spend a lot of time politicking. You go to each agency and talk to the director of research and statistics or whatever. You make sure none of them is going to fight it. And only then do you write a proposal."

By January 1975, Mrs. Mahoney had shepherded the project along far enough to be able to prepare a 1,500-word proposal for Assistant

Secretary William A. Morrill (head of ASPE), who signed it and sent it, along with a sheaf of supporting letters, to HEW Secretary Caspar Weinberger. It said, in part:

The purpose of this memo is to request your approval for a Departmental effort aimed at the development of a new survey to provide improved information on the income and characteristics of the population and participation in Government programs. . . .
  Programs that provide cash, vouchers or services to people on the basis of their income represent, by far, the largest share of the Departmental budget. Both the Executive and Legislative branches are demanding more reliable estimates of future outlays under various program alternatives as well as more sophisticated analyses of program impact. Adequate data are the most important requisites to providing such estimates and analyses.[4]

The memo explained why even an expanded CPS couldn't do the job, estimated that designing the "New Income Survey" would take $3 million to $4 million and fifteen man-years of effort over a two-year period (the figures proved absurdly optimistic), and concluded, "The improved research, evaluation and planning that will flow from the data, I view as a very considerable benefit justifying the investment."

Secretary Weinberger initialed the space next to the word "Approve," adding, however, a scribbled marginal word of caution based on Ford Administration policy: "But I do not believe we can ask for more money ('No new programs'). Let's do as much as we can without new money to start it." His approval was as brief and casual as if the memo had been a request for new stationery rather than the development of a major new tool of social research. Still, when one runs a multi-billion-dollar department, he may well feel that a project costing $3 million to $4 million doesn't merit many words.

The Need for Data in Governance

The creation of SIPP is the latest instance of a practice dating back to the beginnings of history. As societies grew beyond the level of small, close-knit tribes, their rulers could no longer rely on personal observation and hearsay for information on which to base decisions about war and finances. Thousands of years ago, they began to take censuses in order to find out how many men they could call to arms and what tax rates were needed to meet their expenses.

The best-known of these early inventories was made in the thirteenth century B.C., when Moses, leading the Jews through dangerous and unfamiliar territory after the Exodus, found it essential to know how large an army he could raise against any enemy:

And the Lord spake unto Moses in the wilderness of Sinai . . . saying,
    Take ye the sum of all the congregation of the children of Israel, after their families, by the house of their fathers, with the number of their names, every male by their polls;
    From twenty years old and upward, all that are able to go forth to war in Israel: thou and Aaron shall number them by their armies. . . .
    Even all they that were numbered were six hundred thousand and three thousand and five hundred and fifty.
                                                            —Num. 1:1–3,46

Years later, a second such headcount enabled Moses, weighing war against the Midianites, to learn that he could call up an army of 1,000 men from each tribe, or 12,000 in all—enough, he seems to have known, to overwhelm the enemy, as in fact they did. After this victory, Moses at once called for a census of the prisoners, cattle, asses, and sheep seized, in order to divide the booty appropriately among the warriors, the people, and the priestly oligarchy (Num. 26:1–65; 31: 3–5, 26–47).*

Almost as well known as the Mosaic numbering is the Domesday Book, a census of conscriptable males and taxable property ordered by William the Conqueror in 1085–86. William, struggling to create a strong central government in the years after the Conquest, saw that to do so he needed two kinds of information, and sent teams of royal officers around England to gather manpower figures for every town and to record every manor's plow-teams, meadows, pastures, fisheries, and other sources of taxable revenue. With these data, the King could calculate, rather than guess, the size of the forces he could put in the field and the tax rates he needed to set.

---

* Even if, as some scholars maintain, the statistics in Numbers, first set down centuries after the events, are gross exaggerations, it seems likely that censuses were indeed taken by the wandering Israelites and were of great value to them.[5]

In subsequent centuries, limited censuses of one kind or another were made elsewhere, from time to time, in response to particular crises. The first regularly repeated census of an entire nation, however, was established by the Constitution of the United States, whose unique federal structure necessitated a periodic national census to reckon and regularly adjust the number of congressional representatives allotted to each state. Moreover, the population count would determine how much each state had to contribute to the common defense and general welfare.

The first such census, taken in 1790, was limited to the name of the head of each household and the number of persons in it, with a special accounting of how many males there were of sixteen and older who could perform military service.[6] No other data were collected—not even on occupations, because some members of the first Congress considered this an invasion of privacy and others thought such a question an unnecessary expense. Enumerators, traveling on horseback and foot, and compiling handwritten lists and tabulations, took over a year to count what proved to be a population of 3,929,326—a number that disappointed many patriots, including Thomas Jefferson, who had pridefully expected it to be larger.[7]

From that limited beginning the scope of the U.S. Census expanded in response to the new nation's growth and the increasing need of its leaders for information with which to run it. For as the nation developed and the number of matters requiring federal control correspondingly multiplied, legislators repeatedly found themselves unable to act wisely, or sometimes at all, for lack of relevant information. Again and again, therefore, Congress extended the scope of the Census.

By 1850 enumerators were gathering information about occupation, school attendance, physical disabilities, pauperism, and the value of real estate, plus a variety of economic and social data about manufacturing and other businesses, educational establishments, crop data, crime, taxes, and so on. "The census of 1850," writes the sociologist Philip M. Hauser, "may appropriately be viewed as the first census of the United States attuned in a major way to the statistical needs of the emerging mass society and providing information for at least a crude form of 'social accounting.' "[8]

Thereafter, although some new questions were added and old ones dropped as conditions changed, the basic pattern remained much the same for nearly a century. But in 1940, after the worst depression in the nation's history had caused social and economic problems of unprecedented severity, Congress sharply expanded the census to gather information essential to dealing with them.

It had not, however, been able to wait for the information; society, like an accident victim bleeding to death, required emergency surgery and Congress hastily operated, via the New Deal, without having done a workup on the patient. The work-relief programs, for instance, were started in the absence of statistics about unemployment; only estimates existed, but they varied by many millions.[9] Congress acted nonetheless, but some lawmakers were troubled at being asked to take drastic action on the basis of guesswork. As Congressman William R. Poage of Texas said during a 1939 discussion of public housing for low-income and poor people, "We do not know what the housing situation is in the United States. . . . We are spending the Government's money in total blindness."[10]

From 1940 on, therefore, the decennial census included questions about housing, employment and unemployment, internal migration, income, years of education, and even the presence or absence of private toilets and baths in housing units, all to give Congress a clearer idea of the need for further intervention in the new social and economic problems of the nation. Not all legislators, to be sure, favored gathering such information; typically, one southern member of the House objected to questions about income and years of schooling as "socialistic New Deal inquiries designed to get the niggers dissatisfied."[11]

While most Congressmen did want such data, censuses collecting them once every ten years could hardly meet the urgent need of the legislators and program administrators for a continuous flow of essential, up-to-date information. As if providentially, social researchers were at this very time developing a radical new approach to the gathering of national data—the sample survey—that would provide data comparable to those of censuses but at a tiny fraction of the time and cost.

In a sense, the sample survey was not a new approach at all but, according to the survey researcher Howard Schuman, a deeply rooted intellectual inclination, probably built into us by evolution, to regard samples as representative of wholes.[12] Our precivilized ancestors undoubtedly took a sip of any unfamiliar pond before drinking deeply. In bazaars, since time immemorial, buyers of grain have dug a handful out of the sack, scrutinized it, and decided whether or not to buy. Today's shoppers are no different: They assume that the grape they taste indicates what the bunch is like or that the spot-check of a company's ledgers shows how well the business is faring.

To be sure, not every sample is representative: As shoppers know, the top layer of strawberries is often a poor guide to the rest of the boxful. But beginning in the mid-1930s, social scientists, public opinion pollsters, and technicians in the Bureau of the Census had been developing a methodology of sampling a population, or any segment of it, that produced samples very nearly representative of the whole. (There are, however, problems inherent in the technique that we will look at in a later section.)

On the basis of mathematical theory and empirical testing, they had shown by the end of the 1930s that a sample of 1,000 or 1,500 people, properly drawn from the entire population, would yield fairly accurate national estimates of presidential preferences; attitudes on such matters as national health insurance, whether wives should work, and the importance of virginity in a first-time bride; and similar issues. For more complex studies, and for fine-grained analyses in which the results are broken down according to many criteria (five-year age groupings, years of education, income brackets, race, and so on), larger samples were necessary; even so, a sample of 50,000 or 60,000—about 1/2,000th of the population at that time, 1/4,000th of today's—could yield very precise, reliable, and highly detailed data on unemployment, family matters, illness, working conditions, and other multifaceted issues.[13]

Congress and many government agencies soon came to depend on the data of sample surveys for many legislative and administrative decisions. Two early examples: (1) With funds from the Department of Defense, a group of sociologists headed by Samuel Stouffer used sample surveys to study the morale of soldiers during World War II and to find out what demobilization rules at the war's end would create least resentment and social disruption (the result was the point system, which released earliest those with longest and most arduous service); and (2) a sample survey in the 1950s by sociologist William Sewell and others, called *Farmer's Plans for Security in Old Age,* provided Congress with grounds for expanding the Social Security Act to include the farmers.

From 1942 on, the Bureau of the Census increasingly relied on sample surveys to provide Congress, the agencies, and the business community with up-to-date statistics on a number of topics. As the role of government grew ever larger in the postwar years, the Bureau expanded its survey activities, and today it conducts more than 250 surveys in a typical year, some of which are regularly repeated, others of which are one-time specials. These cover an enormous range of topics—everything from birth rates to crime statistics, from the number of housing starts to the prevalence of specific diseases, and from the volume of gasoline sales to the incidence of artificial limbs.[14] The 1980 Census itself was largely a sample survey: It asked only a score of questions of everyone in the country but more than forty others of one person out of five.

The advent of sample survey research had two other significant social effects—one commercial and the other scientific.

Beginning in the latter 1930s, public opinion measurement and market research based on sample surveys grew enormously. Today it is a multi-billion-dollar industry, and a great many businesses and a majority of incumbents and candidates for office depend on sample surveys and polls to guide them in their day-to-day operations. Whether this is wholly beneficial to society or not is arguable; what is unarguable is that continual scrutiny of opinion and preference has become a major factor in decision-making processes of the American people, political leaders, and power groups.

On the scientific side, in the 1940s several university-affiliated research groups—the Bureau of Applied Social Research at Columbia University, the Survey Research Center at the University of Michigan, and the National Opinion Research Center at the University of Chicago—began refining and perfecting sample survey methodology. They also started conducting surveys, some on behalf of commercial clients, and others funded by foundations or the government and devoted to basic research on a wide variety of social topics.

So wide is the variety, indeed, that a list would be virtually coterminous with the whole field of social research. Since many social phenomena do not lend themselves to experimentation easily or at all, and since field observation always runs the risk of subjective bias, the sample survey has become one of the most important tools of social research. One recent study showed that between one quarter and one half of the articles recently published in core journals in sociology, political science, and economics used survey data; another showed that for sociology alone, the figure is 80 percent.[15] Professor Herbert Hyman of Wesleyan University, a long-time survey researcher, says that the survey is "without question the most widespread, most used, tool of social research today. Survey research is the Queen of Methods."

While sample surveys are a major source of data in basic research, they exert their most direct and profound impact on daily life through the social programs that are shaped and implemented by the data they provide. Again, it is not feasible to list these many applications here; Philip Hauser's *Social Statistics in Use* takes nearly 400 pages to do so and, at that, has to summarize or merely mention many of the uses. But here, by way of illustration, are a few examples of what the federal and state governments rely on surveys to provide:

- the data used to calculate the Consumer Price Index, which, among other effects, brings about cost-of-living adjustments in Social Security and other program benefits;
- economic indicators, which influence many governmental operating policies, including Federal Reserve Board actions to control the money supply, curb inflation, and fix interest rates;
- sickness rates and the data on the age composition of the population, which enable Congress and the agencies to plan for the future needs of health services, retirement programs, nursing homes, and other facilities;
- poverty and unemployment data, which trigger a number of governmental actions, including the extension of employment benefits when needed and the allocation of redevelopment grants to areas of chronic unemployment.

Hauser, whose career has spanned service in the Bureau of the Census (where he rose to be Acting Director) and academic sociology (he is a past president of the American Sociological Association), has eloquently summed up the value of survey research to contemporary American society:

Many years ago at a meeting of the Census Committee of the House of Representatives in Washington, a congressman inquired of [me] . . . : "If American business has been able to get along for 150 years without statistics, why does it need them now?" The congressman might well have included— in addition to business—government, labor, education, the church welfare agencies, civic agencies, recreational agencies, voluntary organizations, and the general public. . . .

In 1789 when this nation was launched under her new Constitution and before the first census was taken, the citizen was not subjected to the present number of questionnaires. But, also, he was not constrained by traffic lights at street intersections; he was not compelled to go to school; he was not required to make a contribution for the Social Security system; he did not need a license to conduct his business. . . .

The proliferation of census questions and surveys and the conversion of their findings into statistics is only one of the many changes which have accompanied the transition of America from "the little community" to the "mass society.". . . As unprecedented problems emerged, government functions expanded to deal with them. When functions increased, the need for hard information as a basis for policy formulation, planning, administration, and evaluation of programs became apparent. In consequence, censuses and surveys and administrative records were increasingly used to compile needed statistics.[16]

Even as modern society could not survive a large-scale reversion to preindustrial or feudal simplicity without a devastating famine and other apocalyptic results, so would any major reduction in the flow of survey research cause the machinery of modern society to falter, shudder, and disintegrate. Like Pope Gregory, watching sixth-century Rome deteriorate around him, we ourselves might cry: "Everywhere we see mourning and hear groans. Cities are destroyed, strong places are cast down, the fields are depopulated, and the land is become desert."

"It's Working!"

The development of a new scientific methodology, in popular fancy, involves white-coated researchers who tensely peer at banks of dials or flickering video screens and now and again leap to a console to twist a knob or flip a switch just in time.

Nothing like that, however, was to be seen in the several offices of the HEW North Building on Independence Avenue, where the development of SIPP got under way in 1976. At first, half a dozen, and soon twice that many, survey researchers and social scientists, most of them in their late 20s or early 30s, did nothing more dramatic than sit at desks and pore over technical papers on survey design, stopping sometimes to jot down notes, tap out a few lines on a typewriter, stare bemused at the wall, or wander off into someone else's office for an impromptu conference.

Yet they found their work exciting, not only because it was of importance to both the government and the social-science establishment, but because it involved a number of gamelike and intellectually challenging activities. For instance:

- Fine-tuning the wording of each of the hundreds of survey questions, the sequence in which they are asked, and the choices offered the respondent calls for psychological tactics as subtle as those of a family counselor or interrogator.
- Working out the "skip" patterns—the instructions to the interviewer to bypass questions that earlier answers have made irrelevant—is somewhat akin to solving the problems of logic involved in writing a computer program.
- Gathering a sample large enough to yield reliable data for every region of the country and every economic group, and organizing a corps of interviewers to locate and talk to all those people, is a task almost as complex as planning and commanding a military landing on an unfamiliar shore.

For such reasons, the handful of people working on ISDP—the Income Survey Development Program, as the SIPP project was called—felt like a team of pioneers bound to each other by a shared great adventure and mutual commitment to a noble goal. Dawn Nelson, who spent three years in the ISDP, says, "We had a very close relationship, a real bond that grew out of working together so intensely. We felt—well, *dedicated*."

These feelings were intensified by the close, collective nature of their problem-solving. Developing a new survey requires so many specialized skills that no one person at HEW (or at the Bureau of the Census, which later joined the project) was SIPP's architect. As the director of ISDP, Paul Planchon, a young sociologist, kept track of its activities, but by and large it functioned rather like a hydra, that organized mass of cells whose specialized parts serve a common end without commands from a central cortex. Reminiscing, Planchon says,

We all kept thinking about the overall design of the survey but each one did whatever he or she could do best. Denny Vaughan and Bruce Klein spent most of their time drafting different parts of the main questionnaire. Dawn Nelson kept reviewing it to make it all hang together. Other people worked on special questions for the later waves of the survey, since we'd agreed that respondents should be reinterviewed every few months for a total of five or six times. Still others were drawing up plans for the field tests and the kinds of samples we'd need, and others were thinking about what kinds of data-processing and statistical methods we'd use to make sense of all the data that came in.

His own job, he adds, was mainly one of combination—he doesn't say "control"—of what the others were producing.

Bette Mahoney, who had gotten ISDP started, was the project's administrator. She did little hands-on work, but she and Assistant Secretary Morrill made certain key decisions, one of which was to farm out contracts for studies of certain technical problems; a good deal of longitudinal survey technology, available in academic research centers, was unfamiliar to the ISDP staff. Much of it was also unknown to the Bureau of the Census, but that organization had other assets the ISDP task force needed, and Planchon began conferring with various branch heads at the Bureau to work out terms for its collaboration in the project.

"A few of us at HEW did cling for a while to the idea that maybe we could do it all ourselves," he recalls, "but most of us felt that sooner or later we'd have to work with the Bureau. They were the biggest survey organization around, they were highly professional, they had a wealth of experience, and we could pay for their work—we had a million our first year and three million by our fourth year."

Small cadres of people in the Bureau's Population and Demographic Surveys divisions soon began working for ISDP, but the collaboration was often contentious. "When we began to work with them," Planchon says, "we found that they thought some of our newer ideas, such as tracking people longitudinally, were off the wall—difficult and impractical—and that many of our new questions, like those about the cash value of noncash program benefits, were awful and wouldn't work." More than that, the conflict expressed two different interests: The HEW group wanted a survey focused on a wide range of HEW's social programs, while the Bureau, serving many other clients within government, preferred a general-purpose income survey.

The Census group's criticisms may, in part, have been sharpened by their resentment that the new survey hadn't been given to them to develop. They saw themselves as realistic and experienced survey researchers and the HEW group—long on Ph.D.s—as novices and ivory-tower types who, one Census researcher acidly says, "wanted to reinvent wheels that we already had rolling. Or invent new ones that couldn't roll—they were trying to act like Nobel Prize winners, and half of what they thought up was blue-sky stuff that wouldn't work or wasn't important. We told them so, but it was no use. So we'd say to ourselves, 'Well, it's just a test. We'll have to do it their way, and when we do the real survey we'll cut this junk out.' "

In October 1977, 41 part-time Census employees in San Antonio, Dallas, Houston, Peoria, and Milwaukee, after receiving special training in the SIPP questionnaire, set out to track down and interview the members of some 2,400 households. The sample was not only small but unrepresentative of the nation: It came from only those five cities and consisted largely of names drawn from lists of persons receiving AFDC (Aid to Families with Dependent Children) or SSI (Supplemental Security Income—a benefit paid to aged, disabled, or blind persons who, despite other benefits, remain below the poverty level). Because what these people were getting was on record, the ISDP team could use the figures to see whether the questionnaire did or did not elicit accurate information.[17]

That was only one of several major issues the Site Research Test, as it was called, was intended to illuminate. Planchon's team and the Census groups headed by Roger Herriot (who was more open to "blue-sky" ideas than many of his subordinates) had agreed, after some thrashing around, on a research program using two versions of the questionnaire and two schedules of interviewing in an effort to answer these other questions:

- How much less accurately would people recall their income and program benefits of six months ago than those of three months ago?
- Would the "Short Form" on income questions work as well as the "Long Form"? The Short Form, modeled after the Annual Demographic Supplement of the CPS, asked about each type of income, and the amounts received, one by one. The Long Form first asked a series of questions that gave a general picture of the individual's income sources and only then asked how much had been received from each of them.
- Would people be able to identify the specific programs they were getting money from, or would many of them, especially those with little education, call both SSI and Old Age benefits "Social Security" or be unable to distinguish one welfare program from another?
- Would too many people refuse to say, or pretend not to know, how much money they got from various sources to yield usable data?
- When would it be best to ask for social security numbers? The Census view was that many people felt their SSNs were a private matter; in the CPS, enumerators did not ask for them until deep in the interview so as not to risk having respondents break off, and even so they got SSNs for only 70 percent of the people. That did no harm to the CPS, but in the ISDP test, where the SSN was the only means of checking interview answers against known figures, it might mean that over a quarter of the interviews would be useless. Should the SIPP interviewers risk asking for SSNs early, or would the break-off rate be too high?

During the interviewing, which went on over a five-month period, members of the HEW and Census teams went out as observers with the interviewers to learn whatever they could. They soon saw that interviewing people at length about income and program benefits was a difficult and touchy job, particularly when the people were elderly or, like many of the poor, lived in urban slums or rural shanties. Some excerpts from the observers' reports:[18]

This household consisted of a 75-year-old man and his 68-year-old wife. The husband was somewhat agitated at the repetitive nature of the questions. The interviewer moved quickly through the form, admitting later that she missed a few inappropriate questions in order to placate the respondent.

*

The household consisted of a 72-year-old widow who could not speak English. A neighbor acted as translator. The interview was conducted over a chain-link fence amid the largest swarm of mosquitoes that I have ever been in.

*

Virtually none of the respondents knew the difference between Medicaid and Medicare. The interviewers would suggest that what they had was probably Medicaid. It always *was* Medicaid. If the interviewers had followed their training, a lot of wrong responses would have been sent in.

*

The apartment was up some steep, unlit stairs with a very pungent odor. At the top, not only the stairway window but the frame had been knocked out. This made it possible to see well enough to step around the numerous lumps of canine excrement. A voice through the door told us we could find the occupants at home after 8:30 P.M. The interviewer told me that while she'd go anywhere during the day, she wasn't crazy enough to go back there after dark.

Despite many such difficulties, and indications that some questions worked either poorly or not at all, there was a growing sense of excitement among the observers in the five cities and at staff meetings in Washington. "We'd get back from the interviews and talk among ourselves," John Coder, a member of the Census Bureau team, remembers, "and we'd say how surprised we were that things went as well as they did, with a questionnaire that was so long and mostly about money. We'd say things like, 'We're really getting answers,' or 'Not bad!' "

To be sure, these were only impressions, and possibly subject to wishful thinking. But as the interviewers turned in their questionnaires and a Census processing center transformed them into data tapes that could be run on Census computers, the early tabulations looked encouraging. The day a few sheets of the first printout by a Census computer arrived at ISDP headquarters, Planchon and his team gathered around and pored over the pages, making small pleased noises. As he recalls, "Even though it showed only how many people in the sample were able to answer each question, how many didn't know, and how many refused, it was exciting to see. We could tell that the survey was working."

In reality, all they could tell at that point was that interviewers were getting answers to the questions. How good the answers were, though, they would not know until they and their outside contractors had made detailed analyses of the data, a process that would take many months.

A second field test, however, was scheduled to start in April 1978, only two months after the completion of Site Research interviewing. Indeed, shortly after that test had gotten under way, Planchon, Herriot, and their respective teams started planning the second and more advanced test. Researchers normally don't perform a follow-up experiment before studying the results of the first one, but in an experimental program that has to be funded anew each year by Congress, one cannot be so orderly; to justify each year's budget request, one must show budget committee members evidence of activity. The HEW group and their Census counterparts therefore decided to push ahead on the basis of the impressions they had gained in the field rather than wait for analytic results.[19]

The 1978 Research Panel, as the second test was called, would come closer to the final form of SIPP than had the 1977 test. Though a small part of its sample would come from Social Security records, the larger part would be nationwide and include people from every economic level and age group. The Census team, using Census records, would randomly pick a couple thousand households from 60 of its "Primary Sampling Units," or PSUs. (For its many sample surveys, the Bureau of the Census keeps a file of 1,924 areas, each consisting of a county or group of counties, that collectively make up a sample of every part of the nation and its population.) To be sure, a subsample of this sample, drawn from only 60 PSUs and limited—by a budget pinch that year—to 2,358 households would not be truly representative of the nation or allow of precise and detailed analyses; it would, though, permit a good test-run of the new survey.[20]

The 1978 test would also be a tryout of a crucial element of SIPP, namely, the use of the sample as a panel—a fixed group of people who would be reinterviewed at regular intervals to learn what happened to individuals and their households as a result of changes in their income and benefit receipts. There were a number of questions about panel design that had to be answered before SIPP could be considered workable. Among them:

- Refusals: Would a substantial percentage of the people in the selected households decline to participate when they learned it would mean five or six interviews over a year and a half?
- Attrition: If they agreed, would they grow impatient during the second and later visits and drop out? If any sizable percentage of the panel was lost between the first and last interviews, how could the integrity of the sample be preserved?
- Missing data: If a panel member was unreachable for one or two of the interviews, or refused to answer certain questions on some visits that he or she had answered on others, how should the incomplete record be handled? Adding such interviews to complete ones would give a distorted overall picture, but discarding incomplete interviews would leave a truncated sample that might not represent the national population.
- Linking: How could individuals, families, and households be kept track of in an era when there was so much fluidity to living arrangements? As members of a household left it and others joined it, when was it no longer the same household—and what then was its place in the survey? If the survey followed what happened to households, how could it simultaneously follow individuals who switched to another household—if, say, Mr. AB and Mrs. CB split up, each taking one child and moving in with a new partner, which was now the B household? How could the survey do any of this without violating confidentiality regulations that forbade using names or SSNs in the published records or research tapes?

In April 1978, interviewers set out on the second field test. Many were somewhat concerned about having to visit each household five or six times, about the lengthier questionnaire to be used this time, and about the several versions to be mastered. (After the first visit, many questions would be reworded to avoid repetition and certain new topics would be added.) But as research team observers soon saw, most of the interviewers, though they found the task difficult and beset with problems, also found it both challenging and feasible.

The experiences of Mrs. Patricia Valle, who handled fifty households in various Long Island towns and parts of New York City, will give some sense of how things went for many of the interviewers. Mrs. Valle, a white former office worker, was 34 years old at the time, a homemaker, and mother of two children. For several years she had worked part time as an interviewer in the CPS and the Annual Housing Survey. These are her recollections of her year of ISDP interviewing:

The questionnaire was very long and complicated, but the instructions were quite clear. I did the prescribed home study and then went to classes in New York City for several days. The training was excellent, especially the practice interviewing.

I was concerned about the length of the questionnaire, but as soon as I went out I found that if people were at all cooperative, the length didn't really matter. What did matter was that I had to keep visiting them and putting them through it again and again. They'd be cooperative at first but later they'd often get resentful. "Look," they'd say, "I've answered a lot of these questions time and again, and now I've had it." Or I'd have a hard time pinning them down to a day and time when I could come. Or if they had moved and I tracked them down, they would sometimes feel I was "following" them and act downright hostile. But in the end, almost all of them would cooperate.

The biggest problem was to make them feel that the survey was important. With the CPS, it's easy to get people to see the value of it—it has to do with employment and unemployment—but the ISDP was so broad and inclusive that they couldn't see why all that information was necessary. I had to keep explaining the many purposes it would serve.

Oddly enough, it was poor blacks who were most willing to talk and middle-class whites who were most often suspicious or difficult. One time I went to some awful place in the South Bronx; I parked my car in a dark bombed-out looking street with piles of rubble and men lounging around in groups, and I had to make my way up a rickety staircase in the dark. I was really frightened. At the top there was a black woman in an apartment with no heat and no furniture, nothing but a mattress on the floor, and mice running around—but she welcomed me and was very friendly and willing to answer all my questions and interested in the survey.

The middle-class homes were more pleasant to go to but many of the people, though they were okay on the basic questions, were difficult to deal with when I asked them to name amounts. They'd say, "I'd rather not say." I'd ask, "Well, was it more than $30,000?" Long pause. "Well, yes." "More than $40,000?" A longer pause. "Yes." It was like pulling teeth.

But some of the people, poor and middle-class alike, actually seemed glad to see me when I came back the fourth or fifth time. We'd gotten to know each other over the course of the year. Maybe they'd been pregnant when I first met them, and now they had a baby. Or maybe they'd moved into a new home and I'd say something nice about it and they liked that. It was a real relationship.

The questionnaire was very good. I had flash cards, for instance, showing colors of checks, to help the people know where their benefits came from. And for the later visits the questionnaire was so written that I didn't have to probe for all the information each time; I'd read off something like, "Last time you said you received X dollars from such-and-such a source in the previous three months. Is that correct for these past three months?"

Mrs. Valle's work for the Bureau of the Census since the end of the 1978 test in April 1979 has been on easier surveys, but she looks back on that year wistfully. "It was special," she says. "It gave me a sense of responsibility, a sense of *mission*."

After the first wave of interviews, the members of both research teams again waited tensely for results to come in. Evan Davey, a small, neat man who supervised much of the work of the Census team and today, as Assistant Division Chief of Special Surveys, continues to be actively involved with SIPP, speaks of that time with remembered excitement filtering through his restrained manner:

The Census center at Jeffersonville would process the questionnaires and get the raw data onto disks that they'd send to us in Washington. Then we'd hang around on the doorstep of our programmers, waiting to see what they could get out of them. Sometimes we'd think, "Nobody'll answer *that* question; it'll never work"—and then we'd see on the terminal screen that people *had* been willing to answer it. That's when it got really exciting. But other times we'd see that something had failed abysmally—in one batch of questionnaires maybe a hundred people answered a certain question but only eighteen of them answered the next one. Why? What went wrong?

By and large, though, we *were* getting answers. And even though our sample was small, when we compared those first figures to the March CPS, we could see that we were very close, and we said, "We're doing something! It's *working!*"

Later, as the HEW team, the Census team, and their outside contractors analyzed the data of both the 1977 and 1978 field tests in detail, some interesting specific results began to appear. Among them:

- Only 6.6 percent of the households in the 1978 panel were "noninterviews," most of which were refusals. This was low for a new survey, though not low enough to avoid some bias in the results, but it could be brought down by more dogged approaches by interviewers.[21]
- When the amounts of benefits people reported getting were compared to Social Security and other records, it appeared that asking about the last three months worked better than asking about the last six months; they were able to answer more of the questions and their answers were more accurate.[22]
- The Long Form, though it took more time than the Short Form, was less annoying to respondents and resulted in less error and more complete responses. Moreover, it turned out to have tactical value: People freely named the sources of their income when not asked for the amounts, and then were trapped when the interviewer did finally ask how much. The Short Form, which asked for amounts from the start, forewarned respondents; many, after the first such question, replied to others by saying that they didn't know or couldn't remember whether they got any in that category.[23]
- In the 1977 interviews, up to 14 percent of the people who said they received program benefits misidentified the program it came from. In the 1978 panel, the use of flash cards with color samples matching those of various program benefit checks substantially reduced the error rate.[24]
- Fewer than 1 percent of respondents refused to say or didn't know whether they had any income, and fewer than 10 percent couldn't or wouldn't name specific amounts. Interest income was a serious exception: Roughly half of those who said they received interest refused to say how much.[25]
- Although in the 1977 test the question about the respondent's social security number came at the very end, it met with less resistance, for some reason, than the same question did in CPS; perhaps people felt more strongly motivated to cooperate with SIPP. In the 1978 panel, therefore, the question was asked early in the first interview; 87 percent of the respondents gave their number, and only 2.5 percent refused. (The rest were "Don't Knows" or interviewer errors.)[26]

There were no answers in these first results to several complicated problems inherent in the survey's longitudinal design, namely, what to do about attrition, missing data, and linking. These methodological problems could take years to solve—but once again the researchers had to push ahead without answers. They launched a third and far larger test of SIPP, with a national sample of over 11,000 households, in February 1979, two months before the last wave of interviews of the 1978 panel began. If they were delighted that the questionnaire itself seemed to function satisfactorily, they were deeply concerned that this third and most ambitious test was going ahead and that SIPP itself was scheduled to go into operation by 1981, even though they still had no perfected methodology with which to turn the raw numbers into what they hoped would be the most valuable data base created in decades.

Survey Technique: From Intuition to Science

Like the buyer mentioned earlier who appraises a sack of grain by looking at a handful of it, many a ruler of society has judged how things were in his land from what his undercover agents could learn by eavesdropping in public places. Some heads of state even did this sampling themselves: Haroun al Raschid, Caliph of Baghdad in the eighth century, and Akbar the Great, the sixteenth-century Mogul Emperor of India, are said to have wandered the streets at night in disguise and to have based some of their state decisions on what they saw and heard.

The flaw in this simple-minded method is apparent to us today: Unlike the kernels of grain in a sack, people differ greatly according to their education, economic level, age, sex, and other factors, and those who are in the streets at any given time are a happenstance sample that may be quite untypical of the whole population.

The intuitive feeling that one can gauge the national condition from any chance sample of people persisted until recent times. In this country, preelection straw votes were conducted by many newspapers from early in the last century until well into this one. Some papers printed ballots in their pages, thus getting tallies that consisted only of those who cared enough to mail in their vote; other papers sent reporters out to ask anyone they met on street corners whom they intended to vote for. Hundreds of such sample surveys were conducted over the decades and were very popular, even though they were hardly more accurate than the candidates' own predictions.[27]

But between 1916 and 1932, large-scale polls conducted by the *Literary Digest* regularly picked the winners of the presidential elections. The sample was huge but wonderfully simple in design: The magazine mailed out postcard ballots to some ten million residential telephone subscribers (and, in later years, automobile owners), a couple million of whom voted and returned the cards. The size of the sample was thought to explain the success of the poll, which was called "uncanny," "amazingly accurate," and "infallible." But in 1936, the poll's reputation, and existence, came to an abrupt end when its 2,376,523 ballots indicated that FDR would get a mere 41 percent of the popular vote (he got 61 percent) and that Alfred Landon would win 32 of the 48 states (he won only 2).[28]

What went wrong? In retrospect the error was glaringly obvious: In that Depression year, people who had telephones or automobiles were predominantly middle class and upper class, and the *Literary Digest's* sample thus was drawn from an untypical minority of the population. Size alone did not make for good sampling; more than two million ballots from a biased sample could give a highly inaccurate picture of the national mood—yet a genuinely representative sample as small as 900 ballots could produce estimates nearly certain to be within three or four percentage points of the correct figure.[29]

In fact, in that same election, three surveys using just such small numbers—the Crossley poll, the *Fortune* survey, and the Gallup poll—all came close to the final result because they painstakingly assembled samples that included proper proportions of persons of every economic level, major age category, and region. Moreover, all three polls had low nonresponse rates because interviewers had sought out the people in the samples; in the *Literary Digest's* mail-in poll, in contrast, only one quarter of the persons in the sample bothered to vote, and even had the ballots gone out to a representative sample, those that were returned might have come from a highly motivated and unrepresentative minority.

Although the three small polls did not use true random sampling, they did gather samples that matched the composition of the national population; this was a major step toward scientific, rather than intuitive or common-sense, sampling. By the mid-1930s, a number of the basic principles of scientific sampling had been worked out by mathematicians and were beginning to be applied by avant-garde public opinion pollsters, market researchers, and social scientists.

A key tenet of scientific sampling is that a street-corner or other chance sample, seemingly gathered at random, is not necessarily representative. True randomization requires rigorous technique. A sample of 100 names picked from a large urban phone book by letting it fall open anywhere and spinning a pointer to pick one of the eight columns is not random so much as accidental and probably unrepresentative. If the column consists of names beginning with Sz-, it will be disproportionately Polish, Czech, and Hungarian. If it consists of Smiths, it will fail to have a proper proportion of Jews. But a sample of names randomly chosen one by one from throughout the book will be representative of the names in that phone book.

To choose randomly without being influenced by subliminal habits or preferences, one would use a table of random numbers to dictate what pages to turn to and which names on them to choose. This method gives every name in the book an equal chance; the result, a "probability sample," is truly representative and has neither the accidental nor the purposeful biases of the street-corner sample, mail-in volunteer sample, or "convenience sample" (one's friends, or the members of a club, and so on). It is for good reason that William Kruskal, dean of the Division of Social Sciences at the University of Chicago, has called randomization "one of the greatest ideas of the century."[30]

Probability is not, however, certainty; there is always a chance that any probability sample will be somewhat unlike the population it was drawn from because of the vagaries of chance distribution—the phenomenon that makes most bridge hands mediocre but some noteworthy and a few unforgettable. By pure chance, therefore, a correctly drawn probability sample of people may have somewhat more or fewer in any age, economic, or other category than it should have.

These errors are calculable and controllable. According to mathematical theory, a probability sample of 1,500 is 95 percent sure, in simple breakdowns such as voter preferences, to yield percentages that are no more than 3 points off in either direction from what a total census of the nation would have revealed. The sample must be larger, however, to yield greater reliability (a better than 95 percent chance that the results will be no more than 3 points off either way), or greater precision (a range of possible error narrower than 3 points one way or the other); and as mentioned earlier, it has to be larger to permit a detailed breakdown of the results according to multiple criteria.[31] To achieve high reliability and precision, and to permit fine analyses, many Bureau of the Census surveys use samples of 25,000 to 66,000. Even so, they consist of only one person or household out of every several thousand in the nation.

The probability sample is thus an economical and immensely powerful instrument for examining social reality, a microscope with which to see the world in a grain of sand. The simplest way to gather such a sample is, as in the phone book example, to use some rule that allows every person in the group being surveyed an equal chance to be chosen. For some groups—licensed physicians, for instance—this is a relatively easy matter. But for surveys of the national population or any segment of it, there is no easy way to gather a representative sample, since there is no one directory in which they all are listed. Nor, even if there were, would this be a feasible approach; many categories of people are too hard to reach—trappers, merchant seamen, and drifters are cases in point—to make simple probability sampling feasible. Over the years, therefore, survey researchers developed sophisticated ways of cheaply constructing probability samples.[32] Among them:

- Sampling "frames" can be used in place of the nonexistent universal directory. A frame is any list of people or institutions having certain known characteristics—a register of voters, a directory of students enrolled in a university, and so on—from which a probability sample can be easily drawn. Such frames can be used by themselves for surveys of special groups or combined for broader surveys. Frames made up of geographical areas can be used to sample the population at large; the researcher, using random methods, picks a few small subdivisions within each area, a few smaller ones within each of those, and finally a few households within each of the smallest of them, thus getting a representative sample.
- Within any homogeneous small area, "clustering" saves time and money at a slight cost to the reliability of the sample (an increase

in the probable error). In a housing development, an interviewer might approach four families on one floor instead of four families throughout the complex.

- If the basic characteristics of the particular population being surveyed are already known from Census or other records, it can be "stratified" or sorted out into groups by income, urban-rural residence, or other dimensions. Some strata have relatively few members; to gather enough representatives of such strata to permit reliable analysis, the overall sample would have to be very large and costly. Instead, surveyers limit the size of the overall sample but "oversample" the small strata (choose members at a greater rate than elsewhere). This gives them enough members of such strata to do reliable separate analyses of them, but in order to analyze the overall sample, they reweight these oversampled strata to their true proportion.

Sample design is only one of many sources of potential error in survey research. From the 1930s to the present, survey researchers both in academic centers and in commercial public opinion firms have been investigating others and developing methods for dealing with them. Some of the chief ones:

- Interviewers, because they vary in appearance or manner, may produce somewhat different effects on their respondents. Opinion surveys are particularly subject to interviewer effects; a notable example is the tendency for many black respondents to give different answers on racial questions to white interviewers than to black ones.[33]
- Whatever their color, interviewers, despite careful training, may bias the answers they get by their unwitting use of tone, inflection, facial expression or body language, or the way they interpret what is said to them. A classic example: In 1940, Gallup interviewers asked people which was more important—to help England, even at the risk of getting into the war, or to keep out of the war. Interviewers who themselves favored helping England reported that 60 percent of their respondents did so too—as against only 44 percent for interviewers who felt that we should keep out of the war.[34]
- Some interviewer effects are even more subtle and easily missed: One recent study found that interviewers who expected to have

difficulty getting answers to certain questions did, in fact, report somewhat higher nonresponse rates to those questions than interviewers who expected no trouble.[35]

- The very presence of even the best-trained and most neutral interviewer can skew some kinds of survey material: Many respondents answer questions about racist views or unusual sexual attitudes more honestly on questionnaires they fill in privately than in face-to-face interviews. The same is true even of questions dealing with facts: A recent Census study found that a higher percentage of respondents said they were unemployed when interviewed on the telephone than when interviewed in person.[36]
- Apart from interviewer effects, respondents may give distorted answers for other reasons, among them misunderstandings, language difficulties, forgetfulness, psychological defensiveness, and various motives for lying or withholding information.[37] An example of the latter: In sex surveys, husbands and wives often report somewhat different frequencies of intercourse; recall of the facts has been distorted by such influences as distaste, wishful thinking, and machismo.[38]

Despite all this, survey researchers are in broad agreement that most respondents are cooperative and try to tell the truth. Yet apart from interviewer effects, respondents' answers may be significantly influenced by the wording of the question or the range of answers from which they may choose. A few of the many findings on this score:

- The same question, worded in two different ways, can produce sharply different results. In 1974 Howard Schuman and Stanley Presser of the Survey Research Center at the University of Michigan replicated a Roper experiment of 1940 with the following results:[39]

  "Do you think the United States should forbid public speeches against democracy?" *Forbid*: 28%; Not forbid: 72%
  "Do you think the United States should allow public speeches against democracy?" *Not allow*: 44%; Allow: 56%

  The word "forbid" apparently raises the hackles of a large minority of people, tilting the result far more in the liberal direction than when the same view is worded "not allow."
- When respondents are offered a set of choices ranging from one

extreme to another, a considerable number will choose the middle alternative, if there is one; if none is offered, most will choose an alternative to one side or the other rather than make no answer or choose "Don't know." Thus, by deciding whether to offer a middle alternative or a "forced choice," the researcher may importantly influence the results.[40]

- Merely adding the words "or not" to the end of a question increases the number of people who answer it in the negative.[41]

- Poorly educated respondents seem more easily influenced than better-educated ones by emotionally loaded words or by the order in which alternatives are presented. Yet Schuman and Presser recently found that this tendency is variable: In some kinds of questions, the educated, too, tend to be swayed by the form of the question.[42]

These and other difficulties have led some social scientists to see the survey interview as an inherently defective method. Their chief criticisms are that the interchange between interviewer and respondent is unnatural, being fixed by the form of the questions and answers; forced choice, for example, eliminates "Don't know" even when the respondent really doesn't know.[43] But on the other side, forced choice often reveals an underlying preference that the respondent would have hidden if possible. For such reasons, researchers are inclined to try to minimize the chance of neutral answers or none.

Nonresponses are especially damaging: In sufficient number, they make the results of any question or even a whole survey unreliable or meaningless, since those who fail to answer any question or the entire interview may differ from the rest in unknown ways, with the result that those who answer are an unrepresentative sample.

Nonresponse may, in fact, be the most serious problem that confronts survey researchers today. Federal law requires everyone to answer the questions asked on the decennial census, but in most surveys cooperation is voluntary. In the past, researchers were rather easily able to get nearly all persons in their sample to cooperate, but in recent years refusals (which account for most nonresponses, the rest being those people who couldn't be found) have been climbing alarmingly, especially in big cities. This has been laid to public overexposure to surveys and market research, the fear of the erosion of privacy, the changing nature of central-city populations, or all of these.[44]

Data from the Survey Research Center show the magnitude of the problem: Two of its major ongoing surveys had refusal rates of 4 or 5 percent in the early 1950s but three times that by the late 1970s.[45] Total nonresponse rates, including people who can't be reached or found, are still higher. Schuman noted in the *American Sociologist* in 1982 that "many surveys today lose roughly a third of their sample to nonresponses, thus compromising the essential character of probability sampling. . . . It can hardly be assumed that the loss is conveniently random, and particularly with the fast growing practice of telephone surveys, there is evidence that low-SES [socioeconomic status] persons are especially likely to be omitted."[46]

Survey researchers can, however, take certain steps to minimize nonresponse. Follow-up phone calls and visits are one way; some survey research organizations make five to ten call-backs until they find the respondent at home or get him or her to agree to a time for the interview. Others make persuasive appeals (the general welfare, the cause of science); still others offer benefits or rewards; and some eschew the telephone survey altogether in order not to miss the low-SES people.

Finally, sophisticated mathematical techniques are used to correct for the missing interviews. Weighting is the principal such device: If major traits of the nonresponders are known, these can be used to adjust or correct the data gathered from those who did cooperate. A National Health Survey conducted for the Public Health Service in the early 1970s consisted of both a physical examination and an interview. Since only 75 percent of the sample agreed to be examined, national estimates of disease based on the examined people might be seriously biased. But 98 percent had agreed to be interviewed, so researchers compared interview data collected from both the examined and unexamined people and found them very similar; this meant that there was little difference between the two groups and that the examination results probably held good for the entire sample. Analysts concluded that weighting the examination data to make for a normal distribution would yield an accurate picture of the health of the entire population.[47]

Although survey technique became increasingly sophisticated over the years, the sample survey remained essentially a snapshot—a cross-section of the opinions, income, health, and other characteristics of the population at the time the survey was made. By grouping the data in various ways it could even show correlations that suggested cause-and-effect relationships. Yet many such correlations are not causal relationships but the common by-products of other causes. Juvenile delinquency, for instance, is more common in homes lacking a father than in intact ones, which might imply that separation or divorce is a chief cause of delinquency. But by grouping the data according to socioeconomic level, it becomes clear that the highest rates of delinquency occur at lower socioeconomic levels—where, concomitantly, there is a high rate of marital breakup. However, the rate of delinquency is high at those levels whether or not the family is intact; apparently, therefore, poor socioeconomic conditions, not father-absence, is chiefly to blame.[48]

The observation of change over time would be far more persuasive than such analyses. If a group of families from the lower socioeconomic level rose in the scale due to some event or social development, and delinquency in those families decreased, one would have evidence more like that of an actual experiment. Accordingly, survey researchers long ago saw that longitudinal studies—surveys repeated at intervals over a period of time—would be far more revealing of cause-and-effect relationships than one-time cross-sectional surveys.

Public opinion researchers applied this technique in a limited fashion from the early years on, repeating certain questions from time to time in order to show how national attitudes were shifting on such matters as women's working, civil rights, and social programs, and to link those shifts to events or social changes that had taken place.

A more sophisticated and far more costly procedure was the "trend study" or cross-sectional time series—the same survey, repeated from time to time, using similar samples drawn from the same population. Although the people in each wave of the series are different, the samples are drawn in the same way and therefore indicate changes taking place within that population. The decennial census provides just such a record of certain changes (as already noted, most of its data are based on a one-fifth sample of the national population). Since the 1940s, and particularly from the 1960s on, many other time-series studies have been conducted by the government and by academic and commercial researchers with major grants; such studies have explored everything from election behavior to church membership, from work history to health and aging. The importance of the data bases built up by these ongoing surveys has been summed up by Richard C. Rockwell of the Social Science Research Council:

Repeated measurement is important to government and to the democratic process for two main reasons. First, social change, about which repeated measures can provide a set of signals, is often the instigator of questions about policies and programs. . . . Second, time series provide partial measures of the effects of governmental action. . . .

Social scientists [have] a third interest in repeated measurements. Much of what social science studies occurs on large scales, over long periods of time, and involves complex interactions of individuals, organizations, and governments. These processes cannot be brought into the laboratory and manipulated at the will of the investigator, but must be patiently observed.[49]

As useful as time series are, it was apparent from the first that the most informative kind of time series would be a "true longitudinal"— one that followed a given sample of the same people, or panel, over a period of time. The use of panels over a short span (a year or so) began with a study of voting behavior in the 1940. By the 1960s other social phenomena were being investigated by some two dozen ongoing national panel studies of various durations.[50]

A panel study can give a very different and much more accurate picture of change over time than a time series. A single cross-sectional study in 1975 would have shown that 9 percent of the American people were below the poverty line, and other such surveys in the preceding eight years would have given somewhat similar figures, suggesting that America had a substantial subculture of the chronically poor. But the Panel Study of Income Dynamics conducted by an inter-university consortium followed a single sample over those years and found that only 1 percent of its members had been in poverty for the whole period 1967–75. Evidently, most of the poor are so only temporarily or intermittently rather than continually.[51]

Such surveys, however, pose severe technical problems.[52] One is how to keep track of all the things that happen to any person and simultaneously maintain a usable record of the places he has worked, the households he has lived in, and so on. Methods of doing so, that is, of "linking" the data along multiple parameters, are currently being developed but the best of them are extremely complicated and wasteful of computer storage space.

Another problem is "panel bias"—the tendency, already mentioned, of panel members to answer questions somewhat differently the second time even if nothing has changed since the first. A draconian remedy is to throw away the first interview; a less costly one is to use outside information, if it exists, to see which interview has more accurate answers, and then apply mathematical corrections to the other data.

A third problem is attrition—the loss of persons who die, or move, leaving no trace, or become resistant to questioning. A related problem is that of gaps in information: A panel member may be unavailable for one interview or choose on occasion not to answer all the questions. To use incomplete interviews makes nonsense of the trends being followed, but to discard such cases is worse.

To repair these gaps in the data, statisticians use "imputation," a series of mathematical techniques for filling in the missing answers based on other existing information. Respondent J. S., for example, tells the interviewer all about her income, marriage, and job in three interviews but declines to reveal her income in the fourth; if all else in her life is the same, including her job, one can reasonably assume that her income had not materially changed. Or if she disappears from the sample before the final interview, one can look at those panel members who are most like her as to age, education, income, and so on, see how their average income changed between the third and fourth interviews, and arbitrarily assign that average change to her, too.

Imputation is sometimes said to "manufacture" data but its data are no more fictional than those physical scientists create when they plot scattered readings on graph paper and then draw a smooth curve that best fits them. Nearly all the points on such a curve are artifacts of the fitting process, not actual experimental data. Such curves are generalizations that reveal laws at work, and the points along them, though artifactual, represent the truth of that law. In much the same way, imputation fills in average values from existing data points in order to perceive social laws at work.

This is but one of the ways in which social science has a fundamental kinship to the natural sciences. Nonetheless, outsiders—including people in the natural sciences—sometimes question whether the former are "really" sciences, though they are often vague about their reasons. As Richard Feynman, a distinguished physicist and Nobel Laureate, said during the Nova broadcast of January 1983:

Because of the success of science, there is a kind of, I think a kind of pseudo-science that . . . Social science is an example of a science which is not a science. They don't do scientific . . . they follow the forms . . . or you gather data, you do so-and-so and so forth, but they don't get any laws, they haven't found out anything. [53]*

What may account for such a comment is the fact that to a physical scientist, "law" means an invariant regularity (the speed of light, the relation between mass and energy), while in the social sciences laws or regularities are often strongly conditioned by time and place (love is a widespread phenomenon, but its forms and meanings have varied greatly over the centuries and among cultures). People who make statements like Feynman's seem not to recognize that, within a given society or group of related societies, social science does make sense and order out of bewildering complexity and discovers laws of great intellectual and practical value to contemporary humankind.

Trial Run

Since social research is more cerebral than physical, the launching of SIPP's first large-scale test in February 1979 was externally an undramatic affair, without crowds, cameras, bright lights, or countdowns. Indeed, nothing anyone would have noticed took place; all that happened was that here and there throughout the nation a man or woman (193 in all) sallied forth by car to look for addresses, ring doorbells, talk to people, and make little marks on sheaves of questionnaires on their laps.

Nor had there been anything visually striking about the work of preparation that had gone on for months preceding this event. The staff had grown to fifteen at HEW and twenty-five at the Bureau of the

* The ellipses mark hesitations, not omissions.

Census but, as before, these people spent most of their time reading, thinking, writing, mapping out plans, and endlessly conferring with each other, academics working for them under contract, staff aides of OMB and various congressional committees, and officials in eleven federal agencies and departments. Most of the latter wanted questions of their own added to SIPP, overloading and muddying the questionnaire but giving SIPP a broad base of support for future budget hearings.

The only moments of visible drama in the preparatory work had been the many heated discussions of purely methodological issues between members of the HEW staff and the Census staff. Meetings of committees of the two staffs were often deadlocked by their incompatible views as to how to develop a major new survey. "The main controversy," says Dawn Nelson, who has worked on both sides, "was the ambitiousness of the project as envisaged by the HEW staff versus the Bureau's desire to be practical." As one HEW staffer recalls, "Our side kept saying 'We should—' and 'We ought to—' while they kept replying, 'But we've never—' and 'It's not practical because—.' "

The HEW staff, for example, wanted to run experiments on the accuracy of proxy responses (information given by someone in the household on behalf of an absent member); Census said it wasn't necessary—they'd gotten a fairly high proportion of direct interviews in the earlier tests—and would only be a waste of time and money.

HEW wanted to add many more questions and make SIPP a multipurpose scientific survey; Census argued strenuously that too long a questionnaire would alienate respondents and increase the nonresponse and dropout rates.

HEW wanted each wave of interviews to be completed within one month, with waves three months apart, in order to keep statistical comparisons as clear as possible; Census wanted the interviews staggered and spread out over each three-month period in order to keep the interviewing staff steadily employed.

And so on, and on.

Dr. Wray Smith, the HEW administrator in charge of ISDP (Mrs. Mahoney had left for another job), felt that his side might lose fewer of these battles if its director was older and had more clout. He therefore replaced Paul Planchon with Dr. Charles Lininger, an expert in survey research who brought more academic weight and a tougher style of debate to the conference table. Lininger fared somewhat better than Planchon in the methodological pushing and pulling, but Census, like a massive sumo wrestler, was hard to move. Roger Herriot of Census, recalling the conflict about staggered interviewing schedules, says, "There was a lot of back and forth, and we just could not agree. Eventually we had to go before a steering committee of three top people from the two agencies. It was toe-to-toe for about two hours to see who blinked first, me or Chuck Lininger. Finally, the panel decided it our way." But Lininger, who won a number of other fights, says, "SIPP would never have been as good as it is except for our insistence that Census do things more ambitiously than they were used to doing." With a sour smile, he adds, "I'm not very popular over there."

In this strenuous fashion, compromises were hammered out under the unremitting pressure of deadlines until the design of the 1979 field test was complete. Some of its major features were as follows:[54]

THE SAMPLE.   Starting with a sample previously gathered for another national survey, Census staff selected 130 Primary Sampling Units from their national list of 1,924 PSUs. From each of the 130, they chose smaller areas, and from 1970 Census lists of "housing units" (places of residence) in those areas they had computers randomly pick a total of 9,300 households. This yielded a national probability sample, but one that, by their choice of areas, they had intentionally overweighted at both the low and high ends of the income scale in order to gather enough such cases to make detailed statistical analysis possible. Later, before using the survey findings to make national estimates, Census statisticians would reweight the sample to make it comparable to that of the national population.

Another 2,000 households in those areas were added from lists of people receiving SSI benefits or Basic Educational Opportunity Grants, to permit further comparisons of the questionnaire data with information already on record. The total panel thus consisted of 11,300 households, or some 21,000 people, but Census analysts would use only the probability sample when estimating national rates of poverty, income recipiency, and other core findings.

INTERVIEW TIMING.   The total panel was divided into three groups; each group would be interviewed six times, once every three months, but the interviewing would be staggered, as the Census wanted it to be. The first group's first-wave interviews would be conducted in February 1979, the second group's in March, the third group's in April; the first group would get its second interview in May, and so on.

A different questionnaire would be used on each wave of interviews; some topics, such as income, would be repeated every time but others would be omitted and new ones added in later waves. In the first interview, the major areas covered would be household composition, labor-force participation, and income. (On income alone, interviewers would ask about fifty different sources one by one.) During the next five interviews, they would explore scores of other topics ranging from the cost of shelter to marital history and child care expense, and from educational attainment to assets and net worth.

QUESTIONNAIRE LENGTH. For the first interview, the questionnaire was a thick booklet of legal-size sheets. Sixty pages long, it contained hundreds of questions, some with numerous subquestions, and had space for over 1,650 possible answers, many of which offered multiple choices; for some later waves, the questionnaires were even longer. Fortunately, not all the items would apply to any one person. The questions ranged from the factual and simple:

During the period outlined on this calendar, did you [or the person for whom the respondent is answering] do any work at a job or business?

to the factual and complicated:

I would like you now to think about all the household furnishings that are owned by the persons in this household—things like furniture, televisions, stereos, and appliances. If all of these items were to be sold, could you give me a rough estimate of the amount you could get for them?

and the subjective and difficult:

As far as you can tell, how do people in this community seem to feel about persons who receive welfare? Do they seem to have less respect for a person because he/she needs and uses this kind of help?

TESTS AND EXPERIMENTS. A number of formal experiments and several tests of new techniques were built into the questionnaires or the scheduling.

The two most important experiments concerned who was asked for income information. In some households, one person could answer such questions for the whole household, while in others the answers would have to come from each person who received income; the purpose was to see if the quicker first method yielded data as good as the slower second one. In a related experiment, self-response would be compared for accuracy and completeness to proxy response (in which any adult member of the household could answer for someone who was absent). Two other experiments would measure how accurately people remembered the details of last month's income as compared with that of earlier months.

The major new techniques being tested included the staggered interviewing scheme, an attempt to collect self-employment income data by means of a mail-in form completed privately after the interviewer had left, and the use of social security numbers to link the survey data to information in Social Security Administration files. (This was no simple task: If the names, birth dates, or other details didn't match, clerical mistakes or name changes might be to blame—but it might also be that the cases weren't the same. The solution to be tested was a computerized sixteen-step program that would note all discrepancies, weigh them against similarities, and then make an overall decision as to the validity of each such match.)

There were, however, certain problems of major importance that neither staff had time to solve, most notably how to link the persons and the households of each wave to successive waves, and what to do about missing data and attrition during the series. Ideally, these matters should have been worked out before the interviewers got started, but February 1979 had long been the target date for the start of the third field test of SIPP and the momentum of the planning was such that there was no stopping it now.

In the earlier tryouts, the percentages of households that couldn't be found or wouldn't cooperate had been smaller than feared but larger than are usually achieved on Census Bureau surveys. This time, Census supervisors sought to cut down the nonresponse rate by spending more training time on the problem. They taught interviewers to plan their work by means of road maps, to tackle the difficult cases at the most advantageous times, and to schedule adequate time for call-backs and night visits. Interviewers were taught what to say and how to say it when the door was first answered, and how to establish a pleasant relationship with respondents. They were told how long to persist in trying to "convert" refusers or track down those who had moved, and how to assure respondents who found some questions too personal that Census information can never be given out in a form that would allow any individual to be identified.

The interviewing went much as before, except that it was on a far larger scale and reached more unhelpful kinds of interviewees, including, as Martin David bluntly puts it, a certain number of "dumb, lying, and crazy people."[55] As before, many others, though normally intelligent, honest, and sane, had trouble identifying the programs their benefits came from, while many of the better-off people tried to evade or flatly refused to answer many income questions, particularly those about interest.

Fairly soon most of the interviewers grew skilled at dealing with such difficulties. Supervisors who reinterviewed a sample of households to check interviewers' work found that errors dropped sharply after Wave 1, and by Wave 2 only about 2 percent of the interviews they verified contained any. Most important, the researchers' fear that many interviewees would drop out rather than tell about income and assets, or become increasingly reluctant to spend time on later interviews, proved to be exaggerated. Interviewers were able to collect data from more than six out of seven households throughout the six waves—a distinctly better ratio than in the 1978 test—and the rate of noninterviews actually declined after Wave 3.[56]

For a year and a half, nearly a thousand questionnaires from all over the country arrived each week at the Jeffersonville, Indiana, processing center of the Bureau of the Census. To transform the marks made on the pages of individual interviews into a data base useful to social researchers takes many steps of data processing: some are simple (checking things over, or "editing"), others more involved ("coding"—turning the answers into a form that can be read by the computer; and inserting "identifiers"—code numbers—for each individual so that names and social security numbers can be removed), and still others are quite high level (combining data from different questionnaires, weighting, and imputing). The raw data, on reels of tape, arrived at the

Census Bureau's Suitland, Maryland, headquarters, just outside Washington, D.C. There, in a huge, humming computer center, the reels were popped into machines where, in fitful jerks and spins, they sent their information to Census programmers seated at terminals in offices upstairs. As numbers flooded onto their screens, the programmers would study them and type instructions on their keyboards; down in the computer center the machines would leap to life and shunt their information—now neatly organized by the programmers' instructions—to nearby printers, which would churn out scores of pages of tables in a minute.

Month by month results would arrive at the desks of the HEW and Census researchers. As new batches came in, staffers would hold impromptu meetings to crow about the successes and groan at the failures that the numbers revealed. A list of the memos, reports, and analyses in which, during the next several years, they recorded what they found in the numbers runs to several hundred titles; here are a few of the main points in them:[57]

- When one person was spokesman for the entire household, the data collected were almost as complete and reliable as when each individual was interviewed directly; disappointingly, however, the spokesman method saved only one minute per person covered. When anyone in the household could be a proxy for any other member, the answers on some topics were less complete than those of persons speaking for themselves; on the other hand, proxy respondents were less likely to refuse to answer questions about assets. On balance, staffers concluded that the best scheme might be a mixed approach relying on whatever method was most suitable in each situation.

- Although the staggered interview design complicated the work of assembling the data, it proved feasible and made efficient use of the interviewing staff. It also permitted analysts to determine the accuracy of short-term and long-term recall of income: By comparing the income reported by the third group for three months ago with what the first group reported for that same period— when, for them, it was the past month—they could measure the amount of distortion and forgetting that took place. (All three groups were random subgroups of the sample, so their income distribution was sure to be the same.) Knowing this, analysts could apply corrections throughout, making the month-by-month and annual income data far more accurate than those of the CPS Annual Demographic Supplement.

- The mail-in report of income by self-employed persons was a failure; half the respondents never sent it.

- The computer procedure for matching interviews to Social Security Administration records validated 92.6 percent of the social security numbers taken down by interviewers; manual matching validated another 3 percent. Evidently, future SIPP studies would be able, if necessary, to confirm survey information by comparing it to administrative records.

- In the later waves of the survey, interviewees reported less income than they had at first, but since the nation's economic indicators showed no such drop in the same time period, it seemed clear that some respondents were growing weary of the lengthy questioning and cutting short their answers. Among other bad effects, this exaggerated the poverty rate by several percentage points, which would seriously affect major social programs. But the distortion, being measurable, could be mathematically corrected; how best to do so, however, was not yet clear.

- One alarming finding was the poor result of questions on the value of assets and holdings. Refusals and "Don't Knows" amounted to 20 percent on questions about savings accounts, 30 to 40 percent on property values, and two thirds or more on stocks and securities. The missing values were supplied by imputation, but analysts were uneasy about having so large an imputed factor. The problem, staff observers felt, was that interviewers hadn't pressed hard on questions about assets, since these came after many others about more essential matters—employment, income, and program participation. The solution might be to shorten the questionnaire or to specifically warn interviewers of their tendency to let up.

- The number of female-headed households found by the survey was much smaller than it should have been, even after reweighting; the result, projected to the national population, showed a million fewer such families than were known to exist from AFDC records. Oversampling the high and low ends of the economic scale and rebalancing them later hadn't worked well. Fortunately, when SIPP went operational a simple, more accurate sampling procedure could be used because the sample, five times as large, would include enough poor and well-to-do people for fine breakdowns.

Despite its shortcomings, the 1979 Panel did produce a fair amount of the kind of information it was hoped SIPP would provide, especially income data that were more complete and reliable than comparable data from the annual CPS supplement.[58]

ISDP data showed that CPS had been overstating poverty by more than 9 percent because its once-a-year measurement was crude and prone to memory error. Conversely, ISDP data showed about 5 percent less average monthly earnings and nearly 20 percent more recipients of unemployment compensation than CPS.

For the first time since the social programs of the 1960s had been created, the number of households receiving benefits from more than one program could be estimated. These were the results:

- In a three-month period of 1979, some 30,000,000 households—more than 1 out of every 3 nationally—received benefits from 1 or more of 5 major programs selected for study.
- Over 21 percent (6,383,000 households) received 2 or more types of benefits.
- 5.6 percent (1,657,000 households) received 3 or more types of benefits.

Interesting light was shed, too, on the food stamp program. About 5,100,000 households with income so low as to qualify for food stamps were excluded from the program because they had more assets than were allowed; if the asset limitation was removed, about 8,000,000 more persons would get food stamps, at an additional cost of nearly $3 billion. That is exactly the kind of information legislators need but have seldom had.

Clearly, there was much to be jubilant about—and much to be concerned about. Many changes and corrections were obviously needed to improve sampling, questionnaire design, weighting of the data, and imputation methods. Under contract, four research centers—the Survey Research Center at the University of Michigan, the Survey Research Laboratory at the University of Illinois, and the Urban Institute and Mathematica Policy Research, both of Washington, D.C.—were doing advanced work on a number of the outstanding problems, including the most serious one of all: the lack of a longitudinal linking system. This technical problem had been simply too difficult for the HEW staff to tackle, and although the Census staff thought they could work it out, they had not had the time. As a result, government and academic researchers working with the data tapes being processed from the 1979 test would be unable to trace individuals or particular families and households to see what happened to them as members left or entered them or as their economic situation changed during the series of interviews.

Nonetheless, while the 1979 test was under way, OMB began to urge the HEW and Census staffs to have SIPP "go operational" as soon as possible so as to get on a regular budgetary footing. Both staffs, knowing how many difficult technical problems remained to be solved, reluctantly agreed under pressure to have SIPP start up by January 1981.

A quite different kind of problem soon proved far more serious. Because ASPE was relatively small and specialized in function, it was not a suitable home for the greatly expanded ISDP or for the far larger SIPP. HEW administrators had long intended the survey to be eventually moved to the much larger Office of Research and Statistics of the Social Security Administration, the agency operating many of the programs SIPP was concerned with, and now pressed for such a move. But the top administrators and the research office of SSA were not at all pleased to have the survey thrust upon them and paid for out of their budget (it cost some $4 million in 1979 and would run several times that when it went operational). SIPP hadn't been their creation, and they preferred to see it housed elsewhere.

Nevertheless, they dutifully included a figure for the SIPP startup in the budget for fiscal 1981 they submitted to the House and Senate Appropriations subcommittees in the spring of 1980—but listed it as a separate item that was highly visible, and therefore vulnerable in a presidential campaign year when spending was a major issue. The House subcommittee, not surprisingly, struck it out. There would be no SIPP startup in 1981.[59]

Many members of the HEW and Census staffs were panic-stricken, but older hands reassured them, saying things like, "That's just the way the game is played," "Next year SIPP will be back in the SSA budget and it'll go through," and "We still have funds to continue development and an extra year is all to the good." Everyone settled down, the startup was rescheduled for February 1982, and the work went on.

By the spring of 1981, however, the Reagan Administration was in power and cutbacks were the order of the day. John Svahn, soon to become SSA Commissioner, was then special assistant to Reagan appointee Richard Schweiker, Secretary of Health and Human Services (successor to HEW), and he wanted no part of SIPP. It did appear in the budget request that spring, but the rumor flying up and down HHS and Census halls was that when the budget came before the subcommittees, SSA's representative would not back SIPP. Roger Herriot got a phone call from his old sparring partner, Charles Lininger, who said in a shaken voice, "Roger, they're not going to support it." Herriot was thunderstruck. Everyone on both staffs had known that SIPP was in danger, but no one had really believed that six years of work and $20 million would be thrown away, and the most important new survey in decades abandoned, in order to save a tiny fraction of 1 percent of the SSA budget.

When the House Appropriations Subcommittee heard what the SSA representative, Robert J. Myers, had to say, it unhesitatingly cut out SIPP, and later, in conference, its view prevailed over that of its pro-SIPP Senate counterpart. The ISDP was now a terminal case, destined to expire by the end of the year when its funds ran out, and its fetus, SIPP, would die with it in the womb.

At HHS and Census, staffers, looking as if they had just had news of a death in the family, sought each other out and asked again and again what they could have done to forestall this outcome. A group of them got together one evening for a sort of wake, praising the departed and reassuring each other that somehow they would live on.

Outside of the government, the scientific community was dismayed (it had much to be dismayed about that year). The Social Science Research Council called an emergency conference to consider how social research might best make good the loss of the information it had been expecting from SIPP. The Committee on National Statistics of the National Academy of Sciences, a nongovernmental agency that advises the government on scientific matters, wrote to Secretary Schweiker expressing its deep concern and saying that SIPP was much needed to fill important gaps in existing data about assistance programs, their effects, and participation in them. Schweiker's office acknowledged receipt of the letter but made no comment.

Lininger and his staff gave up their developmental work and halfheartedly turned to analyses of the 1979 data in an effort to salvage something of value during the remaining months. By the end of the year, when the money ran out, one by one they cleared out their desks and departed for other jobs within HHS or elsewhere. The ISDP ceased to exist, and the SIPP questionnaires, test results, and operational plans were entrusted to the Bureau of the Census for safekeeping and whatever use historians of social science might want to make of them.

Survey Research and Social Science

SIPP's untimely demise at the hands of budget-cutters was only one of the ways in which scientific research can be blocked by the government. At the extreme, the leaders of the state may dictate what may or may not be investigated: Stalin's ban on genetics research and the Nazi condemnation of research in physics based on relativity theory are cases in point. Compared with these, it may seem only benign neglect when agency heads and legislators cut off public funding for a project that promises to be valuable both to government administrators and to academic social scientists. The end of funding does not forbid social scientists to think and work as they like; they remain free to continue exploring the questions that interested them.

But where are they to get the data with which to do so? Low-budget methods of social research lend themselves to the study of small-scale phenomena or to limited levels of analysis, but many subjects are so complex and involve so many interacting forces that only expensive research methods will serve. To explore such social problems or phenomena requires the use of sophisticated questionnaires, intricately constructed samples, a sizable field staff, and costly data-processing procedures; only these can yield the large, complex data bases in which analysts may be able to find the co-variations that suggest cause-and-effect relationships. Without such methods, which are beyond the scope of most nongovernmental sources of funding, freedom to do research on these topics is meaningless. To cancel SIPP was tantamount to saying that social science should no longer pursue that line of inquiry.

While academic researchers need the kind of data major surveys furnish in order to do their analytical and theoretical work, the relationship is reciprocal; without the guidance of hypotheses, survey designers can produce only revisions of old data, not the new kinds that yield new knowledge. Organizing concepts or principles do not emerge of themselves from haphazard observations but in response to hypotheses and conjectures that direct and focus our vision; to see evidence of some regularity, we have to suspect that it exists and look for it. As Einstein succinctly put it, "It is the theory which decides what we can observe."[60]

Thus, there is a symbiotic relationship between those who do survey research or data-gathering and those who statistically analyze the data to test hypotheses about cause-and-effect relationships among the variables. Despite this symbiosis, however, the two groups are often critical of and even faintly hostile toward each other.

In every science there is a dichotomy between the technicians of observation and the analysts, between the experimentalists and the theoreticians. But in the physical and biological sciences the division has narrowed; in particle physics, astronomy, and biogenetics, for instance, where theories have become fairly precise and closely tied to empirical details, the best theoreticians are often the best methodologists and vice versa.

In the social sciences, however, there remains a wide gap and a marked status difference between the two poles. In part this may be due to the relative immaturity of these sciences, but in part it is a legacy from the distant past, when the philosopher, speculating about timeless principles, had far greater prestige than the physician or astronomer who observed the facts. Aristotle, scanting observation but relying on the theory that women were naturally inferior, asserted that they had fewer teeth than men; he never deigned to look.

Looking at social phenomena, in the form of designing instruments and collecting data, is still viewed with a touch of condescension by some social scientists; they say things like, "Surveys are descriptive; they're not really social science." That tone pervades certain articles in the *International Encyclopedia of the Social Sciences* which characterize survey research as mere data-gathering and survey analysis as the scientific search for causal relationships in those data. Charles E.

Lindblom and David K. Cohen, of the Institution for Social and Policy Studies at Yale, are even more snide about survey research in their study *Usable Knowledge:*

We now know as never before just who the poor are, where they are, and what it is they lack. More than ever before, we know which parts of the nation are growing and which are not; which parts of our cities are less or more troubled by street crime or urban decay; who among the nation's children are or are not learning to read. Without deprecating this great accomplishment, we take note that it looks more like reporting than science.[61]

But if such reporting is directed by scientific hypotheses and conducted according to scientific procedures, it deserves the name of science; without that empirical base, causal explanations are little more than wise intuitions or seminal but unverified hypotheses. On the other hand, when survey research is not adequately guided by theory, it is often poor science or even nonscience; such is the case with the informal street-corner samplings discussed earlier, and with many minor surveys of a supposedly scholarly sort that ask the wrong questions or fail to ask some of the right ones. Thus, fact-gathering and analysis are not discrete activities but part of a continuum; despite the status differences that remains between them, they are both aspects of social science. A list of leading social-science achievements in the first two thirds of this century, published in *Science*, rated methodological advances equally with theoretical ones.[62]

A large share of the substantive discoveries and formulations of the social sciences in the past half century have been based on major and minor surveys. Without those survey data, what we know about many social phenomena—ranging from race relations to family dynamics, from economic processes to voting behavior, and from crime to fertility—would be far more impressionistic and speculative, and far less verifiable and useful, than is the case.

Because surveys and censuses capable of producing such knowledge run to hundreds of thousands or even millions of dollars for a large cross-sectional study, and far more than that for a longitudinal one, most larger surveys have been funded or conducted by the federal government. The government's aim has been to get the information it needs to deal effectively with practical problems, but some government officials have recognized that long-term and far-reaching benefits might come from academic analyses seeking deeper understanding.

The first such recognition came in December 1929, when President Herbert Hoover, faced with a collapsing economy, asked the social science community "to survey social changes in this country in order to throw light on the emerging problems which now confront or may be expected to confront the people of the United States." Toward that end he named a Research Committee on Social Trends; it obtained financial backing from the Rockefeller Foundation, got the Bureau of the Census to agree to make its 1930 data available to scholars before publication, and supported a group of distinguished academics in writing thirteen major monographs based on Census data on such subjects as rural life, city life, problems in education, population trends, and the conditions of the races (these were summarized in a volume called *Recent Social Trends*).[63]

No such monographs were produced from 1940 Census data because of the pressure of historical events, but prior to the 1950 Census a new committee, formed at the suggestion of the Social Science Research Council and funded by the Russell Sage Foundation, again got Census cooperation and sponsored eleven analytical monographs. These, written by such experts as Paul Glick, Otis Dudley Duncan, Albert J. Reiss, Jr., and Eleanor H. Bernert (Eleanor Sheldon), dealt with the family, children, housing, and immigrants, among other things; many are rated among the most important pieces of post–World War II social science research.[64]

Again in 1960, but not in 1970, volunteer efforts and foundation funds made monograph studies of Census data possible. Currently, the National Committee for Research on the 1980 Census, funded largely by the Russell Sage and Alfred P. Sloan foundations, is backing monograph studies by Reynolds Farley, Glen Cain, Mark Rosenzweig, and two dozen others on the family, aging, housing, black-white differences, and fourteen other subjects.[65]

Under other auspices, hundreds of other studies in many areas of social science have been, and continue to be, based on the many surveys conducted by the Bureau of the Census and on research center surveys funded by the government.

Until the cancellation of SIPP in 1981, therefore, the pattern had long been for the government to pay for the decennial census and for scores of surveys that served both its own purposes and those of American business, and at the same time made data bases available to social scientists which they could use as raw material for fundamental research.

No one can guarantee that major social benefits will result from such fundamental research, yet history suggests that they will. Newton, in his work on the laws of motion, was looking for generalizations that fit what he observed; he had no thought of the practical applications that engineers and technicians would make of those laws in the following centuries. Einstein, trying to understand the relationship between mass and energy, sought only to make sense of the universe; he did not foresee nuclear weapons or atomic power generation. Congressmen looking for ways to cut the budget may see no reason to pay for a survey from which they expect academics to extract only ivory-tower conclusions (or, as some legislators fear, dangerous social reforms), but if the history of science is any guide, some of those conclusions are very likely to be the basis of practical policy decisions in the future.

All of this seemed to apply to SIPP and to justify its cost. It would have enabled a number of federal departments and agencies to operate more intelligently, fairly, and perhaps more economically than they had been; at the same time, at little or no extra public expense it would have provided social scientists with a store of data with which to search, far more effectively than ever before, for fundamental understandings of the relationships between income and program benefits, health, child care, housing arrangements, and marriage and divorce. But none of that mattered to the budget-cutters in the spring of 1981.

"Good Decisions Require Good Data"

Bruce Chapman, a Reagan supporter and politician from Washington State, was appointed director of the Bureau of the Census by the President in early 1981. It was a time of drastic budget-cutting by the new administration, and the first order of business for Chapman, a lean, suave, well-tailored executive, was to see which Census programs could safely be dropped and which could not. Having been a member of the Seattle City Council for three years and Secretary of State for Washington State for six, he was keenly aware of the importance of good data to government administrators. This not only made him cautious about pruning but led him to take the politically awkward stand of fighting for a substantial sum of new money for a pet project—the revival of the defunct SIPP. "It caught my eye," Chapman recalls,

because there was more gnashing of teeth by my professional staff about the termination of SIPP than about the cutting back or ending of most other programs. So I asked to be briefed on it. When I'd learned what SIPP was about, it stuck in my craw that something we at Census would *never* have cut—a general-purpose survey that would fill a major void and benefit many agencies—was being eliminated because HHS wouldn't support it. Those were wild times in terms of the budget process; programs were being slashed right and left without anyone's taking an overall view.

So as soon as I could, early in 1982, I went to my superiors at the Department of Commerce and said, "We've got to look at SIPP from a policy standpoint. We're going through tremendous changes in this country—in its economy, in government funding—and we've got to have a better understanding of what's happening than we can get from any existing database." It took a long time to persuade them that I should ask OMB to reinstate SIPP and should say to them, "Give *us* the money, not HHS—this is a general-purpose survey that will benefit a great many agencies."

It may have seemed outrageous, after all this budget turmoil, for anybody to go ask for money to be restored—especially money that hadn't even been his to begin with. But I stressed the point with OMB that good policy decisions require good data, and that they at OMB were going to need the SIPP data and so were Congress and the American people. I talked about the deficiencies of our present information system—how little we know about poverty, for instance—and how, if you're going to fine-tune your programs and still serve the ends of justice, you have to have sound information. [It was not all an uphill fight; a number of "budget examiners" in OMB and people on the White House and cabinet staffs were aware of the need for SIPP and in favor of restoring it, if possible. And at about the same time, a report by the Joint Economic Committee of the Congress urged that the quality of the nation's statistical data be maintained.][66]

In the end, OMB recommended that SIPP be revived and that the funds for it be added to the Census budget. By midsummer, 1982, Congress appropriated $2.7 million to enable us to start cranking SIPP back up and getting it started by the fall of 1983, and by 1985, when SIPP is in full swing, its budget will be about $18 million.

At a time when the National Science Foundation's funds for social-science research were being cut by 38 percent[67]—the administration sought even deeper cuts, but Congress balked—the revival of SIPP at the urging of a Reagan appointee was a triumph of common sense over politics.

The choice of a 1983 startup date may, however, have owed more to politics than to common sense: The prospect of early tangible results made it easier to get the money and Chapman even promised that the first published reports based on SIPP would come out by the fall of 1984 (at the height of the next presidential campaign). Some social scientists were distressed; at a Social Science Research Council confer-ence on SIPP in December 1982 a number of participants pointed out the flaws and omissions that still existed in the survey and stressed the need for further developmental work. Statistician Stephen Fienberg of Carnegie-Mellon University, who chaired the conference, felt then and still does that the revived SIPP was simply not the one originally planned and that "the timing of the start of the new survey was politi-cally motivated and went counter to the advice of most knowledgeable experts."[68]

At the Bureau of the Census, the people who had worked on SIPP, delighted that it had been resurrected and was now all theirs, were unflapped by the 1983 startup date. Accustomed to having deadlines imposed on them for political reasons, they took a businesslike view of SIPP's existing imperfections and the brief time remaining to fix them. William Butz, associate director of the Demographic Fields section, explains: "The main purpose of SIPP is to answer real-world questions about what people do when you offer something to them. The other research outputs are by-products. If you listen to all the people with special interests, the program will never be ready to run. We want to make use of the input of the academics, but we're not able to give them everything they want."

The Social Science Research Council, however, felt that SIPP would be so important a scientific resource that it behooved them to seek to influence the design and content of the new survey and its "data products" (the reports and tapes through which the data are made available to users). Accordingly, in November 1982 the SSRC named a working group on SIPP composed of half a dozen respected social scientists who would monitor developments in SIPP and transmit the views of the academic world about it to OMB and the Bureau of the Census.*

Immediately after Congress acted, several dozen Census staffers, most of whom had previously been part of the SIPP project, got busy. Working singly, in small teams, and in large staff meetings, they began making major decisions and spelling out details to implement them.

The first major decisions concerned at what intervals and how many times each panel would be interviewed. To stretch the funds, the staff chose to have interviews take place every four months rather than every three, but to cover all the topics in the overall plan, each panel would be interviewed seven times, and in some cases eight. (From 1985 on, all households will be interviewed eight times.) Each panel would be followed for about two and a half years, and a new panel—a fresh sample—would be started each year while earlier ones were continuing. Thus, after the first year there would always be at least two panels running, and part of the time three, each of them a multiframe national probability sample of 40,000 households.

With these decisions made, several staffers got to work on the questionnaires, of which there would now have to be eight versions. But since much of the work had been done in previous years, most of what they now did was pruning and revising. "At least a third of the basic questionnaire went out," Evan Davey estimates. "Most of that material was impractical and hard to deal with, and if we were no longer forced to do it, we weren't *going* to do it." Still, all the major topics covered earlier remained, including income and program benefits, assets, education, work history, marital history, fertility, disability, migration, and child care.

To enable interviewers to keep all this straight, other staffers worked out a series of aids including reminder cards summarizing the income and benefit data gathered on earlier interviews, a card showing the age of a person born in any given year to enable the interviewer to verify the answers to age and birth-date questions, flash cards showing a

---

*The working group is chaired by Martin H. David; its other members include Philip E. Converse, University of Michigan; Harvey Galper, the Brookings Institution; Daniel G. Horvitz, Research Triangle Institute; Graham Kalton, University of Michigan; and Seymour Spilerman and Harold W. Watts, both of Columbia University.

Medicare card and Social Security check colors, and a detailed, question-by-question instruction manual as thick as a book.

Only half a year after SIPP had been revived, the SIPP Planning Group—some fifteen of the people working on the project—was able to run a small pretest of the revised Wave 1 and Wave 2 questionnaires. For two days, a dozen interviewers were intensively trained in a hotel in Atlanta; then, accompanied by observers, they took the Wave 1 questionnaire to about 200 households in that city, and a month later went back with the Wave 2 questionnaire. Afterward, staffers John Coder and Angela Feldman wrote an interoffice memo compiling problems that needed attention. These ran the gamut from the trivial:

—More space is needed to fill names in item 18a.
—Codes 20–21 for [ethnic] origin do not match on Flashcard D.

to the substantial:

—Many high income respondents are unwilling to report amounts of asset income.
—The 21 per cent nonresponse rate for hourly earnings is much higher than we would like to see for SIPP.

Most of the snags encountered in the pretest were of the first kind and easily remedied; the memo cheerfully concluded that "there were no 'general' problems with administering the questionnaire" and that, as one interviewer confidently said, "the questionnaires will no doubt be perfected in the next months."

Certain old problems, however, outside the scope of the pretest, were both serious and bound to be slow in the solving. In two cases—the procedures for weighting and imputation—details were still being hammered out when SIPP had already taken to the field and the first data were being compiled for the reports promised for late 1984.

The toughest problem, however, remained the matter of linking, the key to longitudinal analysis. By the time the interviewers began sending in completed questionnaires in the fall of 1983, the Census staffers, drawing on both their own expertise and work done previously by HHS and its contractors, had readied a way of making a "linking index" for each wave. This was a set of rules for constructing a code number for each individual that would not only identify that person's "file" (all the data gathered about him or her) but, through several of its digits, would link him or her to a particular household and family.[69] The linking index would enable analysts to pull together whatever data, within any wave, they needed. If they wanted to know the income sources of all married men of a given age and educational background, they could tell the computer to extract those cases and compute the answers; if, then, they wanted to know which of them were stepfathers who supported their stepchildren, they could ask for that information and the computer would pick it out.

This system would not enable researchers, however, to follow households or families from wave to wave to see how economic or other changes affected them and their members. It is very difficult to devise a way of tracking individuals and at the same time following the households or families they are part of, given the many changes in the membership of households and families over two and a half years due to separation, divorce, death, marriage, birth, adoption, the moving away of grown children, and so on.

If Family B, whom we referred to earlier, consists of four persons—call them AB, BB, CB, and DB—and AB dies or moves away, is it still the same family? If AB's place is taken by EF (a new husband) or if someone else such as an adopted child joins the family, is it still the same family? If, over two and a half years, it has come to consist of EF and three others but none of the original four, is it the same family?

These questions are reminiscent of that old classroom exercise, the Problem of the Philosopher's Socks. The Philosopher, being poor, darned the holes in a pair of socks again and again until none of the original material was left and the socks consisted entirely of darns. Were they the same pair as at the outset, or a different pair? At what point, if any, did they become different? Anywhere along the line, the Philosopher could have said, "I know which pair of socks these are," implying that they had a continuous identity—yet how could they be the same if eventually none of their fibers had been in the original pair?

The linking problem is even worse than the Philosopher's: Researchers want to follow not just the socks but discarded fibers that become darns in other pairs of socks. In academic centers, researchers had already worked out methods of tracking individuals longitudinally in other surveys, and before the 1981 cancellation of SIPP outside contractors had done a good deal of work on a longitudinal linking system for SIPP, but it was still far from ready to function when the revived SIPP went into the field in 1983. The Census staff felt sure, however, that the linking index numbers that it was assigning to people, families, and households could be converted later to a longitudinal linking index. "By the time we've completed the first panel in mid-1986," Evan Davey confidently says, "we'll be able to link the files longitudinally. We're not worried about it."

If so, SIPP will achieve not only its goal of providing needed data to the makers of policy and the directors of government programs— twenty-two government agencies will directly benefit from it—but it will, the Social Science Research Council believes, become "an especially important source of information for research on American social conditions and trends."[70]

A single example will suggest what social scientists hope for from it. Arthur Norton of the Population Division of the Bureau of the Census, an energetic tousle-headed man in his 40s, is both a Census demographer and a family sociologist; his enthusiasm about SIPP stems more from the latter of these roles than the former. "The lack of longitudinal data thus far," he says,

has meant that we haven't known what factors are involved in household and family compositional change. What we deal with normally is cross-sectional survey data showing the numbers of types of households and families at different times, and the changes in those numbers. Based on statistical associations, we've hypothesized why the observed changes in the numbers took place. If an increase in income level correlated with a decrease in marital dissolution, for instance, we speculated that they were related. But it was only a speculation, because we had no idea whether the *same* people or families were involved.

With SIPP, however, we'll be able to look directly at the changes and connect them with events in the lives of specific individuals and their families. For the first time we'll begin to get at cause-and-effect relationships. We'll be able to project future numbers of households and families, to predict changes in the fertility level, and to see how such factors as work history, migration, education, marital status, and so on, are interrelated. We'll finally be able to confirm or deny the validity of our hypotheses. In short, SIPP has wonderful possibilities for increasing our understanding of the processes involved in family life today.

SIPP will serve researchers in many areas other than family life, but its ultimate value is likely to be larger than the sum of its obvious and predictable applications. As William Butz says, "There's no way to predict all the ways in which SIPP data will be used. The marketplace of ideas will take up the data and use them in ways we can't foresee." Whatever those unforeseen uses of SIPP, they seem sure to make us less ignorant and myth-ridden, more truly knowledgeable, about the human condition in contemporary America.

Postscript: Half a year after the first SIPP interviewers started out in October 1983, data compiled at the Bureau of the Census showed that response rates were running satisfactorily high (about 95 percent) and that the survey was working.[71] The first actual report, "Economic Characteristics of Households in the United States: Third Quarter 1983," was published in late 1984.[72]

ONE THING AT A TIME

A Series of Laboratory Experiments Explores the Antisocial Tendency of People Working in Groups to Secretly Do Less Than Their Best

A Problem Worth Exploring

At Ohio State University in Columbus, one fall morning in 1975, the quiet inside the football stadium building (whose rooms were mostly assigned to subdued academic uses) was shattered by an uproar; somewhere, a number of students were shouting at the top of their lungs. In the social psychology office, a startled secretary scrambled to her feet, but the bedlam abruptly broke off. She sat down again, only to have the shouting burst forth anew—the voices seemed to be yelling "LEEE-ON!"—then stop, then start yet again.

Finally, she went out into the hall to investigate. The intermittent uproar was coming from a seminar room where Professor Bibb Latané was teaching a graduate course in social psychology. During a lull, the secretary gingerly opened the door; nothing was amiss, but at the sight of her concerned face the students were convulsed with laughter. Latané, a tall lean man of 38 with a stiff thatch of straw-colored hair, grinned and told her that all was well; the students were merely helping him pretest a technique to be used in an experiment. Reassured, she headed back for the office; behind her, the outcry broke out once more, though now the students were bellowing "RAAAH!"

They were helping Latané try out an experimental task that he hoped to use to investigate what he called "social loafing," a phenomenon, in his opinion, of considerable scientific and practical importance. When advising graduate students casting about for a research project, Latané often says something to this effect: "There are a hundred million things you can do, but most of them are trivial. You want something that's worth doing for a number of different reasons. If it addresses an interesting theoretical question, *and* involves an advance in methodology, *and* lends itself to an elegant experiment—*and* has social relevance—then it's a problem worth exploring."

In choosing social loafing as a research topic, Latané was taking his own advice: It met all these criteria, especially that of social relevance. A major premise of social life is that by cooperating with others we can achieve our personal goals more efficiently than we can alone; we therefore band together in teams, committees, armies, parties, cooperatives, and so on. Moreover, some desirable activities and products absolutely require team effort; sailing a ship, running a university, and removing a gallbladder are obvious examples.

The problem, as Latané saw it, is that according to both general belief and sociopsychological theory, the team spirit engendered by working in groups should make individuals try harder than they would alone, yet in common experience the opposite often seems true.[1] In many a group, one suspects that most members make a show of effort but actually do less than they would if working for themselves. How often we sense this is suggested by the number of terms we apply to such behavior: *shirking, slacking, lying down on the job, sleeping at one's post, goldbricking*, and *not pulling one's weight*, among others. A typical social psychologist, trying to avoid such value-laden terms, might speak of this as "the social inhibition of performance"; Latané, a nonconformist who likes to use colorful phrases and even jokes in his professional articles, prefers his own candidly pejorative term.

Social loafing is no joking matter; it can be costly to society. In Russia, the average *kolkhoz* (collective farm) yields only two thirds to three quarters as much fruit and vegetables, and only half as much pork, beef, milk, and eggs per acre as the one-acre plots that peasants are allowed to tend as private entrepreneurs.[2] Capitalist institutions can be similarly afflicted by social loafing: At least one cause of the comparatively low productivity of many American factories is said to be the lack of motivation of the workers. Yet there are institutions similar to the kolkhoz and the American factory, namely, the socialistic *kibbutz* (collective farm) of Israel and the capitalist factory of Japan, whose members, far from loafing, appear to work at a high level of effort.

Since collective effort is essential to social life, especially in a complex modern society, the tendency of members of many groups to do far less than they could is a serious matter. Quite possibly, Latané felt, the standard of living in a society can be depressed as much by social loafing as by insufficient investment capital, excessive population growth, or a shortage of skilled researchers and technicians.

For such reasons, it seemed to him, experimental research on social loafing would both address a significant issue of theory and have considerable social relevance. He did not yet know whether it would also involve an advance in methodology but suspected that one might emerge along the way as the need for it became clear.

The first methodological question that had to be resolved was what kind of group activity to use in the experiment. Such complex tasks as assembly-line procedures or vegetable farming would obviously not be feasible in the social psychology laboratory, where each run of an experiment typically lasts no more than an hour. Latané had therefore been considering far simpler activities, among them collective noisemaking such as cheering or applauding. He had spoken about this to his students that morning and they had raised a number of technical questions.

Would people willingly shout or clap (they asked) when there was nothing to cheer about or applaud? Would so pointless an activity fail to produce real effort, or would volunteers, knowing they were contributing to a scientific inquiry, do their best? On the practical side, would the participants be able to sustain steady sound long enough to make good measurement possible, and how hard on them would repeated rounds of shouting or clapping be?

"Well," Latané said finally, having hooked his fish, "let's try it. Who's willing?" No one volunteered. "Come on," he said, "I'll give a quarter to anyone who will." A number of hands went up.

"But what should we shout?" someone asked. One wag suggested that in honor of Leon Festinger's historic experiments on cognitive dissonance, which they had recently been discussing, they use his first name. But "LEEE-ON!" they discovered, did not make for uniform sustained sound, so they switched to "RAAAH!" which did. After ten minutes of trials, everyone was satisfied that shouting would be a practicable group task. Latané, of course, had no way of knowing whether or not it would elicit social loafing; that could be determined only by the appropriately designed experiment.

Latané could hardly have chosen a more classic—or resistant—research problem. The first known experiment in social psychology, conducted by an American psychologist named Norman Triplett in 1898, had been an attempt to see how an individual's normal level of performance is affected by the presence of other people. Having noticed that bicycle racers reach higher top speeds when paced, Triplett created an analogous experiment: He had children wind fishing reels alone and in pairs and found that many of them did better in the presence of another child.[3]

The influence of observers or collaborators on an individual's performance long remained the central problem in social psychology; the psychologist Gordon Allport even said that it was "the only problem studied in the first three decades of experimental research."[4] But although a vast number of experiments were conducted, they yielded conflicting results. Many researchers found evidence of "social facilitation" (the enhancement of the individual's efforts by the presence of others), while others found the very opposite.[5]

No doubt most social psychologists would have preferred to see proof of social facilitation, a tendency that supports an optimistic view of humankind and society. But the evidence of a less altruistic, more individualistic bent to human nature could not be wished away.

One notable experiment yielding such data was conducted in the early 1920s by a German psychologist named Ringelmann. He never managed to get his work published—or his own first name recorded—but his results were summarized by another German psychologist and became a springboard for much further research. Ringelmann asked volunteers to pull on a rope as hard as they could, alone and in groups of two, three, and eight. His subjects, who must have been husky workmen, were able to average 63 kilograms (139 pounds) of force when pulling alone. When they pulled in groups, however, there was not only no increase due to team spirit but a marked drop-off—small for pairs, larger for trios, and largest for groups of eight, the latter averaging only 248 kilograms, or less than half the sum of their individual performances.[6] Apparently, something about pulling together kept them from doing their best.

Latané's interest in this problem was an outgrowth of a body of earlier research for which he and a colleague, John Darley, had been widely acclaimed by their fellow professionals in the late 1960s. In it they had reported a discovery that Latané now thought might apply to, and account for, the phenomenon of social loafing.

In 1964, a young woman named Kitty Genovese had been murdered on a sidewalk in Kew Gardens, New York, by a man who strangled and stabbed her repeatedly for half an hour while thirty-eight residents of nearby apartments watched but did nothing. Commentators spoke scathingly of the brutish New York character, of alienation in contemporary America, and so on. But Latané and Darley, both young assistant professors of social psychology (at Columbia University and New York University, respectively), were unconvinced and disturbed by these glib condemnations, and decided to do experimental research on the matter.

For the next four years they conducted a series of studies in which they led naive (unknowing) undergraduate volunteers in their experiments to believe that a stranger was in distress. On closed-circuit TV the volunteer might see someone apparently receive a powerful electric shock, or on an intercom overhear someone in a neighboring room suffer an epileptic seizure.[7] Latané and Darley found that when naive participants were alone, they would generally rush to the aid of the seemingly afflicted stranger, but if other people, especially strangers, were present, they were much less likely to do so. From interviews with the students afterward, Latané and Darley deduced that the presence of others weakened the impulse to help, chiefly by "diffusing" the individual's sense of responsibility. They concluded that the failure of witnesses of the attack on Kitty Genovese to act was due not to callousness but to the inhibiting effect on helping behavior of that pervasive aspect of big-city life, the presence of strangers.[8]

Now, years later, it had occurred to Latané that the diffusion of responsibility might also explain social loafing. He invited two young social psychologists who had come to Ohio State University to study with him, postdoctoral fellow Stephen G. Harkins and doctoral candidate Kipling Williams, to join him in a program of experimental research on the matter, and since Latané, though then only 38, already had a considerable reputation for doing original and important work, they leaped at the opportunity.

For several weeks, Williams and Latané met day after day in Latané's office to plan the research; Harkins, who had another project going, joined them part of the time. The team decided to do a series of laboratory experiments in which volunteers would perform some task both alone and in groups of different sizes, first to establish the existence of social loafing under laboratory conditions, and then to identify the circumstances that promoted it and those that inhibited it.

Their first order of business was to decide what experimental task might best serve their purpose. For a time, they considered using an improvement of Ringelmann's rope-pulling procedure and planned to build a large apparatus with which they could mislead volunteers into thinking that others, in line behind them, were pulling with them, when in fact the others were only grunting. This ploy would reveal how much less effort each individual exerted when he thought he was part of a team than when he was on his own. (Ringelmann had calculated the average amount of loafing in groups but had had no way of sorting out individual efforts from the group result.)

Just before Latané and his partners began work on the rope-pulling machine, they discovered in the *Journal of Experimental Social Psychology* that another research team had recently used a very similar piece of apparatus. They promptly scrapped the idea—with some relief, since it bade fair to be a slow and cumbersome way to gather the data. They then spent a number of brainstorming sessions thinking up other tasks such as turning cranks to generate electricity, blowing air into balloons, and sorting IBM punch cards. Each had flaws: overly complicated apparatus, unduly strenuous effort required, too much time needed, and so on.

Then one day Harkins came across a sound meter that he had stuck in a desk drawer, and asked his colleagues whether perhaps sound or noise of some sort made by their subjects might not be an easily measurable product of joint effort. Latané and Williams responded with instant enthusiasm and within minutes had come up with half a dozen suggestions for noisemaking activities, two of which—clapping and shouting—seemed simple, cheap, and easy to manipulate and measure. Furthermore, both could be presented to volunteers as meaningful tasks, since cheering and applause are part of cultural, and especially undergraduate, tradition. The next day Latané tried out group shouting in the classroom; afterward, satisfied with the results, he and his collaborators got to work in earnest on the details of their first experiment.

In it, they would try only to reconfirm Ringelmann's basic finding of social loafing. Student volunteers would come six at a time to the laboratory and there either clap or shout as loudly as possible, singly and in groups of various sizes. The results would be measured by a sound-level meter; the decibel readings, converted into dynes/cm^2, would represent the actual effort the students had exerted.

If this first trial did demonstrate social loafing, Latané and his colleagues would be justified in going on to advanced experiments that would be far more difficult to conduct and require more apparatus. For in the first experiment the six participants, seeing and hearing each other, might indulge in less social loafing than they would if their individual contributions to the team effort weren't being observed. In later experiments, therefore, the researchers would need to develop procedures and equipment to isolate participants from each other's observation and yet allow them to function in teams of different sizes.

One other preparation was necessary for the first trial: The team had to concoct a cover story—a plausible account of what they were doing—to distract the volunteers' attention and keep them from suspecting the real purpose of the experiment. For if the volunteers knew that the researchers could detect their antisocial behavior, they might try to suppress it—or, perhaps, exaggerate it for the researchers' benefit. The one thing they probably would not do, to judge by many other socio-psychological experiments, would be to act exactly as they would if they did *not* know the truth.

After discussing a number of possible cover stories, Latané, Harkins, and Williams decided on a very simple one: The notices they posted asked for volunteers, who would earn partial course credit in psychology by signing up, to take part in "a study of judgments of how much noise people make in social settings, namely cheering and applause, and how loud they seem to those who hear them." (Such descriptions of experiments are always purposefully vague.) They then prepared a little script consisting of a pitch or explanation, along with appropriate stage directions, to be memorized and delivered by Harkins and Williams. (Latané would direct the project but leave the hands-on laboratory work to his junior colleagues.) The script, like the notice calling for volunteers, stated that the aim of the experiment was to see how well people can estimate the magnitude of the noise produced by social clapping and cheering.

Finally, all was ready: Latané had booked a large laboratory room in the university's stadium building; a microphone and sound level meter had been delivered and tested; Harkins and Williams had run through their script a few times; the notices had been posted; and scores of volunteers had signed up, of whom eight groups of six, all undergraduate men and mostly sophomores, had been notified of their appointments. Early one winter evening in 1976, the researchers met in the laboratory, rechecked their equipment, and waited for their first volunteers to arrive and, with luck, demonstrate under laboratory conditions a tendency toward social loafing that might lead to discoveries casting light on an important, socially harmful, and perhaps controllable, tendency of humankind.

Unambiguous Evidence

The investigation of human social behavior by means of laboratory experiments such as the one Latané's team was about to perform is a recent development, historically speaking; research of this kind, most of it conducted by social psychologists, has taken place largely within the past four decades.

At the turn of the century, social psychology, then in its infancy and deficient in investigative methodology, was more like a species of philosophy than a social science; its practitioners could do little but try to offer insightful and plausible theories to account for the social behavior they saw around them. But as psychology, of which it was an offshoot, became increasingly experimental and methodologically sophisticated, social psychology followed suit, and since the 1940s its characteristic mode of research and chief source of new knowledge has been laboratory experimentation.[9]

Social psychology is unique among the social sciences in this regard. Most of the others study phenomena as given in nature in order not to tamper with the complex integrity of events; social psychology deliberately simulates nature in the laboratory in order to be able to experimentally vary conditions one by one. The chief reason this approach is feasible in social psychology is that its province lies largely between psychology and sociology in a zone where many of the phenomena are small in scale and easily simulated in brief, inexpensive, controlled trials. Most other social research is concerned with mass effects or large-scale phenomena, such as systems of governance, economic behavior, and social stratification, that can rarely be manipulated in real life or simulated in the laboratory; as with astronomical events, efforts to understand them are largely limited to inferences based on observation. One cannot perform experiments on the power structure of American society, nor can one study it by having six sophomores sit around a laboratory table and carry out some assigned group activity.

In contrast, the territory of social psychology is the interaction between the individual and others: how we perceive or misperceive them, respond to them, and are affected by them in social situations.* The phenomena in this area, most of them amenable to experimental investigation, include the common proclivity for overrating or under-

---

* This is the classic textbook definition of the field; some social psychologists, however, maintain that their discipline includes far larger phenomena.

rating others on the basis of cues and labels; the ways we attribute others' actions to various causes; the tendency to modify our views to conform to those of the group we are in; the ability to perform better in cooperative groups than competitive ones; and dozens of comparable matters, including attitude formation and attitude change, the effects of cognitive dissonance (conflicts between our beliefs), helping behavior, aggression, group dynamics, persuasiveness, and interpersonal attraction.[10]

These subjects can also be, and sometimes are, explored by nonexperimental methods like those used by other social sciences: survey research, field studies, archival research, and so on. But the evidence yielded by these methods lacks the clarity and the before-and-after character of experimental evidence.

When we observe any form of social behavior in a real-life setting, we find many factors that are correlated with it; oral sexual practices, for instance, are more common among young Americans than middle-aged ones, better-educated people than ill-educated ones, the white-collar class than the blue-collar class, and so on. But since we cannot remove or add age, education, or socioeconomic level, one by one, to see what happens, we are hard put to know whether any of them is the cause, or a contributing cause, of the behavior, or whether both of them are concomitant effects of something else.

Again: The American divorce rate has more than trebled during the past half century at the same time that increasing numbers of women have gone to work, organized religion has declined, most of the farm population has moved to the cities, average real income has risen, the findings of sex researchers have been widely publicized, and divorce laws have been liberalized. Did any of these factors, or several of them acting together, increase the divorce rate? Or was it that the growth of divorce caused one or more of them? (The more ex-wives there are, the more women are forced to work.) Or were divorce and these social changes the side-by-side effects of some other cause, such as the growth of manufacturing and retailing, which shifted the major function of marriage from production to emotional satisfaction?

Correlations thus show association—if A exists, B is likely to coexist with it (or, conversely, to be absent)—but what they imply about causation is ambiguous.[11] Yet if we are to understand social behavior, especially if we are to use our knowledge to solve social problems, we need to know what is cause and what is effect. *

There are, to be sure, nonexperimental ways, some of which are discussed elsewhere in this book, of inferring with some degree of certainty whether factors that correlate with a piece of social behavior are likely to have caused it or played a part in its causation. For one thing, if a given correlation suggests a cause-and-effect relationship, other information, including common-sense knowledge of the real world, may tell us which factor is likely to be cause and which effect.

An example: If the grade averages of students at a university are correlated with their use of marijuana—that is, if the more frequent the use, the lower the grade averages—it is probable there is some connection between them. In technical terms, the use of marijuana is the "independent variable," the grade average the "dependent variable" (its state varies according to the state of the independent one). But researchers are cautious about claiming that such a relationship is one of cause and effect; they prefer to say that the correlation "suggests" a cause-and-effect relationship. To the extent that it does, however, real-world experience tells us which is the likely direction: Conceivably, students who get low grades might as a result seek consolation in marijuana smoking, but that seems farfetched compared with the possibility that the smoking results in the low grades.

Even so, the correlation suggests causality only to the extent that other factors which might cause both low grades and marijuana use can be ruled out—personal problems, peer group pressure, the influence of background and upbringing, and so on. To exclude such other possibilities, researchers might use multiple regression analysis to determine the relative connection of every such factor with grade averages. As we saw in chapter 2, this is a statistical manipulation that equates two or more groups of individuals in every respect except one,

---

* Nowadays some social scientists are reluctant to speak of causes and effects since these terms imply more than we really know—which is only that the appearance of one event is always followed by the appearance of the other. Accordingly, they use such expressions as "If A is increased, then B can be expected to increase." But since even they, like the rest of us, live their lives as if they believed in causality, let us call a cause a cause, an effect an effect.

plus the behavior under study, thus revealing the degree to which a variation in that one respect goes hand in hand with a variation in the behavior. The stronger the connection, the more likely it is that the two are causally related.

A third approach, discussed in chapter 1, is the study of natural experiments—changes in social behavior occurring after clearly defined events such as a disaster. In addition to occurrences of that kind, historical events, including the passage of new laws, are natural experiments, though it is hard to separate out the effects of any one such event from concurrent happenings. An example might be the recent change in Social Security rules enabling widows who remarry to retain widowhood benefits. Prior to that change, an increasing number of widows were said to be remaining unremarried, even though living with male partners, in order not to lose their benefits. If future survey data provided by SIPP, the survey discussed in chapter 3, do show an increase in the remarriage rate of such widows, it would seem to be the result of the new rule, particularly if the remarriage rate of widows not receiving such benefits did not also rise.

In contrast to these several approaches, researchers using the experimental method create a desired situation and set up two (or more) versions of it by altering a single factor, the independent variable, X. They then put participants in each version of the situation, randomly deciding who goes into which one so as to balance out all other differences among the participants. If the people in one version behave differently in any way from those in another—this behavior being the dependent variable, Y—the researchers can assert with considerable confidence that since everything but X was the same in both cases, X causes Y, at least under these experimental conditions.[12]

The great appeal of experimental social psychology is that it discloses principles of behavior with a simplicity and rigor analogous to that of a chemical experiment in which drops of a reagent, added to a solution, produce a precipitate. As Elliot Aronson and J. Merrill Carlsmith state in *The Handbook of Social Psychology*, "The major advantage of the laboratory experiment is its ability to provide us with unambiguous evidence about causation."[13]

The psychologist Kurt Lewin, who had immense influence on the direction social psychology has taken in the past four decades, went even further, claiming that "laws can be established in psychology only by an experimental procedure."[14] While recent developments in survey analysis and other nonexperimental methods make this dictum doubtful, it is true that experimental evidence is more nearly definitive about causation than any other kind. No wonder it has been and still is the favored and characteristic research method of social psychologists.

But this emphasis has had certain drawbacks. In the opinion of some social scientists, the devotion of most social psychologists to small-scale experiments testing specific hypotheses has kept them from paying much attention to the development of high-level theory that could offer a unifying explanation of social influence. A number of such theories do exist—Gestalt, psychoanalytic, field, exchange, and attribution theories, among others—but most of the creative effort of social psychologists has been directed toward experiments testing microtheories applicable to narrowly circumscribed phenomena.[15]

Yet even minute and seemingly trivial research may have broad implications. Some years ago a team at Kent State University had students learn a series of nonsense syllables, then try to read images being flashed on a screen for 1/100th of a second. If other people were watching, the students often mistook meaningless patterns for syllables they had learned, but if the bystanders were blindfolded, they did not. The experiment yielded a generalization of seemingly minuscule import: "Dominant responses" (well-learned ones) are made more likely by the presence of an audience.[16] But this trifling finding has larger implications: While dominant responses are often the right ones, whenever we are apprehensive in a social situation we may react to stimuli in familiar but inappropriate ways. This goes far to make sense of many otherwise baffling kinds of behavior ranging from gaffes and slips of the tongue to the chronic rigidity and mutual incomprehension of arms-control negotiators.

What motivates many social psychologists is thus the conviction that through small laboratory experiments they will be able to discover principles underlying major social problems, and that this knowledge can lead to social change. As Morton Deutsch, a major figure in contemporary social psychology, cautiously put it in a recent address, "The games people play as subjects in our laboratory experiments may have some relevance to such important social concerns as war and peace and social justice."[17] That is the promise and the allure of experimental social psychology.

A Really Clean Experiment

The sophomore men arriving one by one that winter night to take part in the experiment had no idea what to expect as they made their way through the gloomy corridors and stairways of the stadium building to the higher floors up under the stands. But the laboratory, when they found it, was reassuring. It was a large, brightly lighted room with soundproofed walls and doors; the floor was carpeted, and several one-way mirrors on the walls were framed by curtains. A number of chairs and a couple of tables were arranged for the evening's work; others were stacked in the corners. The only equipment, on one of the tables, was a simple omnidirectional microphone and a bottle-shaped object of black plastic with a dial on its face; this, the students learned, was a sound-level meter.

Each arriving volunteer was greeted by the two junior researchers—Harkins, slight, dark-haired, and 27, and Williams, broad-shouldered, blonde, and 22—who introduced themselves and made small talk while waiting for the others. Latané, meanwhile, was stationed out of sight in an adjoining observation room where, through one-way mirrors, he could observe the goings-on without his senior presence distracting the participants.

When all the students had arrived, Harkins asked them to take their place on six chairs arranged a yard apart in an arc at one end of the room. He stood alongside the table with the sound-level meter, a dozen feet from the students; Williams sat behind it, ready to record sound levels on a worksheet.[18]

"As you know," said Harkins, "we're interested in judgments of how much noise people make in social settings, namely cheering and applause, and how loud they seem to those who hear them. We want each of you to do two things—one, make noises, and two, judge noises. There will be a number of trials, some using only one of you, others using two, four, and six at a time. On each trial, I'll tell you who is to perform and whether you are to cheer"—he demonstrated with a bellowed "raaah!" and the students laughed delightedly—"or clap. When you're to begin, I'll count backwards from three and raise my hand. Continue until I lower it. We would like you to clap or cheer for five seconds as loud as you can." To help them in estimating the loudness of the sounds, he named the decibel levels of some familiar noises.

"Okay, let's try it once or twice with 'rah,'" said Harkins. "Three . . . two . . . one," and he raised his hand. The students yelled rather feebly. "Oh, come *on!*" he said, "that's all you've got?" He turned to Williams, who, as planned, made a sour face and shook his head. The students laughed; their next try was somewhat lustier. After a few rounds of yelling and clapping, interspersed with jocular remarks and praise, Harkins professed himself satisfied and ready to start.

From then on, working from a schedule, he kept things moving swiftly: He'd announce who was to shout or clap, give the countdown, raise his hand, and, after five seconds of bedlam, drop it. Each student shouted and clapped twice alone, four times in pairs and in foursomes, and six times in groups of six. After the first few rounds, the trials went smoothly and swiftly; thirty-six bouts of yelling and thirty-six of clapping took only a little over half an hour, though by then the students were exhausted and had raw throats and sore palms.

At the end of the session, Harkins spent about fifteen minutes debriefing the group. (In debriefing, researchers tell the participants, by way of reward, something about the covert goals and scientific value of the experiment. If it was psychologically stressful—the shouting and clapping experiment was not—the researchers give a full and reassuring explanation in order to relieve any distress the volunteers may be feeling.) After thanking the students for their hard work, Harkins confessed that the experimenters had been looking for something other than they'd said they'd been, and explained the phenomenon of social loafing; he also asked them not to tell other students any of this in order not to jeopardize future trials. In order not to confront the students with any unpleasant truth about themselves, he said that he and Williams wouldn't know until they had analyzed the results whether that evening's trials had revealed any social loafing; actually, he thought it possible that Williams already knew from the meter readings whether or not they had.

The students were intrigued but not discomfited; it was plain to them that even if any of them had loafed, his part in the group result couldn't be identified. But to judge by their questions and comments, none thought that he himself had loafed, though each was ready to believe that his fellows might have. Satisfied with what they'd been told, the students left.

Harkins was glad to see them go; neither he nor Latané, who now came in from the observation room, had any idea what the carefully noncommittal Williams had seen on the meter. Williams beamed at them. Even without having had the opportunity to convert the decibel readings to dynes/cm^2, it had been obvious to him as he jotted down the peak readings of the dial that two, four, or six students making noise together produced distinctly less than two, four, or six times as much as individuals did.

The results of one session weren't, of course, conclusive; the experimenters ran a total of eight such sessions, two per evening, Harkins and Williams alternating as leader and recorder, before they had a pool of data large enough to ensure that what they were seeing were not chance variations. Then, at Latané's direction, Harkins and Williams used a terminal of a mainframe computer to convert their 576 sound-level readings to energy output figures and to compute averages for the whole series of sessions. In addition, they ran an analysis of variance to make sure that the decrease in average sound output was correlated more strongly with increases in group size than other factors. Finally, they made a "confidence level" computation and found that there was less than a one-in-a-thousand chance that the trend they had seen could have occurred by pure chance.

They then burst into Latané's office. "We've got it!" they crowed, handing him a sheet of paper containing numbers arranged in a table. Latané studied the data briefly, then fished graph paper out of a drawer and swiftly sketched a graph based on the numbers. In its later, polished form, it looked like this:[19]

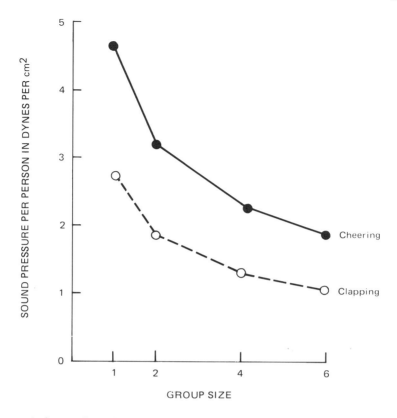

GROUP SIZE

Latané's long plain face was transformed by a radiant smile. "That's it," he said, "that's the Ringelmann effect. Now we can get moving."

The next step, Latané told Harkins and Williams, was to clean up the experiment: The results, though impressive-looking, might well have been distorted by the fact that the students had done their yelling and clapping in each other's view and hearing, and might therefore have been influenced by embarrassment, a tendency to conform rather than outdo each other, and other such factors. Even more important, the noise produced by two or more persons might not add up in any simple fashion; Latané, recalling something he'd learned long ago in high school physics, said it was possible that some part of the missing sound wasn't due to social loafing but to sound cancellation: Sound waves from several sources, out of synchronization, could interfere with and partly cancel each other. If so, not all of the sound loss had been due to social loafing. Their next goal, therefore, was to eliminate, or at least control, these extraneous variables.

To check out the question of sound cancellation, Harkins and Williams took the sound-level meter to the student house Williams lived in and ran a little test: Each of two television sets, turned on full volume, produced 90 decibels, but, to their chagrin, the two together yielded distinctly less than 180. Harkins then hurried to the physics department, where he learned that sound produced by pairs of clapping hands, and even more so by multiple voices, would definitely suffer losses due not only to the interference of sound waves with each other but to other "coordination losses"—moment-by-moment variations in individual output and minute differences in the direction in which the sounds were projected.

The two young men then met with Latané in a series of brainstorming sessions to consider what to do about the several extraneous variables. Neither he nor they can say today who came up with the solution, since their thinking in these meetings was as intimately conjoined as—well, as pulling together on a rope. Says Latané today: "I like to think I was responsible for the climate of discussion, but a lot of the ideas just came out of the back-and-forth. I'd have a hard time naming the source of the ideas, because identifying an idea as a good one is at least as important as thinking it up."

What follows is a composite version of the three men's recollections as to how their collective problem solving proceeded:

- Problem: First they'd have to establish how much of the drop-off was due to coordination losses; then they could subtract that, and the rest would be what was due to loafing. But how could they measure the coordination loss?
- Solution: Sidestep the coordination loss problem by using individual microphones to measure sound at the source, before coordination loss occurred.
- Realization: Better yet, individual miking would enable them to compare each volunteer's output when he shouted alone with his output when he shouted with others—the difference being a direct measure of social loafing.
- Problem: But each man's microphone would pick up the others' yelling; the measurements would be inaccurate.

- Solution: Station each man in a separate cubicle.
- Problem: That would prevent them from acting as a team.
- Solution: Give them earphones so they could hear each other.
- Realization: The students didn't really need to hear each other. Since the experiment sought to eliminate audience effects and group norms, the researchers could pipe in prerecorded group shouting, over the earphones, to drown out the real thing but give them the sense of team effort.
- Elaboration: In that case, why not have only *one* man shout at a time, while thinking he was shouting in groups? He wouldn't know the difference, and the research team would be able to measure each man's output uncontaminated by sound from the others.
- Defining of the construct: Although the volunteers would be shouting alone, they would *think* they were shouting in groups—and therefore they would behave as *if* they were. As Gordon Allport said, social psychology is the study of the influence not only of the presence of others but their imagined or implied presence.[20]
- Conclusion: This design would yield a really *clean* experiment. And a simple one—because separate mikes or separate cubicles would be unnecessary, after all; the students could be blindfolded and all in one room, but since they'd be shouting one at a time, there wouldn't be any wave interference and a single microphone would do.
- Elaboration: Still, it would be a far better experiment if the students also shouted in actual groups, so that the researchers could compare the sound level of each actual group with the total sound produced by the same men shouting in pseudogroups. There would be less sound from the actual group, due to coordination losses, and the researchers would thus get a direct measure of coordination losses that they could use as a correction factor in future experiments they hadn't even thought of yet.

All three researchers, at this point, were jubilant and excited. As Latané recalls, "We knew that the design of the first experiment was preliminary, but when we came up with the design of the second study—pseudogroups, masking noise, and all that—there was a wonderful moment of feeling that this was a *neat* design, that there was a *rightness* about it."

In a fever of excitement, they worked days and nights to set up the next experiment. Williams enlisted the help of five roommates in his house to record the sound of group shouting; he and Harkins then copied this sound again and again, adding to it the lead-in and ending cues suitable for every actual group and pseudogroup, and assembled them on two tracks of a stereo master tape.

Part of the time—for the real groups—both tracks gave the same instructions. But for pseudogroups, they differed: For a two-man pseudogroup trial, for instance, one track would announce, "This time, A and D shout," while the other track said, "A alone shout." Both tracks then gave a three . . . two . . . one countdown, then five seconds of the group shouting, and finally a loud bell signaling time to stop.

In the laboratory, Harkins and Williams set up a switchbox with which they could plug each of the six subjects in to one track or the other. They could thus make each student in turn think he was part of a group when, in fact, he was shouting alone, while to keep the students from catching on, all six would hear, every time, the 90-decibel bellowing of Williams and his roommates.

When all was ready, they again set up nighttime sessions with volunteers. This time, they used a different cover story, to avoid the inhibiting effect the earlier one might have had due to its emphasis on judging the noise people make in social settings.[21] "In our experiment today," Harkins told the students, "we're interested in the effects of sensory feedback on the production of sound in social groups." But since sensory feedback was the crucial element, he said, the experimenters wanted them not to see or hear each other, or hear themselves; accordingly, they'd be blindfolded and would wear earphones through which they'd be told what to do and would hear prerecorded shouting. Since their fellow students wouldn't see or hear them, they could feel free to shout their loudest. "There's no reason not to do your best," he said. "Really give it a try!"

Harkins and, in later sessions, Williams, carried this off easily enough. Both of them, in their previous research, had found they disliked using deceptive methods to impose stressful experiences on naive participants—long a standard practice in social psychology—but they felt comfortable with this experiment since concealing the pseudogroup design worked no hardship on their volunteers. Latané, moreover, maintained that the pseudogroup design was nothing more than "impression management"—much the same as the perfectly acceptable practice of adopting a façade of behavior, in a social situation, intended to make one's self appear particularly charming, suave, decisive, or knowledgeable. Indeed, he added, the researchers' impression management was needed to prevent the volunteers from doing some of their own, since if they knew the whole truth about the experiment, they would undoubtedly exhibit their best (but not usual) selves.

Latané also urged his colleagues, in debriefing the students afterward, to reveal the goal of the experiment but not the details of the pseudogroup design that revealed each student's behavior to the researchers while each thought himself safely concealed in the group. Latané's rationale: "If you debrief in such a way as to make plain to participants how they've been tricked and made fools of, and how badly they behaved, you're being intrusive and gratuitously damaging their sense of self-esteem. I think that kind of debriefing is more unethical than the harmless deception involved in stage-managing an experiment."

Harkins called no cues this time; instead, he and Williams plugged and unplugged patch cords for each trial, connecting each student in turn to either the first track or the second track of the tape. It was a tension-inducing chore: They had to be accurate yet quick lest their subjects become suspicious of the crackling sounds made on the headsets by the movement of the jack-plugs. Both researchers kept making excuses to the students through a microphone and worrying that their cover was being blown. (Later, Williams built a switchboard with silent switches, making it possible to connect any headset to either track instantly and soundlessly.)

For all their anxiety, everything worked remarkably well. When actual groups were to shout, each student heard on his headset the identification letters of those who were to perform—one, two, or all six students (to simplify the experiment, the research team had omitted four-man groups); each time, the right number shouted. Alternating with these trials were the pseudogroup trials in which one student heard that he was to perform either alone, with one other, or with all five others, while the others all heard that he would be shouting alone. This, too, worked as it was meant to.

It worked so well, indeed, that Harkins, Williams, and Latané (who had come into the laboratory once the students had their blindfolds on) knew at once that the experiment was a success. "We could see it on the meter immediately," Harkins recalls. "We'd see, for instance, that subject A shouted at 95 decibels when he thought he was shouting by himself but only at 85 decibels when he thought he was in a group. There was even one guy who shouted lustily when alone, but when he thought he was shouting with others would screw up his face exactly the same way and make a tiny bleat that hardly registered on the meter. He nearly broke us up."

Despite their amusement, both of them were keenly aware how unfunny and even painful it would have been for that student had the researchers told the whole truth in the debriefing. "But we never did tell them about the pseudogroups," Harkins said, discussing the experiment not long ago. "The aim of debriefing is to bring your subjects back, in terms of self-esteem and self-concept, to where they were when they came in. So if you haven't done them any damage by deceiving them, it isn't necessary to tell them that you did. In this case, it was only proper to tell them the purpose of the research, but it couldn't help them to know that we had recorded them singly when they thought they were in groups, and it could even have harmed them—and us, if it got around and everyone was on to what we were doing."

(Some social psychologists disagree with this approach, arguing that unless subjects are fully debriefed and thus motivated to be part of a conspiracy of silence, their own erroneous version of the experiment is very likely to get around and do even more damage to later trials.)

After running six groups of six male sophomores through the experiment, Harkins and Williams again fed the data into the computer. Gratifyingly, it reported that when shouting in pseudogroups of two, each student had averaged only 82 percent as much noise as when alone, and in pseudogroups of six only 74 percent as much. They proudly handed Latané another pageful of numbers which he again immediately transformed into a penciled graph; in its later, formal embodiment, it looked like this:[22]

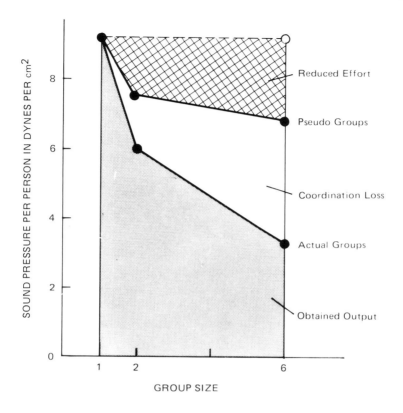

GROUP SIZE

It showed that the larger the group, the less sound was produced, on the average, by each person—and that the curve for the pseudogroups, where none of the decline could be attributed to coordination losses, cleanly demonstrated social loafing. Moreover, since the second experiment had been so different from the first in its cover story and other circumstances, the phenomenon appeared to be "robust"—not idiosyncratic or limited to a particular experimental situation.

Latané, deeply pleased, congratulated his colleagues, although, having already successfully completed some three dozen publishable experiments, he was understandably less exuberant than they. "I felt a sense of real satisfaction," he recalls, "but not excitement so much as the warm feeling, 'This has paid off—we've gotten hold of something solid that's amenable to further work—it's like money in the bank.'" Later, a paper that he, Williams, and Harkins wrote about the experiment spelled out that feeling in more elevated terms and even suggested that what they had observed in the laboratory in small groups of young Americans might prove to be relevant to human groups of many kinds throughout the world:

> These [and other] experimental findings have demonstrated that a clear potential exists in human nature for social loafing. We suspect that the effects of social loafing have far-reaching and profound consequences both in our culture and in other cultures . . . . Although some people still think science should be value free, we must confess that we think social loafing can be regarded as a kind of social disease . . . [with] negative consequences for individuals, social institutions, and societies. . . . We think the cure will come from finding ways of channeling social forces so that the group can serve as a means of intensifying individual responsibility rather than diffusing it.[23]

A double paradox: an important social principle demonstrated with admirable rigor—by a method somewhat akin to a magician's trickery; an ethically lofty aim—furthered by concealment and pretense. Such is often the nature of experimental research in social psychology.

Research Through Deception: An Ethical Dilemma

Latané, Williams, and Harkins, in misleading their students as to what was going on, were doing nothing unusual—for social psychologists; deception of volunteers has long been an integral part of most experimental research in their field.

Nearly half a century ago, when social psychologists sought to make their discipline an exact science by means of laboratory experimentation, they ran into a serious problem: Human subjects, unlike rats or pigeons, can understand what is going on, and their understanding is likely to affect how they respond to the experimental situation, defeating its purpose. If they know that researchers want to see how they react when they are asked to choose teammates from a mixture of whites and blacks, or overhear a stranger in distress, or see someone pilfering petty cash, they are almost sure to behave more admirably than they normally might.[24] An analogy: In the military exercises called "war games," it is easy to be brave; one knows that the "enemy" is not really out to kill.

Social psychologists soon realized that they would often need to disguise the real goal of an experiment from the participants in it. How best to do so became one of their dominant concerns as they strove to develop the methodology of their burgeoning discipline.[25] For there was little to be gained by refining their techniques of observing behavior and statistically analyzing their data if what they were seeing was largely the result of the participants' awareness of what the researchers were up to.

A case in point, say Aronson and Carlsmith in *The Handbook of Social Psychology*, is Solomon Asch's classic and seminal study of conformity, reported in 1951. Asch invited student volunteers to take part in what he told them was "an experiment in perceptual judgment." In the laboratory, his volunteers were asked to say which of three straight lines displayed on cards before them was the same length as a standard line on another card. In each trial, a naive (unknowing) volunteer would hear several others, all of whom were confederates (stooges), name a line that seemed clearly longer or shorter than the standard. The naive subject, faced with unanimity on the part of his or her peers, would sweat, squirm, and about a third of the time go along with the majority vote. Asch's study and many others like it have added greatly to our understanding of conformity but would have been impossible without the use of deception; if the target volunteers had known the truth, they would have been under no social pressure to deny the evidence of their own senses.[26]

Once established, deceptive methodology rapidly began to yield rich scientific rewards. Using it, various researchers were able to show that the tendency to conform is significantly related to specific personality traits and to the composition of the group, that violence seen in a movie increases the chance that viewers will afterward react violently to provocations, that teachers led to believe (incorrectly) that certain of their students have unusual latent ability will favor them and so produce the educational result they expected, that people faced with conflicting feelings reduce their cognitive dissonance by rationalizing (after having chosen between two desirable alternatives, for instance, they tend to think even better of the one they chose and to devalue the one they gave up), and to make many other discoveries of comparable importance across the range of social psychology.[27]

Deception soon became the method of choice whenever the subjects' awareness of the researcher's purposes could spoil the experiment. By the late 1960s, according to some estimates, it was being used in four tenths of all sociopsychological research, and of the studies meriting publication in the most prestigious journal in the field, the *Journal of Personality and Social Psychology*, fully two thirds involved deceptive methods.[28]

In specific research areas, deception was even more prevalent: Four fifths of all laboratory studies of conformity followed Asch's method of using confederates to apply social pressure to naive subjects.[29] In 1963 Stanley Milgram, then at Yale, published a report on a study of obedience to authority in which he had ordered naive subjects to give supposedly painful and even apparently life-threatening electric shocks to other subjects who, unseen, were heard to howl in pain and beg for mercy (the sounds were tape-recorded); the report created a sensation and over the next decade or so spawned some 130 other published and unpublished studies of obedience using the same technique.[30]

According to the social psychologist Joel Cooper of Princeton University, if one classifies as deceptive the mere withholding of a crucial part of the truth—a view taken by some ethicists—perhaps as much as 90 percent of the research published in social psychology journals in recent decades has relied on deception.

But while the use of this methodology is an exercise of the social psychologists' right to seek the truth—and of their obligation to do so in a scientifically rigorous fashion—it deprives the volunteers of *their* right to consent to, or to deny, the use of their bodies and minds by others. Any humiliating, embarrassing, or stressful experience they undergo without having knowingly agreed to do so, but having been misled or misinformed about what would happen to them, clearly violates this right.

Even an innocuous deception does so. A young man who has an attractive young woman flirt with him and then fills out a self-esteem questionnaire—even if he is spared the belittlement of learning that the flirtation was make-believe and his good opinion of himself unwarranted—has had his time, energy, and person used in a way that he might not have sanctioned had he had the choice; to that extent it is an intrusion on his right of self-determination. True, most volunteers in such experiments have agreed to participate in them, but when that agreement is based on ignorance of what will take place, it is the

researcher, not the participants, who determines how those tiny segments of the latters' lives are to be led.

Both the right to free inquiry and the right to self-determination are
deeply rooted in our culture, but the conflict between them did not
become apparent or come under official control until recent decades.
In 1914, the Supreme Court found the New York Hospital at fault for
having subjected a patient to treatment without his permission; the
ruling principle, Justice Benjamin Cardozo wrote, was that "every
human being of adult years and sound mind has a right to determine
what shall be done with his own body."[31]

The ruling applied only to treatment; research remained uncontrolled. But after the atrocious experiments of Nazi doctors on concentration camp inmates came to light at the Nuremberg Trials in 1947, it
was clear that research, too, had to be made to respect the rights of
individuals. As the Nuremberg Code, promulgated by the Tribunal,
put it: "The voluntary consent of the human subject is absolutely
essential. . . . [He] should have sufficient knowledge and comprehen-
sion of the elements of the subject matter involved as to enable him to
make an understanding and enlightened decision."[32] This principle
has become generally known as the doctrine of "informed consent."

In the United States, the pressure of public opinion and congressional concern led to the first formal requirement of informed consent:
In the 1960s, the Public Health Service adopted regulations governing
biomedical research, one of which obliged individuals and institutions
receiving grants to obtain the informed consent of their patients to any
experimental medical procedure. While this was an agency rule rather
than a law, it denied federal funds to those who did not conform and
therefore effectively exerted control over much of the field.[33]

At the same time, a number of lawyers, ethicists, civil rights advocates, and others of varied political views—including some social psychologists—began inveighing against the stressful, anxiety-producing,
and humiliating experiences sometimes visited upon naive volunteers
by researchers and arguing that informed consent should be obligatory
in behavioral science research.[34] One of their favorite examples of
what they considered wrongful treatment of naive subjects was Milgram's obedience experiment and they often quoted Milgram's own
words from the journal article in which he first reported his work. In it
he had described the conflict produced in his volunteers when he

ordered them to give increasingly powerful shocks to the unseen and seemingly agonized subject of the supposed learning experiment whenever he made a mistake:

> In a large number of cases the degree of tension reached extremes that are rarely seen in sociopsychological laboratory studies. Subjects were observed to sweat, tremble, stutter, bite their lips, groan, and dig their fingernails into their flesh. . . . One unexpected sign of tension—yet to be explained—was the regular occurrence of nervous laughter, which in some Ss developed into uncontrollable seizures.[35]

Such experiences, and the risk of lasting psychological damage to subjects who as a result of the experiment saw themselves in a pitiless new light, seemed grossly unethical to the critics and unjustified by any scientific discoveries the experiences might yield.[36]

Partly as a result of this professional debate and partly as a result of the tendency of bureaucracies to expand their own rules, in 1971 the Department of Health, Education, and Welfare extended the PHS regulations on biomedical research to cover research in human behavior, made them stricter, and ordered them put in effect in all branches of HEW. This brought most sociopsychological research under HEW control (since most of it relied on HEW funding) and sharply restricted the use of deceptive methods. In 1974 the regulations were made even tougher; informed consent was defined so stringently as to rule out even minor deceptions unless they were deemed both acceptable and essential by an Institutional Review Board within the researcher's institution.[37] IRBs, however, chiefly concerned with not risking HEW's disapproval and the cutoff of grant money, were hard to convince.

By the mid-1970s, more than half of a large sample of behavioral scientists queried by the Survey Research Center of the University of Michigan said that the regulations, as enforced by the review procedure, were impeding research.[38] Nonetheless, some investigators, who were either particularly bold, canny, or persuasive, or who held a position of power, continued to successfully propose and carry out significant research using deceptive techniques, though not of a highly stressful kind; Latané was one of them.

Many others, however, switched to experiments requiring only minimal deception or none, sharply narrowing the range of behavior they could explore. Still others gave up experiments and turned to other forms of research such as the observation of people in public places, the use of questionnaires asking people how they would feel in hypothetical situations, and so on—methods that are limited to certain kinds of behavior and can answer only a limited number of questions about them.

Many opponents of deceptive methodology argue that limiting its use need not impede scientific research, since alternative and morally acceptable methods are available. Role-playing is one of them: Participants are asked to imagine how they would respond in an experimental situation or even to play-act their response. But while the results sometimes come close to those of the same experiment carried out by means of deception, more often they do not.[39] Latané and Darley did a pencil-and-paper simulation of one of their helping experiments; all their respondents said they'd be highly likely to help, whether or not others were present—a self-image far nobler than the reality revealed when naive participants were actually exposed to the situation.[40] As Dr. Joel Goldstein, chief of the Research Review Branch of the Department of Health and Human Services (successor to HEW), has observed, "What people say or do in role-playing experiments is qualitatively different from what they really do."

Another alternative, "prior general consent," involves asking people to agree to undergo any one of a list of named stimuli without being told which one they'll actually experience; this only leads them to do a good deal of informed guessing, which, one leading researcher sourly observes, "simply gums up the experiment." Much the same is true of still other alternatives.

During the 1970s, as the complaints of the scientific community mounted, some members of Congress became concerned and two special commissions on the protection of human subjects of research began to consider the need of research to be protected from overregulation. If previously the exercise of the right of free inquiry had intruded on the right of self-determination, now the latter was intruding on the former. Society, which stood to benefit from safeguarding both rights, faced a dilemma.

A solution to it, or at least a compromise, lay in the HEW regulations themselves in the form of the principle of the "risk/benefit ratio." As stated, it says that in all research with human subjects, "risks to subjects must be reasonable in relation to anticipated benefits, if any, to the subjects, and the importance of the knowledge that may reasonably be expected to result."[41] While deceptive research offers no benefits directly to subjects, it does so to everyone indirectly in the form of knowledge that may be unobtainable in any other way.

Based on these considerations, the Department of Health and Human Services eased its regulations somewhat in July 1981. Among other changes, informed consent was less rigidly construed; a limited form, allowing for minor deception or the withholding of some information, was deemed acceptable if there was "minimum risk to the subject" and if the research "could not practicably be carried out" otherwise.[42]

Like all compromises, this one has served both sides and satisfied neither. Opponents of deceptive methodology continue to argue against the attempt to weigh scientific benefits against human costs. For one thing, they say, the units of measurement are incommensurable; there are no quantitative measures of risk that can be equated with measures of benefit, and the "calculations" therefore remain only impressionistic. For another, such calculations express an inferior ethic. Diana Baumrind, a developmental psychologist at the University of California, Berkeley, the philosopher Alasdair MacIntyre of Boston University, and the social psychologist Thomas Murray, formerly of the Hastings Center, an institute for the study of ethical problems of the life sciences, are among those who have argued that the risk/benefit ratio embodies utilitarian thinking, since it appraises the morality of an act in terms of its ends rather than its means. Worse, they feel, it weighs both values—scientific knowledge and human privacy—on the same scale, when they are different in kind. Baumrind, for one, maintains that concern for the person is morally superior to the freedom to seek scientific knowledge and should take precedence over it; for her, this invalidates any risk/benefit calculations.[43]

Most social psychologists, on the other hand, feel that legitimate and important research is still severely and unfairly constrained by the regulations and by tedious and obstructive IRB reviews. Stanley Schachter of Columbia University, one of social psychology's most inventive experimenters for thirty years, is among those who has given up doing experiments. "I simply won't go through all that," he says. "It's a bloody bore and a terrible waste of time." Others, though they still do some experiments involving deceptive methods, are disgruntled and pessimistic. Professor Edward E. Jones of Princeton University, a well-known experimenter, says, "Not only have the regulations and IRBs made the researcher's life far more difficult but they've exerted a profound influence on our thinking. You don't even *consider* experiments that would run into resistance—it just doesn't occur to you to tackle a problem that would require deception of a kind that will create trouble with the IRB. Whole lines of research have been nipped in the bud."

Leon ("LEEE-ON!") Festinger himself, comparing social psychology as it had been in the days of his historic studies of cognitive dissonance with what it is now, when researchers are fearful of getting in trouble, writes, "One can stay far away from ethical questions . . . but it seems to me that steering clear of these difficulties keeps the field away from problems that are important and distinctive to social psychology."[44]

Meanwhile, despite the complaints of both sides, laboratory experimentation has been flourishing, even though somewhat tamed and confined, and college sophomores and other subjects are having their rights protected but not to the extent of their being defended from harmless deceptions and the preempting of trifling amounts of their time and energy. The balance now being struck may not be the best and wisest one possible, but it is a sensible attempt to make two opposing cultural values coexist. If it proves to be tilted too much one way or the other, it will doubtless be readjusted but not replaced by a total ban on deceptive methodology or by a return to the laissez-faire policy that existed, prior to the Nuremberg Trials, in the years of our innocence.

Hypotheses and Manipulations

"Like money in the bank," Latané had said of his team's pseudogroup experiment and the solid finding it yielded. Now the three researchers began to invest this intellectual capital by developing hypotheses as to the conditions that favored or counteracted social loafing, and testing them by means of variations of their pseudogroup procedure. So exciting did they find this that, despite their other obligations, they found time by day and evening, to the exasperation of two wives and one girl friend, to think up, plan, and run half a dozen experiments in the next seven or eight months plus several more in the following year.

This intense burst of effort owed much to their feeling that they were onto something important, but a fair amount to a special characteristic of laboratory social experimentation: It is often fun. Creating an experimental situation, planning a cover story, and staging the event is part science, part show business; the experimenter is not only social scientist but dramatist, performer, and illusionist. By way of testing various hypotheses about human behavior, social psychologists have rigged clocks to run twice as fast as usual, collapsed in subway cars with stage blood seeping from their mouths, and piped smoke through a ventilator into a room where a naive student and several confederates were filling out questionnaires.[45]

Latané (who was responsible for the last of these) had begun his career experimenting with rats but soon found doing so with people both more intellectually meaningful and more entertaining. Despite a low-keyed southern-small-town manner, he has a flair for elegant flimflam which, he says, he employs only because it is more likely to get at the truth than such alternative methods, advocated by ethical purists, as estimation or simulation. He demonstrated to Harkins and Williams that this was the case by suggesting that they describe the pseudogroup experiment to a number of undergraduates and ask them how they thought the subjects had performed under the various conditions. The students guessed that subjects had shouted and clapped louder both in the real groups and the pseudogroups than when performing alone; they were, of course, dead wrong, thus making Latané's point.[46] Besides, as experiments go, it wasn't much fun.

The team therefore concentrated on thinking of ways to test their hypotheses in the laboratory by tinkering with the experimental situation, that is, manipulating the independent variable. Here are some of the highlights of the resulting series of experiments:

Latané, conferring with Harkins and Williams, asked the question: "What might counteract the tendency toward social loafing?" The three researchers tossed suggestions back and forth: altruism, ideology, and fear, among others. And, most intriguing, self-interest: Perhaps by setting things up so that everyone directly benefited when the group produced more, they could elicit high-level performance in everyone.

They therefore ran what was essentially a replication of the basic pseudogroup cheering experiment, this time offering the participants a few dollars—it usually doesn't take much to motivate under-graduates—for high performance: The more total sound they pro-duced both singly and in groups, the more money they'd share. Sur-prisingly, the cash incentive made almost no difference; as long as participants thought they were shouting in groups, they loafed.[47] A robust phenomenon, indeed.

Why didn't the money do it? the researchers asked each other. The only answer that made sense was that each one must have been count-ing on his teammates to work hard, and expecting that his own loafing would go undiscovered.

What condition could they create to offset that tendency? After some thought, it occurred to them to tell the volunteers that they were being individually monitored in the groups as well as when they were shouting alone. As Latané pointed out, even the Red Chinese, for all their collective ideology, ask assembly line workers to sign their work.

Measuring the performance of the students both singly and in groups, and both with and without individual monitoring, meant ma-nipulating the independent variable four ways, but the team worked out a basically simple experimental design for doing so. First, as be-fore, the students, thinking they were identifiable only when shouting alone, performed in both real groups and pseudogroups. Then they did so again, this time supposing themselves identifiable at all times; to make students think so, Harkins and Williams handed each student a lavaliere microphone, gestured at complicated equipment in the con-trol room, and told them that they'd be individually monitored under all conditions. In reality, the lavaliere mikes and other equipment were dummies, since the pseudogroup method with one microphone efficiently yielded individual readings.

The results were noteworthy. The students, thinking they could be identified only when shouting alone, made 37 percent less noise in the pseudosixes than alone. But when they put on the lavaliere mi-crophones and thought themselves identifiable at all times, they made only 8 percent less noise; social loafing had been virtually eliminated.

Harkins and Williams, putting the numbers through a probability computation, found that the likelihood that these results had occurred by pure chance was less than 1 in 5,000.[48]

Still, Latané said as they discussed these results, there was one variable they should have controlled but hadn't—they'd used the same people for both conditions. How could that affect the results? Well, for one thing, it was possible that the students had loafed less in Stage Two not because of the lavalieres but because by then they were used to the task.

Harkins and Williams saw other possibilities. Perhaps by Stage Two the students were tired—they couldn't shout much louder when they thought they were monitored than when they thought they weren't, so it looked as if they hadn't loafed. Or perhaps, since the researchers knew from Stage One how loudly they could shout alone, the students felt obligated to do as well when they thought they were being monitored in the groups.

How could the researchers control for this variable? They worked out another and more intricate experiment, this time dividing their volunteers into three sets, each of which experienced a single condition.

The first set had only one microphone; the students had no reason to think they were identifiable except when shouting alone. The second set had individual microphones; they were told that they'd be identifiable both alone and in groups. The third set had only one microphone but were told that their cheering was being recorded and analyzed by a computer and that the researchers wouldn't, and didn't need to, know how loudly any one of them shouted at any time.

The results were as clear-cut as the team could have wished: Each set of participants, responding to a different independent variable, behaved in a unique fashion. Those who thought they were identifiable only when performing alone shouted loudly when alone but loafed in the pseudogroups. Those who thought they were identifiable at all times did no loafing at all and shouted at the same high level alone and in pseudogroups. Those who thought they were never identifiable shouted with limited force when alone and at only about that same level when in groups; they loafed all the time.

That appeared to clinch it: Identifiability was an effective deterrent to social loafing—an outcome the team welcomed not only as the fruit of their labors but also as having larger implications. In the paper in which they later reported this work, they concluded with a little bon mot (the Latané touch), "We believe that the results, like the methods, of our two experiments are cheering, since we regard social loafing as a social disease that threatens effective collective endeavor."[49]

This finding encouraged the team to consider other ways to deter social loafing. Their discussions led them to speculate about why people in groups loaf in the first place. One hypothesis they formulated was that perhaps there is a natural tendency in human beings— assuming the experimental results were generalizable—to exert themselves as little as possible. The team called this the "taking-it-easy" strategy.

But such discussions being dialectical in character, they soon came up with a contrary hypothesis: Perhaps people want to exert themselves as fruitfully as possible, and social loafing is their effort to do the best they can with their resources. Since their supply of energy is limited, there may be a tendency to allocate more of it to those times when their efforts will be identified and rewarded. If so, people will do their best in groups when they have no individual activities to save their strength for. The team called this the "allocation strategy." Maybe, they thought, it explains why kibbutzniks, who have no private plots, work so much harder at communal activities than kolkhozniks, who do.

Out of such discussions grew two more experiments. Harkins, with a couple of assistants, conducted them in the fall of 1977 in a laboratory at Northeastern University, where he had accepted an appointment beginning that academic year. But the discussions and planning with Latané and Williams had taken place at Ohio State before he left, and during and after the experiments he conferred with them frequently by phone, mail, and in person at professional conferences.

Harkins gave undergraduate men and women—a dozen groups of four each—the usual pseudogroup treatment but with a few differences. Because clapping is harder work and produces more social loafing than shouting, he chose clapping as the task; on their headsets, prerecorded clapping masked the real sounds being made. Each group was told that subject C would always clap alone, D would always clap with someone else, and A and B would sometimes clap alone and sometimes with someone else.

The results were both satisfying and disappointing. Satisfying in that they gave further evidence of the nature of social loafing: The Ds, who clapped only in pseudopairs, averaged only 62 percent as much sound as the Cs, who clapped only alone, while the As and Bs, who did both, clapped only 75 percent as loudly in pseudopairs as they did alone. But the data were disappointing in that they backed up the hypothesis of the taking-it-easy strategy rather than the allocating one: Though the Ds clapped only in pseudopairs and had no individual trials for which to husband their strength, they loafed as much as the As and Bs, who did their best when clapping alone but loafed when clapping in pairs. [50]

Latané, Harkins, and Williams also felt they had to test the possibility that these results might be in part an artifact of the experimental design. Perhaps Ds got the idea of loafing from hearing that As and Bs would be switching back and forth from paired to solo clapping. Or perhaps Ds, knowing that Cs were always clapping alone, would be particularly aware that they, by contrast, didn't have to exert themselves.

So Harkins ran a second experiment. It was exactly like the first except that in half the groups the students were told that each of them would clap alone, while in the other half they were told that they would clap in pairs. The results were the same: People clapping in pseudopairs produced only 57 percent as much sound as those clapping alone, even though they neither knew anyone was clapping alone nor had any reason to save their strength for solo performing.

The results hardly justified optimism about the control of social loafing, but Harkins and his colleagues, in a paper in which they reported the experiments, were stoutly hopeful:

Although there are many differences between the kibbutz and the situation we have created in our research, the one that strikes us is the sense of group identity [i.e., in the kibbutz] and faith in the group. Rather than serving as a means of diffusing responsibility, the group seems to intensify it. The success of the kibbutz provides us with reason to believe that we may be able to discover conditions under which people in laboratory groups can also be led to work as hard or harder collectively as individually. [51]

If social loafing seemed a stubborn tendency, the kibbutz certainly showed that under the proper conditions individuals would do their best in a group. Looking for a way to replicate this observation on a small experimental basis, the team came up with an idea born of comments made by several university athletes who had been in their classes, namely, that in athletic contests such as track and swimming, participants do better in relay races than in individual events.

In the spring of 1979, at the researchers' request, the coach of the University Swim Team put on a simulated competitive swimming event featuring both relays and individual heats. The cover story for Williams, his assistants, and Harkins, who came down from Northeastern for part of the trials, was that they were studying "the dynamics of swimming," namely, such matters as water turbulence, starting techniques, and timing procedures. (Latané, as usual, observed and advised from the sidelines.)

Each of sixteen men, divided into four teams, swam two 100-meter individual freestyle races and one lap in each of two 400-meter freestyle relays. Half the swimmers heard their lap times shouted out (as is usual at meets) for all present including their teammates to hear; the winning individuals and teams got prizes. The times of the other swimmers were not called out and those who asked about them were told they were not being made available; the winners did, however, get prizes.

What with whistle-blowing, shouting, splashing, and cheering, it was the most fun-filled experiment in the series. And in one way the most involving: At the end of the trials, Williams and the graduate students, still busy with their worksheets, found themselves suddenly hurtling through the air and into the pool fully clothed, a swim-team tradition no one had warned them about.

The intellectual fun, however, came when they analyzed the data. They found that while all the lap times were fairly close, there were statistically significant differences among them that cast new light on social loafing and its control:

- When swimmers' lap times in the relay races were called out, they averaged 60.2 seconds for their 100-meter stint; when their times weren't called out, they averaged 61.7 seconds. In other words, when their efforts weren't identified, they loafed, team spirit notwithstanding.

- Relay swimmers whose times were called out did a little better (60.2 seconds) than swimmers in individual events whose times were also called out (61.0 seconds). Although swimmers were given personal credit in each situation, they tried harder as team members than as individuals.

Thus, having one's efforts identified when one is part of a cohesive, high-morale group produces even better performance than having one's efforts identified when working for personal benefit. On the other hand, if the contribution of members of a team isn't identified, they will loaf. The findings suggest that both principles—individualism and team spirit—operate and interact in human beings.[52]

Later that year, Latané and his two colleagues put together a forty-four-page manuscript titled "Many Hands Make Light the Work: Social Loafing as a Social Disease."[53] In it they reviewed the seven chief experiments in the series and spelled out the broader social implications of their findings via brief excursions into such diverse matters as the contrast between kolkhoz and kibbutz, the problems of team pickle-packing, and the avoidance of social loafing on football teams (good coaches publicly celebrate the linemen, who, ignored by the media, might otherwise tend, in the paper's breezy language, "not to bust their guts").

In 1980, the paper was awarded the prestigious Socio-Psychological Prize of the American Association for the Advancement of Science. For Harkins and Williams, then only 32 and 26, respectively, and just beginning to publish, it was a triumph. But even for Latané, then 44 and with a long list of publications, grants, and honors to his credit, it was immensely gratifying: He and John Darley had won that same award in 1968 for their helping experiments, and now, in 1980, he became the first social psychologist to have won it twice.

Identity Crisis

Despite half a century of collecting evidence—at least some of it unambiguous—about the principles of human social behavior, and despite the recognition by scientific bodies such as the AAAS of the value of some of these findings, experimental social psychology has been periodically charged with grave shortcomings as a science.

All the social sciences, to be sure, have been similarly attacked. But experimental social psychology, though modeling itself more closely than any of the others on the physical sciences, has been the most sharply criticized, its methods being ridiculed and its findings dismissed as either trivial, irrelevant, or invalid. Yet since those findings often reveal aspects of human behavior that many of us would rather not hear about, it may be that in large part the criticisms of experimental social psychology express distaste and wishful thinking; one recalls the Victorian lady who hoped that Darwin's theory of the origins of mankind was not true but that, if it were, it would not be spoken of.

One common criticism of sociopsychological experiments is that the great majority of them use, as their subjects, college undergraduates, mostly sophomores, who can easily be recruited by offering them modest fees or partial credit toward an introductory psychology course. The critics say that what is true of college sophomores may not be true of the rest of humankind; the findings of such experiments, therefore, are of limited value.[54]

In rebuttal, Festinger and others have argued that for purposes of hypothesis-testing (as opposed to sample-survey research), the population studied is not a critical matter. If variable X produces variable Y, and, in the absence of X there is no Y, then the connection between X and Y is a proven fact in that group, and may point to a general truth, though to establish that, it must be found to hold true in other groups. But even if it fails to do so, that does not disprove the X-Y connection; it means, rather, that one or more other variables, interacting with X, have to be added to the theory. Thus, the use of sophomores is at least a first step toward explaining many a sociopsychological phenomenon.[55]

Another criticism is that many sociopsychological experiments are largely method with little content. Gordon Allport, for one, said that many studies use sophisticated methodology to explore narrow phenomena under highly specific conditions, yielding only "elegantly polished triviality" (or, as someone has caustically put it, "itsy-bitsy empiricism").[56] An example: In a recent experiment, students listened either to a boring reading of a textbook or to a comedy record and then were asked for a handout by a classmate who had "forgotten" his money; the finding was that people (or, anyway, students) who are in a good mood are a little more generous than those who aren't.[57]

Still, even though much published sociopsychological research deals with trivial subjects, this is the normal state of affairs in every science. Most research papers in all disciplines serve chiefly to fatten résumés and inch their authors toward promotion. It is not clear that experimental social psychologists are worse sinners in this regard than anyone else. In any case, even if far too many of their experiments have dealt with trivia, others have contributed a mass of knowledge about substantial and generalizable phenomena. Social psychology, its defenders say, is the study of everyday life—of conversations, anger, love, spite, giving, winning and losing, rationalizing, and the like. When social psychology confirms our common-sense understanding of such events, it is reassuring; when it corrects common sense, it is invaluable.

Related to this issue is another trenchant criticism: During the 1960s and early 1970s, many experimenters were so entranced with the show-business aspects of their research that the ingenuity, intricacy, and boldness of a deceptive *mise-en-scène* came to be valued more than the issues it addressed or its findings. As M. Brewster Smith, a former president of the American Psychological Association, recently wrote:

What students and colleagues seemed to find especially appealing was the Festinger style of experimentation, manipulating "social reality" through clever stage management to create conditions for which testable predictions could be derived. . . . [As a result] the cleverness of the experiments seemed on the whole to exceed the human and scientific significance of the cumulative results.[58]

Those who defend deceptive methodology disagree with this sweeping criticism, though they agree it is true in some cases. They add, however, that after the more extreme forms of deceptive methodology came under attack, the prestige of clever or intricate deception declined and for some time now the guiding view of the discipline has assigned far more importance to the substantive aspects of research than to its thaumaturgic ones. As Joel Cooper, though arguing that deception is often essential, says, "We don't exult in it any more."

Another attack holds that laboratory research may be internally valid (it shows what it says it does) but not externally valid (what it shows doesn't apply to the real world). In this view, many laboratory situations are highly artificial and the conclusions one draws from them are unlikely to explain seemingly analogous phenomena in everyday life.[59] How can a Milgram-type obedience experiment, in which a subject is ordered by an authoritarian researcher to deliver electric shocks to another human being, possibly be compared to the life experience and behavior of Germans who carried out the barbaric policies of their Nazi rulers? Could one really assume that the subjects in an experiment conducted by Philip Zimbardo, who were made posthypnotically deaf for thirty minutes to see whether they would become suspicious of joking and laughing confederates, experienced anything comparable to what happens to aging people who slowly lose their hearing and concomitantly develop paranoid symptoms?[60]

The contention that experiments are artificial and that their findings may be inapplicable to real life, say Aronson and Carlsmith, "is not idle concern; it is simply misplaced. . . . All experimental procedures are 'contrived' in the sense that they are invented. . . . [But they can be] purified through systematic replication." Milgram's original experiment, they point out, may not go far to explain the behavior of Germans under Nazi rule (as he hoped), but a series of later experiments by Milgram employing varying conditions, "increased . . . the extent to which his initial finding can be generalized." The greater the variety of scenarios in which an operational variable is shown to yield the same effect, the greater the likelihood that the laboratory experiments reveal truths about real life.[61]

The severest of the recent assaults on experimental social psychology was an expansion of the last critique. In 1973, in an article appearing in the *Journal of Personality and Social Psychology*, psychologist Kenneth Gergen of Swarthmore College sweepingly asserted that the discipline was not a science but a branch of history. His major argument— an old familiar one—was that while sociopsychological research purports to discover principles of social behavior that are generally true, it actually deals with effects that are time-bound and place-bound and have no relevance outside a given sample of people in a particular setting.

Some of his examples: Milgram's obedience phenomenon "is certainly dependent on contemporary attitudes towards authority"; cognitive dissonance theory asserts that human beings find inconsistency repugnant, yet early existentialists welcomed it; conformity research reports that people conform more to friends than nonfriends, but while this may be true in our society, it may not be so in others, where friendship plays a different role. His conclusion:

It is a mistake to consider the processes in social psychology as basic in the natural science sense. Rather, they may be largely considered the psychological counterpart of cultural norms. . . . Social psychological research is primarily the systematic study of contemporary history.[62]

Gergen's diatribe provoked years of debate, soul-searching, and counterattack; this painful reappraisal won the label, "the crisis of social psychology."

In the end, however, powerful counterarguments restored the scientific image of social psychology. Barry Schlenker of the University of Florida, for one, pointed out in a scathing rebuttal in the same journal that even the physical sciences began with many observations of a limited and contradictory nature and gradually developed larger and more general theories that unified the seeming inconsistencies. The social sciences, moreover, have discovered a number of phenomena that cut across time, place, and culture: All societies, for instance, have incest taboos, some form of the family, and some provision for maintaining order. Social psychology itself has contributed a number of theories that have been found to hold true in many different social contexts and thus have transcultural validity, among them those pertaining to social learning, reference-group behavior, and the maintenance of status and dominance hierarchies.[63]

As for the attacks on laboratory experimentation, they have provoked a good deal of talk about and interest in research outside the laboratory and the use of nonexperimental methods. Yet the advantages of the experimental method remain so great that, according to a recent analysis, it continued to be used in about three quarters of all social psychological research studies during the 1970s.[64] There is no reason to suppose that the situation has changed in the 1980s.

The net effect of the recent challenges to the credibility of social psychology has been to make its practitioners more keenly aware of the danger of overly narrow research, the need for social relevance in their work, and the value of nonexperimental research methods. The discipline has survived the attacks and continued its scientific maturation. In a history of social psychology since 1930 to appear in the next edition of *The Handbook*, Edward Jones offers this summing-up and forecast:

The crisis of social psychology has begun to take its place as a minor perturbation in the long history of the social sciences. The intellectual momentum of the field has not been radically affected by crisis proclamations. . . . The future of social psychology is assured not only by the vital importance of its subject matter, but also by its unique conceptual and methodological strengths that permit the identification of underlying processes in everyday social life.[65]

Testing for Generality

Only something important could have kept Latané from attending the award presentation at the January 1981 annual meeting of the AAAS. Something important did: While Harkins and Williams, in Toronto, were accepting the award on behalf of all three of them, Latané, in Allahabad, Uttar Pradesh, was running the basic social loafing experiment with pairs of 12-year-old Indian boys and girls.

This was the first of a series of efforts to test the generality of the phenomenon. Although social loafing had shown up in the varied experimental situations concocted by Latané, Harkins, and Williams, and by several other researchers, nearly all the participants of this research had been American college sophomores. It remained to be seen whether or not social loafing was a general human tendency, and under what conditions it either prevailed or was inhibited. (Scraps of cross-cultural evidence such as the contrast between kibbutz and kol-khoz, though suggestive, were not sound experimental evidence.) As the team noted in one of their papers, "Cross-national and cross-cultural research . . . would help to determine whether social loafing is limited to modern Western urban cultures and the extent to which social loafing is modifiable by personal values, religious orientation, or political ideology."[66]

Any such effort would take money, but funding for social research in other countries was not easy to come by in 1980 and 1981; Latané therefore looked for ways to piggyback an experiment on trips funded for other reasons. (Academics, often thought of as impractical, can be very canny when research dear to their hearts is at stake.)

Thanks to one of his grants, Latané had funding to attend a social psychology conference in India in 1981. Through an Indian social psychologist he had met at a conference in Poland two years earlier, he obtained a collaborator, Janak Pandey, at the University of Allahabad. Latané and an American colleague, Nan Weiner, brought equipment with them to Allahabad; Pandey made arrangements with two local convent schools and conducted the experiments in Hindi using tapes he had prepared in that language.

Williams, meanwhile, who had taken a faculty post at Drake University in Des Moines in 1980, discussed social loafing with a Japanese social psychologist visiting that school, and, with funds from Drake to attend a conference in Taiwan, worked out a comparable trip of his own. En route he stopped in Japan; there, he and his wife (also a social psychologist) rendezvoused with Latané (who came from India to meet them), and with the help of Williams' Japanese contact and a university student who had corresponded with Latané, they were able to carry out experiments with 7th graders, college students, and a group of Honda executives.

In addition, one of Latané's postdoctoral students at Ohio State, William Gabrenya, went to Taiwan with his Taiwanese wife, partly thanks to money squeezed out of one of Latané's grants; there, with her help in making contacts, he ran the experiment with 12-year-old Taiwanese boys and girls.

Finally, Latané ran yet other experiments while on another junket in Bangkok, Thailand, with 12-year-olds and in Penang, Malaysia, with 14-year-olds. (Harkins was unable to wangle a trip, and played no part in the cross-cultural experiments.)

As of this writing, the data from these five countries have not been fully analyzed, but Latané is pleased with what he has seen thus far. Telling a conference group about it last summer, he said, "We had two logics of design. One was the search for cross-cultural generality, using people of the same age in societies that are very unlike our own. The other was the developmental approach, comparing people of various ages within each of several cultures, as we did in Japan and Taiwan, and in Des Moines, where Kip and Karen Williams tested kindergartners, 4th-graders, and 7th-graders.

The cross-cultural experiments have shown social loafing to be quite general, although I had thought we might get very much less of it in the Oriental societies. As for the developmental studies, in Taiwan and Japan, and in Des Moines, we found that there was less of it in the younger children, suggesting that there may be a learning component in social loafing. Essentially, that's what we'll be saying when we get around to writing it all up.

Thus far, only the Indian experiment has been set down on paper, and then only in the form of a brief presentation made at an American Psychological Association meeting.[67] Latané, who in 1982 became Director of the Institute for Research in Social Science at the University of North Carolina, hasn't had much time for writing of late, and it seems that none of the others has, either. Plainly put, they've been waiting for each other to do the job. As Latané ruefully says, "We seem to be victims of our own paradigm. When it comes to writing up the results, we're displaying some first-rate social loafing."

THE SLOWEST, COSTLIEST, BUT BEST (AND WORST) OF METHODS

Two Long-Term Studies, Tracking Nearly 800 People Over Many Years, Find That Many of Our Beliefs About Human Aging Are Incorrect

A Question That Had to Be Answered

If, in 1948, someone had recommended to young Bud Busse—Ewald William Busse, M.D., then finishing his residency in psychiatry at Colorado Psychopathic Hospital in Denver and planning a career in research—that he commit himself to spend more than a quarter of a century on a single project, he might well have said that the other person should commit himself, in another sense of the word.

Nonetheless, Busse eventually did just that. His dedication, although due in part to his interest in the subject—human aging—was in far larger part the result of the method he and several colleagues employed. This was to observe the physical and mental health, and the social behavior, of a number of middle-aged and older people as they gradually aged and died off, a technique that obviously cannot be hastened by researchers.

It proved a fruitful choice: Busse and the scores of other researchers who, over the years, took part in this project and in a concurrent one on the same subject produced well over a thousand research papers and monographs on aging, a sizable contribution to knowledge in that field, and Busse himself, nowadays Gibbons Professor of Psychiatry at Duke University School of Medicine in Durham, North Carolina, has written or coauthored over ninety research papers on aging, won five professional awards for his work, and long been widely recognized as a major authority in gerontology.

All of which was the unforeseeable outcome of a minor research study Busse began in 1948 that originally had nothing to do with aging. At 31, a dark-haired young man with a soft southern drawl (he'd grown up in Missouri), Busse had just begun teaching at the University of Colorado School of Graduate Medicine and, at its Colorado Psychopathic Hospital, become director of the Electroencephalography Laboratory. In the latter post, he was scouting around for a first research problem to work on.

Reminiscing recently—he's now 68 and somewhat craggy-featured but still dark-haired, and still has a Missouri accent—he mused about how the little problem he found thirty-seven years ago fortuitously led him into the then minuscule, but soon to be major, field of gerontology.

I was doing electroencephalographic research on young people who had epileptic seizures. I was particularly interested in their temporal lobe functioning. The discharges coming from the anterior temporal area of the brain, particularly on the left side, showed "focal" abnormalities—that is, brain waves from that region in these young epileptics were slower than normal and were related to peculiar sensations or movements in specific or focused parts of the body.

By chance, at the same time I was running clinical diagnostic EEGs on a number of other patients referred for different reasons. I happened to notice that many old people had those same abnormalities in their brain waves, even though they never had any seizures. I had no idea why I'd see this in young epileptics, where it was diagnostic of seizures, and also in old people, where it was not. I'd note in my reports of the old people's EEGs, "The focal abnormality present in the record does not appear to be related to the patient's complaint or the diagnosis." But what *was* it related to? What did it mean?

That seemed to me worth looking into, so I applied to the National Institutes of Health for a small research grant, and got it in 1951. I and several colleagues at the University of Colorado began collecting data on older people's EEGs. In 1953, when three of us—Robert Barnes, Al Silverman, and I—moved to Duke University School of Medicine, the grant went with us and we continued working on the problem there.

It had become apparent to us that focal abnormalities in the temporal area grew increasingly common as people got older. But why? What factors were related to it? That was the question that had to be answered before we could answer another and very practical question: What were its clinical effects?

But we didn't know when the abnormality first appeared in any individual, so we couldn't tie it to other factors in that person's life that might have caused the change. What we needed to do, obviously, was observe a number of older people over a period of time so we could see what other things happened to them before and at the same time as these abnormal brain waves appeared, and what changes took place in their behavior as a result. We felt that we simply *had* to do a study in which we'd follow the same people for at least three years and maybe much longer. So we proposed that to the NIH, asking for a rather larger grant, and got it in 1954. That was the beginning of "Long I"—the first Duke Longitudinal Study of Aging.

A modesty in Busse's reminiscing obscures the fact that he was the prime mover in the decisions to research not just an intriguing anomaly of aging but its broad implications, and to use an onerous and at that time questionable methodology. In retrospect, both choices look uncannily prescient.

In the early 1950s longitudinal studies lasting more than a couple of years were not well thought of; they had proven hard to sustain, and longitudinal methodology was still primitive and full of pitfalls. Few social researchers foresaw that over the next twenty-five years long-term longitudinal research, despite its drawbacks, would come to be seen as the best way to investigate some phenomena and the only way to explore certain others.

As for the study of aging, shortly to become a major field of interdisciplinary research, in 1954 it scarcely existed. There were almost no professional gerontologists, no courses on gerontology, and no centers for the study of aging.[1] Virtually the only attention paid to the subject was the study of diseases in the institutionalized elderly, and the prevailing view of aging was that it was a time of slow and inevitable deterioration, decay, disease, and folly,[2] rightly characterized by Shakespeare's cynical Jaques as

> . . . *second childishness and mere oblivion,*
> *Sans teeth, sans eyes, sans taste, sans everything.*

Busse, however, sensed that longitudinal research would prove not only viable but the method of choice for studying aging, a topic soon to be of major interest to medical, behavioral, and social researchers and to the leaders of our society. His most important intuition, however, was that our knowledge of aging ought to be based not on the institutionalized minority of the elderly but on a sample of the great majority who, as he said, "live out their lives in various communities with more or less personal satisfaction and social competence." Busse proposed to view aging not as a disease but a "normal" process, meaning by that term, both healthy and typical.[3] This, according to George Maddox, a sociologist and long-time team member, "was a stroke of genius. Busse was dead right in wanting to see not just those aging people being treated for disease but those who were living in the context of the community. You have to have that kind of normative information to understand aging. It revolutionized our thinking about it."

Because Long I grew out of the EEG research, it was centered about the normal aging of the central nervous system. But Busse persuaded his colleagues to view this goal in broad terms—so broad as to make it the study of how normal adults function in the last quarter of their lives. To plan and carry out this ambitious task, he assembled a team of a dozen people—medical specialists, psychologists, social workers, and others—from the faculties of Duke University and its Medical Center, and called a series of meetings to decide how to proceed.

The first issue they discussed was what hypotheses about the nature of aging they should seek to prove or disprove. Was it a long, inevitable decline, or was it a plateau followed by a rapid descent to death? Was aging a diseaselike process or only a healthy slowing-down? Were the disabilities seen in many aging persons chiefly of organic origin or largely the result of factors such as social displacement and failing self-esteem? But Busse argued that it would be wiser not to decide in advance what to look for.

We tried not to put this in the usual framework of constructing hypotheses but to concern ourselves with what *happens,* what you *observe,* as so-called normal people advance through the latter part of their life cycle. There was no good empirical data with which to construct hypotheses for a long-range study, and nothing like a single dominant theory of aging existed. So we agreed that our emphasis would not be on testing any single theory of aging but that as we went along we'd try to develop hypotheses based on what we'd observed and see if we could answer them from our data. If we couldn't, we'd set up satellite studies—short-term special investigations outside our basic design—to try to answer them.

But is it possible to conduct scientific research without having hypotheses in advance? Karl Popper, the philosopher of science, and certain others have held that the mind does not passively absorb all sorts of data and inductively see connections among them; fruitful perceptions require guiding questions. "All observation," Popper has said, "is an activity with an aim (to find, or to check, some regularity which is *at least* vaguely conjectured)."[4] And in fact Busse and his team had just such vague conjectures behind their planning.

Busse: "It's a question of what you mean by the term 'hypothesis.' We did wonder whether the EEG abnormality was related to biological changes or to socioeconomic level or to other factors in the individual's style of life, and what other changes came about as a result of it. We tried to devise ways of looking at these and other possibilities. But we had no central hypothesis, no basic theory of aging."

From this general perspective, the team discussed and slowly worked out a protocol of tests and procedures that would serve their purposes. Every team member argued for the inclusion of the favorites of his or her discipline—enough, had all been used, to require a week-long examination every two years of every person being studied. But after a good deal of hard bargaining, they arrived at a more feasible list. Volunteers would be scrutinized, questioned, prodded, and poked for two full days every several years: Their vision and hearing would be tested, their blood sampled, their brain waves and heart waves recorded; they'd be asked hundreds of questions about their medical, social, and sexual histories; they'd take intelligence tests, reaction-time tests, and projective psychological tests (the Rorschach and the Thematic Apperception Tests) that would reveal a host of their conscious and unconscious attitudes. In all, 788 pieces of information would be collected about each volunteer: 336 of them medical, 234 social, and the rest neurological, psychiatric, and psychological.[5]

The participants would be normal people of 60 and up living in the nearby community—but how should the team gather a sample of them? Addressing that issue with more enthusiasm than expertise, its members decided to use what social researchers call a "convenience sample" rather than a random or probability sample; the latter, as we saw in chapter 3, yields more trustworthy data but is far costlier and more difficult to collect. As Busse recalls,

Originally, we weren't as sophisticated about how to develop a sample as we later became. We'd go to key people in the community—ministers, physicians, and so on—and say to them, "We're interested in studying so-called normal older people and the normal aging process. We'd like to get a list of individuals past the age of 60 who are reasonably healthy and who are functioning well in the community." And they'd say, "Yes, there are people I see or know who are 60 or older and are going great." They'd give us their names and we'd go to those people and explain our purposes to them.

The only inducements we could offer were a free and very complete physical examination at regular intervals, and a chance to play a part in the scientific study of aging and to learn from us what we were finding out. But most of the people we approached were sympathetic and agreed to take part, and many of them suggested friends or relatives they thought might also be interested. Some would even say, "Look, I can give you a whole list of people in my church who would fit your needs." Our sample grew and grew by the "snowball" process.

We recognized, however, that we had to have a reasonably balanced combination of people, so we began to develop a quota system with which to select from our growing pool of volunteers a panel that would match the older population in and around Durham in age, sex, racial, and socioeconomic characteristics. Later, when we compared the physical and psychiatric characteristics of our volunteers with those in samples selected by random procedures, we found no striking differences between them, although our people did appear to be a little healthier, physically and mentally, than average.[6]

It took us four years to accumulate our basic panel of 270 people ranging in age from 60 to 94. But long before we completed it—in fact, by May 1955, when we had only the beginnings of the panel—we started having them come in to Duke University Medical Center and began our first round of observations.

Neither Busse nor anyone on his team imagined, at that time, that they, or their successors, would still be examining some of those panel members a generation later.

The Case for Longitudinal Research

To understand the special value of longitudinal research for a study such as Busse's, let us briefly recall the virtues and limitations of the leading method of social research, the cross-sectional survey.

We have seen that a properly conducted cross-sectional survey gives a picture of attitudes, behavior, or conditions in a given population at one point in time. But as to how things got that way—what processes produced these conditions—social researchers can only make inferences from the evidence. The same is true in any field where researchers cannot witness the processes they seek to explore: Geologists, for instance, must infer the history of our planet from the sequence in which layers of material were deposited on its surface.

The basic tool for inferring processes from cross-sectional data is correlational analysis. This says, in effect, that if, in a particular sample, individuals possessing more of trait X also have more of trait Y, then one of them may be the cause, or a contributing cause, of the other, though which is which is not always clear. But other sources of knowledge, including common sense and everyday experience, may make this clear. Surveys consistently show that people at higher income levels have more education than people at lower ones, but since people receive their schooling before they start working, it seems evident that education is a contributing cause of financial success rather than the other way around.

Many correlations, however, are spurious: X and Y may have no cause-and-effect relationship but merely be the side-by-side results of some other cause.[7] A frivolous example: Suppose we have data showing that on the average, married males have less hair than unmarried ones; now, since it is absurd to suppose that hair loss causes marriage, we might conclude that marriage causes male baldness. But it would be a rash, not to say stupid, conclusion; we have not taken into account other variables likely to play a part, most notably age. If we divide the males into ten-year age groups and compare the average hairiness of the single and the married in each, it becomes clear that younger males have more hair and are mostly unmarried, while older ones have less hair and are mostly married. In other words, Z—age—influences both X and Y, creating a "spurious" correlation between them.

Accordingly, researchers working with cross-sectional data use multiple regression analysis to hold constant all suspect variables other than the ones being investigated. Yet since it may be impossible to think of or measure all the variables that may play a part, they are wary of concluding more than that a correlation suggests, or strongly suggests, that one factor is a contributing cause of the other.

Another and sometimes more powerful way to infer cause-and-effect relationships from cross-sectional data is by means of a survey repeated at different times, using comparable samples of the same group; any significant change in the data is likely to be the result of events that took place between rounds. A recurrent employment survey, for instance, will show whether unemployment was steady, rose, or fell from one round to the next, and any change can be reasonably ascribed to economic developments or government actions occurring between them.

But such before-and-after comparisons, using new but similar samples each time, show only *net* change, not the flow. If the number of the unemployed remains the same from one time to the next, it may mean that there is a small hard core of chronic unemployables—but it may equally well mean that there is a steady turnover and that many usually employed people suffer from periods of joblessness. Without information better than that of the cross-sectional data, economists and political leaders cannot know the real nature of unemployment and can only guess how best to deal with it.[8]

Longitudinal studies, in contrast, track the same individuals over a period of time, looking for differences or changes in them following specific events. This approach is far more congenial to the human mind than correlational analysis; as developmental psychologists have shown, we have a built-in tendency to intuit causality from before-and-after regularities. In the more formal terms used by Paul B. Baltes and John R. Nesselroade, specialists in longitudinal methodology, the evidence needed to prove a causal relationship between two variables includes both *covariation* (correlation) and *temporal order*—which usually must be inferred in cross-sectional studies but is directly observable in longitudinal ones.[9]

The "trend study" method just described (repeated surveys of a given population at regular intervals) is often considered longitudinal research, even though it deals only in overall change and cannot point to the causes of change in individual cases. (It can suggest, for instance, why the total number of the unemployed has increased or decreased but not why certain people lost their jobs and why others were able to find new ones during the period under study.)

The "true longitudinal," on the other hand, follows an unchanging group of individuals (a panel) over a period of time and can link changes in their condition to events in their lives. Such studies come in many sizes and shapes. The participants may be seen, tested, or questioned only twice, several times, or dozens to hundreds of times. The total period covered may be on the order of a day or two, many months, or one to several decades. A single group of individuals may be followed to see what patterns of development and change its members naturally undergo or may be divided into matched subgroups, one or more of which is given some experimental treatment such as training, therapy, or a subsidy, while another, the control group, is not.[10]

Long-term longitudinal research lasting several decades or even longer is far and away the slowest, possibly the costliest (per individual), and in many ways the most taxing and problem-ridden method of social-science investigation. But for exploring the intricate web of cause-and-effect relationships affecting human development over any major part of the life cycle, it is, at least in its present-day form, the most realistic and hence best approach. As Judith Tanur, a sociologist specializing in survey technique, puts it, "The availability of longitudinal data makes it possible to test which model [among those proposed by social theorists] presents the most accurate picture of the world."[11]

The advantages of longitudinal over cross-sectional data can be seen in these typical examples:

- Often, a small shift in voter preference is shown by two cross-sectional polls or by a poll and a subsequent vote.[12] The 1980 election results, coming a week after a CBS/New York *Times* poll, showed that the gap between Carter and Reagan had widened by 7 percent during that week. But CBS/*Times* pollsters recontacted the people in the survey and asked them both how they had answered the poll and how they had voted, thus obtaining a two-observation longitudinal data base. It was an eye-opener: Not 7 percent but 21 percent of the people polled had changed their minds that week—some toward Carter because of the Iranian hostage negotiations, others toward Reagan because of Carter's handling of the economy.[13] The reality was far more complex than cross-sectional comparisons revealed.

- Cross-sectional samples of older persons taken at various times consistently show that only about 5 percent of people aged 65 and older are institutionalized; this is often understood to mean that there is only a 5 percent chance that this will happen to any given aging person. But Erdman Palmore, a sociologist associated with the Duke Longitudinal Studies, tracked a panel of individuals over the years and found that many people enter and leave institutions several times in their latter years. At any moment, only 5 percent may be in institutions, but there is at least a 20 percent chance that any adult will spend some time in an institution during his or her final years.[14]

- Many studies have portrayed human development during childhood, adulthood, or aging by assembling cross-sectional data on people of different ages. An analogy: One might measure the heights of all the children in a grade school and from these data draw a curve showing the average height at each age. The method is plausible for spans of a few years, but when used over a longer one it commits the "life-course fallacy"—it assumes that people growing up in different times have similar experiences.[15] But they may not have. The children and grandchildren of turn-of-the-century southern Russian Jewish immigrants are distinctly taller than their foreign-born elders, and a composite curve of height at different ages, using data from American-born-and-fed grandchildren, their parents, and their foreign-born grandparents, would be as unreal as the chimera, that Homeric monster with the head of a lion, the body of a goat, and the tail of a dragon.

- The life-course fallacy is well illustrated in the case of intelligence. In the past, intelligence tests given to different age groups have found teenagers scoring highest, middle-aged people not so high, and older people distinctly lower; the conclusion has been that intelligence reaches a peak early in life and declines thereafter, especially in the latter years. Yet the same method showed that middle-aged people had less education than younger ones and elderly people still less, though it would be absurd to conclude that people lose schooling as they get older.[16] Both phenomena, in fact, are "cohort effects," not actual declines. (A cohort is any group sharing a given trait, usually age.) People in their 70s have less education, on the average, than those in their 20s simply because the 70-year-olds grew up at a time when far fewer young people finished school or went to college than half a century later. Having less education (and less experience taking tests), they achieve lower intelligence scores throughout their lives. The younger people score higher because more of them have had college education, not because they're at the pinnacle of their intellectual powers.[17]

Longitudinal studies of human intelligence yield a very different picture. In Iowa, the psychologist William Owens, Jr., and others tracked down a group of men who had taken intelligence tests in college in 1919 and retested them in their 50s and again in their 60s. The findings: By and large, the intelligence of these men did not peak until they were in their 50s and had declined only slightly when they were in their 60s.[18] In Seattle, the psychologist K. Warner Schaie followed the intellectual development of a random sample of members of a health maintenance organization over a twenty-one-year period. Testing their specific mental abilities (verbal, numerical, and so on), he found that some of these increased until middle age while others began to decline by then, but that overall there was no significant average decrease until the late 60s and early 70s. Even at 81, less than half had suffered any important losses.[19]

Curiously, social scientists ignored the longitudinal method long after its value was first pointed out. In the nineteenth century the Belgian statistician Auguste Quetelet and certain others foresaw and made the case for the longitudinal approach, especially in the study of long-term social processes and human development. But neither theory nor method was available, and the concept remained so unfamiliar that the term "longitudinal" did not enter the social-science vocabulary until the 1920s.[20]

Then, however, perhaps as a result of Freud's use of case histories and his portrayal of the various stages of psychological development of the child, longitudinal research suddenly caught on. In the early 1920s, at a series of conferences sponsored by the National Research Council, the psychologist-executive Beardsley Ruml and the educator Lawrence Frank argued that to understand how human beings develop and to distinguish the effects of individual differences from those of environmental influences, researchers would have to observe the same individuals from birth to maturity or even beyond. The time was ripe, the idea made sense to many researchers, and with Rockefeller Foundation and other funding a number of universities set up child development institutes to study groups of children from birth to maturity.[21]

(Short-term longitudinal studies, meanwhile, were catching on in other areas. In the mid-1920s the Public Health Service launched the first of various longitudinal studies of the incidence of sickness in the population to correct the flaws in its cross-sectional estimates, and during the 1930s the Social Security Administration and other government agencies began using longitudinal panels to study unemployment trends.)[22]

Unfortunately, most of the early long-term longitudinal studies of child development did not fare well. The researchers tended to ask highly specific questions at the outset, thus limiting the data they gathered and the kinds of questions they could later attempt to explore. And while the studies were longitudinal in name, the researchers analyzed their data cross-sectionally to obtain norms such as the abilities, height, and weight typical of each age.[23] These were easy to calculate, while in the precomputer era it was immensely difficult to keep track of all the variables in each individual's life and to sort out the effects of different combinations of them over the years. Few researchers, moreover, found it congenial or good for their careers to work on projects that would take one or two decades before yielding publishable findings. Most of the creative researchers associated with the child development institutes therefore left after some years; in consequence, little of value was published by the institutes.[24]

By the 1940s the status of long-term longitudinal research, at least on human development, was at a low ebb. While a few human development studies were being successfully sustained (notably those of the Institute of Human Development at Berkeley and the Denver Child Research Council, and a study of gifted children in California begun in the 1920s by the psychologist Lewis Terman), the larger number were limping along or switching to short-term studies.[25] Lester Sontag, director of the Fels Research Institute, has suggested that the crux of the difficulty was that researchers continued to think in cross-sectional terms, focusing on the compilation of normative data for each age group from which national estimates could be made. In so doing, they ignored the real potential of longitudinal studies, namely, their ability to observe *processes* along the dimension of time and thereby to disclose the factors that cause the lives of different people to turn out differently.[26]

They were, in short, still looking for data answering the question "What exists?" rather than for cause-and-effect sequences answering the question "How does it get that way?" The true value of long-term longitudinal research had not yet been demonstrated, though it soon would be.

Getting Started: The First Dozen Years

The first two volunteers to undergo Round 1 observation arrived at the sprawling green campus of the Duke Medical Center one morning in May 1955. No one at Duke today recalls who they were, but Busse and others on the team well remember the procedures they were put through, since the same routine was followed with all 270 panel members for the next four years. In Busse's words:

In the beginning, most subjects would drive in on their own. But if they were very old—and some were in their eighties or nineties—we'd send a driver for them, and as the years went by we had to do that more and more often.

We'd ask them to be in by 7:30 A.M. without having had breakfast. They'd go to a hospital reception area, where each one—only two came in on any day—would be met by one of our social workers, who would guide them around for the next two days. First, she'd take them to a lab where a technician would draw blood. Then she'd take them to breakfast at the cafeteria. (Later on, we set up a little dining room in our own area and fed them there.)

Then she'd lead them around on a tight schedule that included going to various places for x-rays, an eye exam, hearing exam, and electrocardiogram.

The two volunteers' schedules were different so they wouldn't have to wait at any time.

At some point, a physician, either Claude Nichols or Gus Newman in the early years, would give them a very complete physical, including rectal and pelvic examinations. That wasn't easy on the volunteers, but what was hardest—on the ladies, anyway—was the EEG. Their hair, which they always had had done for the visit, would get all messed up by the ten to fifteen electrodes that had to be placed on their scalps, and a few ladies refused to come back for that reason. Some parts of the psychological and social work-up were quite stressful, too, such as the interview about their sexual histories and activities and the questions about how they felt about sickness and death.

Most of the psychological and social work-up, however, was not so much stressful as arduous; it included the then-new WAIS (the Wechsler Adult Intelligence Scale), the Rorschach, and social adjustment questionnaires, that forced the subjects to think about and to voice many of their hidden feelings about themselves, their friends, their activities, and their satisfactions and dissatisfactions. [27]

Busse: "All in all, it was a long, tiring two days, and many of them complained about it. Some would require time to just rest quietly for a while, so we'd give them regular breaks for coffee and cookies, and we set aside rooms where they could lie down if they needed to." But then came the payoff: Toward the end of the second day, the physician who had examined them would meet them to discuss what he'd learned. Dr. John Nowlin, a large, genial internist who took over the examinations some time later and conducted them single-handedly until the end of the project, says that this almost always seemed an adequate reward for the two days of labor:

The big thing they wanted to know was whether I had found something or not. I always tried to be upbeat; if there was something amiss, I'd tell them about it without sounding alarming. I'd say, "Your right lung's not working quite right" or "There's something wrong with your heartbeat that you ought to take care of." And if there was something urgent, I'd tell them I would get in touch with their doctor. Most of them left the briefing feeling that the two-day ordeal had been well worth the trouble.

The regimen remained basically the same for many years, although at Round 2, beginning in 1959, the Rorschach was dropped (it hadn't proved useful under these circumstances), and a memory test, a reaction-time test, and a forty-five-minute psychiatric interview were added, as was a search of every inch of the subject's skin.[28]

By and large, however, the research team clung to its original battery of tests even when better ones appeared. And for good reason: Changing a test in mid-course would impair the validity of before-and-after comparisons. Any change, indeed, is hazardous; a new interviewer, asking the same old questions, might do so in a way that subtly skews the spectrum of answers. Even minor variations in the way a physician talks to the people he examines can inconsistently distort blood pressure and other readings. Nowlin, keenly conscious of this, scrupulously made exactly the same little jokes in every examination for a dozen years. About to listen to bowel sounds with a stethoscope, for instance, he would always smile and say, in his mellow southern accent, "Let me just take a listen to your breakfast."

Because unforeseen problems slowed the schedule, it took four years to complete the first round of observations of the whole panel, and Round 2 would take two more; only then could the first longitudinal results appear. Clearly, it is a heavy burden to do research when one cannot hope to see the first results for so long—and since the Duke project was testing no specific hypotheses, there was no assurance that anything of interest would show up even then.

Much was happening, however, that made team members feel they were in the right field at the right time and so kept their morale high. Almost as soon as the project started, Duke University set up an interdepartmental Council on Gerontology to conduct seminars, conferences, and institutes, at which the members of the team played a leading part. Two years later, the U.S. Public Health Service designated Duke the first regional Center for the Study of Aging, with Busse as its director, and gave it an initial grant, assuring Long I of continuing support. A few years later, the NIH, the Duke Endowment, and the R. J. Reynolds Company put up money for a new gerontology building—a wing of the Medical Center—in which the longitudinal project was comfortably housed from then on. But the principal means of maintaining intellectual interest and morale on the team were the Monday Night Meetings held at least twice a month at Busse's home. As Busse recalls,

The Monday Night Meetings began even before the longitudinal was running. They were always held at my house, on our large enclosed porch, with food and drink at hand, because I felt it would be helpful to meet away from the hospital in a relaxed setting. Twenty or so of us would get together there after dinner for two or three hours; we'd discuss research problems, generate new ideas, and report our findings to each other. Anyone who was going to present a paper at a seminar would come in with handouts—data, a rough draft, a bibliography—and we'd discuss and critique them.

Although team members could make no longitudinal findings for the first half dozen years, they had plenty to talk about at these meetings. Most of them were making cross-sectional analyses of the Round 1 data; indeed, throughout the long life of the project by far the largest number of reports it yielded were based on such analyses. Not only were these of scientific value but they met the need of team members to publish research while the agonizingly slow longitudinal study dragged on. Here are three typical examples of their cross-sectional findings:*

- Within the Duke sample, lower socioeconomic status was associated not only with a higher disease frequency in the aging years but with greater resulting disabilities.[29]
- Impaired hearing in the aging was linked to lower levels of psychological functioning but impaired vision was not.[30]
- Depression in the elderly was not associated with the turning inward of unacceptable hostile impulses, as often seems the case in younger people, but with a loss of self-esteem.[31]

A frequent topic of debate at the Monday Night Meetings was how to handle the masses of data being accumulated on nearly 800 variables. At first, with only punched cards and sorting machines, it was a Herculean task to extract and manipulate the data for any particular study. But in 1958, when the Center acquired its first computer, the discussions turned to how to store the information in it in a form that would enable researchers to pose longitudinal questions to which they

---

*Because this chapter is concerned with long-term longitudinal research, we will bypass the rest of the mass of cross-sectional studies produced by the project.

could extract meaningful answers. Eventually, specialists elsewhere in the university wrote a program for the Center's computer; thereafter, a researcher, using an instruction manual and a large black code book, could command the computer to display a table of data on, say, "Var:DCHHRTSZ" (variable: change in heart size) and to show how this was related over the years to such other changes in the same individuals as increasing weight, rising blood pressure, or number of social activities engaged in.

Other Monday night sessions dealt with knotty problems of how to extract sense from the data so retrieved; the air was thick with talk of chi-square tests, dummy variables, change-score analyses, stepwise multiple regressions, and the estimation of missing values. For while the members of the team could ask statistical specialists to carry out these and other procedures for them, they had to understand the concepts in order to know what to ask for.

But for a time, it seemed to some of the researchers that they might never need to know all this. As Round 2 got under way in September 1959, the social workers who contacted volunteers to schedule their examinations reported that a distressing number of them were dropping out. Only 182 of the 270 panel members returned for Round 2: Some, as expected, had died and a few had moved away, but a larger number refused to come back or were said to be too ill to do so.[32]

Since these dropouts distorted the sample—which was nonrandom to begin with—Busse was concerned about the credibility of whatever they might find. He therefore invited George L. Maddox, an energetic, articulate young sociologist with a strong methodological background, to join the team to advise them on this critical issue. Maddox, who arrived in 1959 and stayed with the project all the way (eventually becoming chairman of the University Council on Aging and professor of sociology), recalls dealing with the sampling problem at the Monday Night Meetings:

I came on just after Round 2 began. It wasn't clear to the team whether their project could be sustained at all—that is, whether the snowball technique had produced a sample that could yield any generalizable findings, and even if it could, whether the dropout rate would make the sample so unrepresentative that we couldn't say anything about aging in general.

What I said over and over to my colleagues was, " Don't press this matter of generalizing from our data to the national population. You do have a reasonably good distribution of upper-status and lower-status individuals in your sample, but they're not random, so they may not be representative of either. They're healthier and more verbal than average; they're somewhat of an élite. But there are two kinds of issues in research: the epidemiological issue—what's the distribution of X and Y?—and the experimental issue—what's the relationship between X and Y? You can make only very guarded statements about distribution based on this sample, but you *can* identify the important variables in aging and you *can* and *should* concentrate on the relationships between the Xs and the Ys."

Furthermore, Maddox pointed out, each individual's own history was a valid experiment in itself because the researchers could trace the relationship of variables within each life. As he and other team members came to say, "We view each individual as his own control."[33] This was a clarifying and reassuring concept; major findings would be unaffected by sampling problems, since the chief goal was to discover how the Xs and Ys are related within the individual's life and these relationships or processes would be generalizable.

As it turned out, the dropout problem disappeared after Round 2: from then on, though the sample dwindled steadily due to death and illness, refusals were minimal.[34] The continuing but shrinking corps of volunteers were, in fact, a loyal lot. Busse:

Over the years I got to know many of these people, and they would see me on the street and come up to me and say, proudly, "Now, you don't remember me, Dr. Busse, but I'm so-and-so, one of your research subjects." We had many techniques to keep them interested. We'd send them birthday and Christmas cards, and our social workers would call them on the phone to chat. Frances Jeffers and Dorothy Heyman, our key administrative assistants, would periodically have receptions for them in the dining room of the Medical Center and serve them refreshments, and one of us would discuss our findings with them. We showed them that they *mattered.*

So it went, year after year, with the rounds taking ever less time as the ranks of the panelists thinned out. By July 1967, a dozen years after the project got under way, Round 4 had been completed with 110 of the 270 panelists still left. The Duke team and the researchers who temporarily joined it were by this time regularly turning out longitudinal reports; overall, these painted a very different picture of aging from the traditional one. Yet a historian of the project would be hard put to point to memorable moments when members of the team made notable breakthroughs; as is typical of long-term longitudinal studies, the discoveries of Long I emerged slowly and by increments, more like the gradual changes of mind that come with experience than the dazzling moments of illumination dear to biographers. Here are a few of the typical slow-arriving conclusions of those first dozen years:

THE OUTCOME OF HEALTHFUL LIVING.   Erdman Palmore reported that those panelists who, at Round 1, were neither overweight nor underweight, did not smoke, and, most important, exercised regularly were in distinctly better health at Round 2, three to four years later, than those who weighed too much or too little, smoked, and took no exercise. (Health was judged by such criteria as the number of visits to doctors, time confined to bed per year, and whether or not the individual had died before his or her actuarially expected number of years.) Cross-sectional studies elsewhere had already found such correlations but, as Palmore pointed out, one couldn't tell from such evidence which factor caused the other; it is at least possible, for example, that feeling healthy might make one want to exercise, while feeling poorly might drive one to overeat and smoke by way of consolation. But the present study being longitudinal, the health practices were measured at the beginning of the study and the illness and mortality indicators later, so that it was quite likely that the causal connections were in the direction Palmore reported.[35]

AGING AND ILLNESS.   Robert H. Dovenmuehle, a psychiatrist, found that of the panelists who survived until Round 2, only half had undergone changes in health that impeded functioning, and most of these had suffered relatively little limitation; another third remained as physically capable as the first time around; and one out of eight were actually in better health than before. These and other data suggested that though age inevitably brings physical changes, serious crippling illness is not a normal part of the process, and disabilities are neither an inevitable nor an irreversible accompaniment of aging. Most of the ailments of the aging, Dovenmuehle reported, "are in the nature of chronic illnesses, a considerable number of which are partially reversible. . . . Although disease and disability cannot be completely avoided . . . relative preservation of health and of ability to carry out one's life activities can be attained with adequate medical care."[36]

HYPOCHONDRIA IN THE AGING.   Dorothy K. Heyman, a social worker, and Frances C. Jeffers, a research associate in psychiatry, tested the validity of the common belief that as people age they become overly concerned with changes in their health and exaggerate their medical problems. Using data from Rounds 1 and 2, Heyman and Jeffers found that few panelists had become more concerned about their health over the years. Moreover, panelists' own subjective ratings of their health at Round 1 were generally in accord with the overall PFRs (Physical Functioning Ratings) given them by the examining physicians, and this remained so at Round 2. Apparently, most panelists were realistic about their health rather than hypochondriacal.[37]

Further evidence: If people did grow more hypochondriacal as they aged, one would expect their visits to doctors to increase, especially after the advent of Medicare in 1965. But Palmore and Jeffers, using data from Rounds 1, 2, and 5, found no change in the percentage of panelists visiting doctors over a two-year period or in the number of office visits they made.[38]

BODY AND MIND.   A number of separate studies made over spans of three to ten years by several hands—the ophthalmologist Banks Anderson, the psychiatrist Carl Eisdorfer, and others—inquired as to whether certain physical problems of aging caused declines in mental and social functioning. Some findings:

• Decrements in visual function did not interfere with social adjustment, activities, or general level of happiness unless the loss was severe and affected both eyes.[39]
• Over a three-year period, panelists with CVD (cardiovascular disease) had lower IQ scores than panelists free of CVD. But on closer analysis, it turned out that socioeconomic status was the significant factor: Low-income whites and blacks were twice as likely as higher-income whites and blacks to have both CVD and lower IQs. Conclusion: CVD, of itself, does not cause a decline in psychological functioning.[40]
• Despite cardiovascular diseases, and substantial impairment of physical functioning, sight, and hearing, most of these aged peo-

ple remained functioning residents in the community, living fairly mobile and independent lives.[41]

- Panelists who had high blood pressure in their 60s lost a significant degree of intellectual function by their 70s, as measured by WAIS, while those with normal blood pressure remained relatively unchanged, and those with slightly elevated blood pressure actually seemed to have raised their scores. But after allowing for "practice effect"—the panelists took the WAIS four times in ten years and probably gained a few points from familiarity— researchers concluded that the hypertensives had lost a lot, normals had lost a little, and mildly hypertensive people had held their own. Apparently, mildly elevated BP helps aging persons maintain adequate cerebral circulation.[42]

INTELLIGENCE AND AGE. Eisdorfer and research associate Frances Wilkie analyzed WAIS scores of panelists over a ten-year period. Against expectation, the averages rose: People first tested in their 60s averaged 9 points better a decade later, and those first tested in their 70s, 3 points better. However, the many panelists who had died in the interim had had lower scores, on the average, than the survivors; thus, the ten-year rise in WAIS scores resulted from the fact that the survivors had been both healthier and higher-scoring to begin with. But when their records were looked at longitudinally, a more accurate curve resulted: Those first tested in their 60s lost a trifle of their intellectual capacity by their 70s (2.6 points out of a mean of 100), while those in their 70s lost somewhat more (7.3 points) by their 80s.[43]

Various other investigators reported that while the incidence of some degree of mental impairment increased over time, severe impairment remained rare, and that although many elderly people complained of memory decline or other losses of mental powers, they actually performed adequately when tested.[44]

"DISENGAGEMENT" VERSUS ACTIVITY. A widespread assumption, backed by cross-sectional data, held that as people age, they become less involved in social life, work, and leisure pursuits. In the 1960s, many gerontologists thought that "disengagement," as this was called, was a natural and beneficial adaptation to the inevitable changes of aging, maintaining satisfaction with life by bringing one's reach within one's grasp. But Palmore reported that over a period of ten years there was little overall reduction of activities among panelists; moreover, those who did reduce their activities tended to be less satisfied with life than those who remained engaged, while those who actually increased their activities showed an increase in satisfaction. These findings thoroughly contradicted disengagement theory and supported the opposed theory, widely held by those who worked among the aged, that continued activity was better for them.[45]

SEXUAL ACTIVITY IN AGING.   Three psychiatrists, Adriaan Verwoerdt, Eric Pfeiffer, and Hsioh-Shan Wang, reported that the data on sexual activity, if viewed cross-sectionally, showed a steady decline as age increased. But viewed longitudinally, the data revealed a far more complex and diverse reality: Between Rounds 1 and 2, 27 percent of the men had been sexually inactive, 31 percent were active but became less so, 22 percent remained active without any decline, and 20 percent became more active. Of the women, 74 percent had no activity throughout the period (many more women than men were widowed), 10 percent were active but became less so, another 10 percent were active without any decline, and 6 percent had increased in activity.* These data confirmed other Duke findings that aging is not a fixed and inevitable process of deterioration but is a highly individual, often unchanging, and sometimes improving outcome of interactions among biological, psychological, and sociocultural factors.[46]

EEG ABNORMALITIES IN THE AGING.   With so many significant findings having been produced by the first dozen years of work, it was paradoxical that the original question—what do focal EEG abnormalities in the aging brain signify?—turned out to be a dud. Busse, the psychologist Walter Obrist, and various other collaborators never did discover what produced the abnormalities; furthermore, they found no evidence that the appearance of these abnormalities in an aging person portended diminishing circulation to the brain, loss of intellectual ability, failing social adjustment, or any other untoward conse-

---

* The Duke figures are based on heterosexual intercourse, and therefore show lower incidences of sexual activity than the well-known Kinsey data, which were based on all forms of activity, including masturbation.

quence.[47] The original question had thus turned up nothing of real interest—but had led to many other inquiries about aging that had yielded findings of substantial value.

Even as the researchers were harvesting these first fruits of the longitudinal study, they were also becoming painfully aware of certain unanticipated and irremediable shortcomings in its basic design.

The most obvious was that it took too long. At first, Busse and his colleagues had expected to study normal aging for six to ten years, but now it was evident that they would need twenty-five years or more to complete the picture. This exasperatingly glacial pace frustrated nearly everyone and caused far too high a rate of staff turnover. And since donors of grants prefer projects that seem certain to yield results fairly soon, Busse repeatedly had difficulty getting enough backing from the PHS, and went to various foundations—which, similarly, were less than enthusiastic about giving when the intellectual payoff lay so far in the future. The researchers were resolved to continue making the most of Long I but began thinking about devising a shorter second study. And a better one, for as they could now see, Long I had other flaws. According to Busse:

By 1965 we started talking about designing another longitudinal to answer questions that we realized were not answerable in our first one. For one thing, not all the processes of aging begin at sixty or sixty-five; some start earlier, and we wanted to know about them. For another, how could we pull a sample that would be representative enough so we'd have more generalizable data? Could we find and afford a technique better than the snowball one?

And we were also becoming aware of a bigger problem. Our longitudinal study, following one panel from the beginning to the end, was vulnerable to "cohort effect" because it involved a group of people born and raised in a particular era. And it might also be subject to "period effects"; we had no way of knowing how much of any change we observed was due to aging and how much to the stresses and strains of the particular time when we were observing people. So we wondered if there wasn't some combination of different cohorts, observed at different times, or some combination of the cross-sectional and the longitudinal approaches, that would enable us to control for the cohort effect and the period effect.

Busse was speaking of what is surely the most serious defect in the first longitudinal study. It had been called to the team's attention by outsiders—K. Warner Schaie and Paul Baltes, both of whom were doing advanced methodological and theoretical studies of longitudinal design. John Nowlin recalls how they brought the news to Duke:

Schaie and Baltes were very much interested in our project and came to a conference here on longitudinal studies in about 1966. We did nothing but sit around for several days and talk about longitudinal design. They pointed out the built-in flaws of the simple kind of longitudinal we were conducting. They said it was possible to learn as much about aging by looking at a large population over a short time as by looking at a small population over a very long time and to overcome the flaws of our kind of study at the same time.

The crux of their suggestion was to look at different cohorts—groups in their fifties, their sixties, and so on—at the same time, and follow all those cohorts for maybe eight years or so. For each cohort, you could develop a slope for those years—you could see how they changed during that time—and through a series of comparisons you could exclude cohort effects and period effects so you could tell how much of the change was due to aging alone.

Once the team began seriously planning the new project—"Long II" as it was soon known—it took some thirty Monday Night Meetings, over a period of a year and a half, plus an uncounted number of informal get-togethers of the leading staff members by day, to work out all the details and put together a proposal to the National Institute of Child Health and Human Development. By 1967, when Long I was a dozen years old, the grant creating its advanced and sophisticated sibling finally came through and Long II was scheduled to begin in 1968.

Confounded Methodology

It was inevitable that many stubborn methodological problems would plague the Long I study of aging. All forms of longitudinal research are subject to certain of them, but long-term panel studies encounter the largest number and the most troublesome.

Yet because the long-term panel approach has such intuitive and theoretical appeal, many researchers regard it as the best of methods, ignoring the fact that it is also, in some respects, the worst. As the sociologist James A. Davis of Harvard University mockingly observed in a recent article, "If the sociologist's attitude toward longitudinal research is one of religious faith, our feeling towards panels . . . approaches superstitious reverence. If longitudinal studies are Good, panel studies must be Wonderful."[48] He then proceeded to point out a number of the grave inherent weaknesses of panel studies (while admitting their unparalleled advantages); these are chiefly of a statistical and highly technical nature, but two of the most bothersome are easy to understand.

The first: Even if X is regularly followed by Y, that doesn't prove X caused Y unless you also know the "causal lag"—the time required for the influence to occur. You can't prove that having a college degree increases income by means of a correlation existing between the two on the evening of commencement; you have to know how long the effect would take to show up. But if you know that, you already know a lot about why education increases income; the panel study doesn't add much.

The second: Because observing the same people for many years is difficult and costly, most long-term panel studies make do with small samples. This limits the reliability of the findings; the smaller the sample, the more possible it is that the distribution of items in it is due to mere chance. (If you note the hair color of the first three people you see, two of whom are redheads, you'd be unwise to conclude that two thirds of the population is redheaded.) Furthermore, the smaller the sample, the less the precision with which researchers can make statements about covariations. (It doesn't help much to be told that there is a 95 percent chance that an observed correlation is within 15 points, either way, of the true figure.) To put it another way: So many different things happen to each panel member during two or three decades that if analysts sort out all the combinations of the variables, the result may be more a collection of unique cases than a set of subgroups about which they can make statistically meaningful statements.

These are only two of the many difficulties inherent in long-term panel studies. We've already noted some of them, including staff turnover, practice effects, and the need to stick with procedures that become outmoded as the years pass. But certain others are even more pervasive and intractable.

Some involve distortions of the data created by the method itself;

these are termed threats to "internal validity." Here are three of the eight such problems (some of which we heard of earlier) commonly cited by methodologists:[49]

PANEL BIAS.   People often answer certain questions rather differently the second and later times than they did the first, perhaps because they become less inhibited or because they mull over or discuss the questions between times, or for still other reasons. A drastic solution is to throw away the first round of observations; a less drastic one is to "adjust" the first-round data retrospectively, but this involves a good deal of extra work and, to some researchers, smacks of making the data fit one's hypotheses.[50]

OBSERVATION EFFECTS.   Some forms of observation, especially medical and psychological examinations, tend to influence the very phenomena they seek to observe. Specifically, when such examinations discover pathological conditions, this leads to treatment since not to reveal the discoveries is ethically intolerable—but this modifies the natural history of the phenomenon being observed. Such contamination of the experiment can be avoided by using a different subsample of a known sample at each round, but only at the cost of giving up the special advantages of following the same people throughout.[51]

REGRESSION TO THE MEAN.   At the first observation, some panel members will score either higher or lower on some tests, due to chance circumstances, than they normally would. If a panelist has had some bad news that caused him to lose sleep the night before, he may do poorly in an intelligence or reaction-time test but at the next observation come closer to his usual level of performance. This phenomenon, known as "regression to the mean," can easily be mistaken by researchers for an upward trend—or a downward one—depending on whether the individual underperformed or overperformed the first time. The problem can, however, be dealt with by certain sophisticated statistical procedures which create a baseline from later measurements, thereby offsetting the regression effect.[52]

Other vexing problems are the several common threats to "external validity"—characteristics of panels that limit the extent to which what one learns about them can be extrapolated to other groups.[53] Two of these are particularly hard to deal with.

One is attrition of the sample. Whatever the merits of the sample the researchers begin with and however cautious they are about generalizing from it to the population at large, they may still draw wrong conclusions if the sample changes its composition as time goes by. People who move away or drop out, for instance, may be atypical; they may be the least successful, the most upwardly mobile, or have other special traits. What researchers see in the diminished panel may not give them a true view of what has happened to their original sample. Death, likewise, is selective: It tends to weed out the ailing and inferior performers; the panel's average scores rise, since superior members live on, thereby obscuring any actual decline in their performance.[54]

Solutions to this kind of attrition exist, but none is simple or wholly satisfactory. One is to painstakingly track down the dropouts by means of missing-persons techniques, then use moral suasion to bring them back in. Another is to add new members who match the dropouts as closely as possible. A third is to rework the data, charting the survivors of the panel at any point as if they had been the whole panel from the start.[55]

Other causes of attrition are "nonresponses" and "missing data." In every round, some panelists will refuse to answer certain questions or decline or be unable to take part of the examination. In a cross-sectional study, one can afford to throw out a small number of such incomplete cases, but in a long-term longitudinal study, throwing out incomplete cases at each round of observations eventually leaves a severely pruned sample that may have very different characteristics from the original one and yield erroneous conclusions as to how and why people change.[56]

The best present solution is to retain such cases, filling in the missing data by imputation, as described in chapter 3—that is, by estimating the missing values from other information in the individual's record or in the records of other panelists who are like him or her in most respects. But the procedure is laborious and the resulting data, though probably close to correct, are in a sense artifactual.[57]

The second major threat to external validity is even more problematic. To assume that what happens to a particular group of people over time reveals general principles of human development is to commit what the sociologist Glen Elder calls "the fallacy of cohort centrism." The members of a cohort in a panel study all were born in, grew up in, and have lived in a particular segment of history; their experiences and the course their lives take may differ appreciably from those of people born before or after them. This, as Busse had discovered, is the "cohort effect." Moreover, at the time of any particular observation, special conditions may exist—a recession, an international crisis, a new administration—that make their responses on that occasion somewhat different from what they might have otherwise been; this is the "period effect."[58]

Thus, in any long-term panel study, three causal factors—the individual's biological age, the cohort effect, and the period effect—are "confounded," that is, intermingled, making it unclear what part each of them has played in the net result. This three-way confound was long ago said by James Birren, a prominent gerontologist, to cast an "aura of inelegance" over all long-term longitudinal studies.[59]

But a number of methodologists, including K. Warner Schaie, Paul B. Baltes, Erdman Palmore, and John R. Nesselroade, have painstakingly worked out analytic techniques that they maintain can unconfound these three factors and reveal the role of each.

Although their techniques differ in many ways, the central idea behind them was first put forth in a classic paper by Schaie in 1965.[60] He suggested that several cohorts of different ages be observed over a period of time; the observations could then be compared in three ways, each of which controls for one of the three confounded factors, leaving only two to contend with, as follows:

- By noting the changes within a single age group year by year (as in standard longitudinal studies), researchers exclude the cohort effect, since everyone in the group was born in and lived through the same times. Any changes that occur can therefore be due only to their age, or the conditions prevailing during the observation (the period effect), or both. (For simplicity's sake, we will ignore such other, more manageable problems as measurement error, interviewer effects, and attrition.)
- By testing different cohorts at the same time—comparing, say, groups of children aged 9, 8, 7, 6, and 5—researchers exclude period effects, since all groups are observed under the same prevailing conditions. Any differences are therefore due either to age

or to differences in the social conditions in which the groups grew up (cohort effect), or both.

· Finally, by cross-comparing cohorts in successive years, researchers can see whether the members of each cohort reach the same stage of development as members of other cohorts when they arrive at a given age—whether, for instance, the former 8-year-olds and 7-year-olds reach the same level of development at 9 as the original 9-year-olds. These "cross-lagged" comparisons eliminate the factor of age; any observed differences can be due only to cohort effects or period effects, or both.

Having reduced the confounds to two in each case—and having three ways to cross-compare the results—Schaie went on to outline several processes of mathematical juggling, using a number of interrelated equations, to isolate each of the factors in turn. He concluded, "The above considerations show clearly that it becomes possible to unconfound the sources of developmental change as soon as one begins to analyze simultaneously two or more behavior sequences."

He then offered three strategies (later he expanded it to five)[61] for conducting a longitudinal study, each of which would enable researchers to make all three of the comparisons just outlined. The most efficient approach, he said, was to combine the "time-sequential" method (two or more cohorts followed at the same time and for many years) and the "cross-sequential" method (a large number of cohorts, representing all ages, followed for a shorter time—but long enough to permit cross-lagged comparisons for every age).

Schaie's scheme triggered off a long-running debate. Ever since 1965 he and other methodologists have produced a stream of papers, monographs, and books—some improving on his method of unconfounding, others attacking all these procedures. Much of the debate, dealing with such issues as in what sequence to enter the variables in a multiple regression equation, is comprehensible only to statisticians, but the central problem underlying the major issues is not hard to grasp: according to the sociologist Norval D. Glenn, the unconfounding techniques proposed by Schaie and others all rely on certain unproven assumptions, and if these are incorrect, any procedure based on them cannot be trusted.[62]

One of these assumptions is that the period factor (the conditions at the time of observation) affects people of every age and cohort equally—that, for instance, by observing people in their 20s, 40s, and 60s at the same time, one eliminates differences due to period effects. But psychology and common sense tell us that the reactions to any stimulus may differ according to past experience, physical condition, and other factors. (For example, a war would have a different impact on young, draftable men, the fathers of such men, and childless older men.) Glenn's conclusion: Period effects are *not* the same for all age levels and cohorts, and controlling for period does not exclude them.

In the same way, one cannot assume that people in different cohorts age at the same rate during the same segments of their lives; those who grow up in stressful times may mature or age earlier than those who grow up in easeful conditions. Nor can one assume that people of the same age who grew up at the same time have aged in the same way; an impoverished life style and a privileged one yield different results.

But Glenn and other critics did not say that efforts to unconfound the age, cohort, and period factors are inevitably futile, or that longitudinal research is valueless. They said, rather, that researchers must use outside knowledge or theory to make estimated corrections of their unrealistic assumptions. The process of unconfounding thereby becomes more difficult and yields only tentative results—but credible ones. If the weight of psychological evidence is that older adults are less susceptible than young ones to forces that change people's attitudes, estimated corrections allowing for that effect could be made in equations where age was being held constant. Similar corrections based on outside knowledge or theory could be made in other equations where either the cohort effect or the period effect was being held constant. As Glenn concluded:

Mechanical, atheoretical cohort analysis is a useless exercise . . . [and] statistical innovations alone will not solve the age-period-cohort problem. Successful cohort analysis depends at least as much on knowledge of theories of aging and of recent history as on technical expertise. . . . [Analysts] must be willing to draw heavily on theory and evidence from outside the cohort table to arrive at reasonable tentative conclusions.[63]

A few years later Schaie, writing with a coauthor, candidly admitted that his own original rules "were based upon an intuitive rationale for teasing apart effects which, quite frankly, has been shown to be of questionable validity."[64] This did not mean, however, that unconfounding is impossible, but that more complex procedures, using out-side knowledge or theory, are needed to turn each so-called controlled factor into an estimated variable—a confoundedly hard way of uncon-founding the age, cohort, and period factors.

Despite these difficulties, longitudinal studies using more than one cohort and unconfounding the three major factors one way or another have proven the best approach now known for gaining scientific in-sights into the interplay of processes that govern human development from birth to death. It is a complex, difficult, and somewhat uncertain method, but that is because the phenomena under study—primarily, the processes of human development under natural conditions—are by nature impossible to lay hands on and to do controlled experiments with, and can be explored only by means of inferences based on observations of the events.

Of course that is true of many other areas of scientific research. Astronomers can witness sun spots but not tinker with them; oceanog-raphers can observe currents but not manipulate them; geologists can watch the movements of the earth's crust but not experiment with them. It is the very essence of research in these sciences—and of much social research—to infer the nature of the forces under study from what can be observed taking place. We all constantly do the same thing in everyday life; if we reach wrong conclusions more often than scientists, it is because we are less rigorous in our inferential thinking and because our data base so often includes myth, belief, superstition, and prejudice.

Harvest: The Second Dozen Years

In August 1968, a passerby in the first-floor hallway of the Duke Medical Center gerontology building would have seen nothing to indi-cate that two major research projects on human aging were being conducted there, although Long I was even then conducting its fifth round of observations and Long II was beginning its first round. As in the past, only two panel members came in for observation each day, and the sole clue that both projects were in full swing was that on some days a social worker might now and then walk very slowly down the hall with a man or woman of 85 or 90, and on other days move along briskly with a relative youngster of 45 or 50.

Even behind the closed doors of the examination rooms no dramatic scenes were being enacted. In Long II, as in Long I, panel members were only undergoing thorough but standard physical examinations, taking paper-and-pencil tests, filling out questionnaires, and talking to interviewers. Nor was anything more exciting to be seen on the upper floors of the building than a score of researchers closeted in separate offices, staring at sheets of numbers spread out on their desks. Such is the unremarkable picture offered by Erdman Palmore, today a white-bearded but athletic man in his 50s, when he looks back on his early days on the Long I team (he joined the project and the Duke faculty in 1967 and has been both a productive researcher and the editor of the three official volumes of Duke papers on aging):

All you'd have seen was somebody coming out of an office and going down to the computer room, or hurrying back with a sheaf of printouts and poring over the figures in his or her office. Or doodling equations, punching numbers into a desk calculator, or sketching curves on graph paper, by way of looking for meaningful patterns in the data piling up in the computer's memory bank. Or, finally, trying to put down the results in words on paper. But you'd never have seen anybody running down the hall and crying "Eureka!" Our discoveries didn't come in flashes. We'd study tables of figures, rearrange them, run them through statistical procedures to test out some new hunch about them, and only gradually come to a clear conception of what the data meant.

Yet to the members of the team conducting the two studies, there was a great deal of intellectual excitement in what they were doing. Not only was the slow-moving Long I yielding a rich harvest of findings, but Long II, very different in design, bade fair to yield an even higher-quality crop of new knowledge in far less time. And the findings of both studies, as they emerged, seemed sure to play a major role in a widespread revaluation of the meaning and worth of the latter years of human life.

The team had designed Long II to carefully explore certain topics Long I had only touched upon and to make full use of 1968 state-of-the-art methodology. The main features of the study, which had won the support of the U.S. Public Health Service and several foundations, were as follows:[65]

- In order to explore the antecedents to aging as well as aging itself, the team would observe people aged 45 to 70. But rather than follow them for thirty years or more until they were all old or dead, the researchers would group them by five-year cohorts (45–49, 50–54, and so on) and observe the members of the five resulting groups every two years until each panelist had been followed for six years. The research plus the analysis of the data, completed in a mere decade, would yield portraits of five six-year segments of the human life span which, taken together, would portray aging from the upper 40s to the lower 70s.
- Using a modification of Schaie's design worked out by Palmore, the data could, when needed, be cross-sequentially compared to un-confound aging from cohort and period effects. (By the time the data were being analyzed, however, the team knew that this method, though a major advance over that of Long I, would rely in part on assumptions based on outside knowledge.)
- The team now realized that a probability sample would be far superior to one made up of volunteers. But because drawing such a sample of the whole Durham population would be prohibi-tively costly, they temporized: They got permission from the major local health insurance organization to use a random sam-ple of its membership list, which included most of the middle- and upper-income people in the area.

  From that list they chose 502 white people within the desired age range. (A black sociologist and black community leaders had advised them that, given the tenor of those racially turbulent times, they were likely to encounter unmanageable resistance in the black community.) Whatever was true of this sample could be assumed to hold true for the large middle mass of Durham whites in that age range. Since, however, that group was some-what above the national average in income and education, their findings could be applied only with caution to the comparable white population of the whole nation.
- Because the team was now interested less in physical changes than in how people adjust to middle age and aging, they omitted a number of the physiological tests used in Long I, such as those of color and depth perception and the EEG, and added various new

tests and questionnaires measuring psychological adjustment, social adjustment, and mental performance under stress (tests completed under time pressure). By paring down the old list and
using shortened versions of some of the new items, they were
able to cram each Long II observation of each panel member into
a strenuous eight-hour session.

Day after day, for eight years, panel members came in two at a time,
some from the thinned ranks of the now quite elderly Long I group,
most from the large and much younger Long II group. Between 1968
and 1976, the Long I volunteers returned seven more times; each
round required fewer months as ever fewer of the people were left (only
41 of the original 270 completed the eleventh and final round). During the same period, the Long II panelists came in four times, but
because the multi-cohort design required only eight years from the first
observation of the first panelist to the last one of the last, and many of
the panelists had been under 60 to begin with, 375 of the original 502
were still alive and in the study on the final day of observations in
October 1976.[66]

The team, too, changed during the years: Its ranks grew to over two
score for a while and often included young new faces, while old
familiar ones disappeared as people completed special studies and left
for other posts. But a dedicated nucleus of about ten, some of whom
had been with the project since 1955, remained, passing through their
youthful 30s or 40s to their flourishing 50s, and finally starting to look
a little like some of the people they had begun studying long ago.

During this second dozen years of the aging project—a baker's
dozen, since the team continued to actively analyze the data until
1980—the harvest of research findings increased severalfold; many
hundreds of reports were presented at Monday Night Meetings and
conferences, many scores of papers were published in professional
journals. As before, much of this output was based on cross-sectional
analyses, but the unique contribution of the Duke studies was its body
of longitudinal findings; in some of the latter, the confounding factors
had been fairly well disentangled, permitting the researchers to view
the components of aging without the distortions of cohort or period
effects. Here are a few of the findings of Long I and Long II that
emerged during these years.

FINDINGS ON PHYSICAL AGING

REACTION TIME.   In both Long I and Long II, one test employed a display screen on which a series of digits appeared at a rapid pace; panel members, sitting in front of it, had to press a button as soon as they saw two consecutive even numbers or two consecutive odd ones. They proved somewhat slower and less accurate than college students given the same task, but when Ilene Siegler, a psychologist, and her coworkers looked at the results longitudinally, they found that the panel members had actually lost little speed or accuracy over the years. The findings thus resembled those of intelligence studies: Cross-sectional comparisons exaggerated the decline, longitudinal studies gave a truer and more encouraging picture.[67]

BRAIN IMPAIRMENT.   Wang and Busse compared the EEGs and the psychological and neurological test scores of Long I panel members over a fifteen-year period with their longevity. (For those who had died, they knew the length of life; for those who were still alive, they estimated the remaining years from actuarial tables.) Their finding: The greater the degree of brain impairment, the shorter the life span; brain impairment apparently portended early death. But by means of regression analyses, they showed that other factors mitigated this effect: Brain-impaired persons who functioned well physically, were reasonably happy, and were satisfied with their work had good prospects of continued life. Their conclusion: "The common belief that all elderly persons with brain impairment have a poor prognosis is clearly unjustified."[68]

Several other analyses of Long I and Long II data made the related important observation, contrary to that derived from cross-sectional data, that organic brain disease does not always steadily worsen; rather, the mental condition of many aging people with brain impairment fluctuates, showing both sharp exacerbations and distinct remissions due to changes in their physical condition, habits, and socioeconomic circumstances. The implication: Manipulating these factors might restore many people given up as hopeless to relatively good mental functioning.[69]

SELF-APPRAISAL OF HEALTH.   Maddox and research associate Elizabeth Douglass sought to answer an interesting question: How realistic is the judgment of aging people of their own health? They compared panel members' evaluations of their own health over a fifteen-year period to the examining physicians' appraisals over that same time. Surprisingly, the panel members' judgment of their own health was more closely related to how a physician evaluated it three years later than his evaluation was to how they rated their own health three years later. This might mean either that what a person thinks of his health is a self-fulfilling prophecy, or that a person's self-evaluation is influenced by internal clues so subtle that the physician doesn't see them until time has made the conditions manifest. In either case, most aging people in the Duke panel were apparently good judges of their overall physical status.[70]

PREDICTING LONGEVITY.   Analyses of both Long I and Long II data suggested that some twenty factors having to do with the individual's health, habits, and outlook were causally related to how long he or she lived. But existing statistical methods, when used with these longitudinal data, left a good deal of variance unexplained (that is, people with similar histories didn't necessarily live the same number of years). Palmore worked out a new technique, stepwise multiple regression analysis, which greatly reduced the unexplained variance; using this approach, it became clear that, apart from the well-known effects of age, sex, and race, five factors played a major role in panel members' longevity. The most important was the condition of the person's cardiovascular system, but the second most important, surprisingly, was work satisfaction. Apparently, maintaining a satisfying and meaningful social role makes a considerable difference in overall health and length of life. (The three other significant but much less influential factors were cigarette smoking, general physical functioning, and overall happiness rating.)[71]

FINDINGS ON MENTAL AGING

CARDIOVASCULAR DISEASE AND COGNITIVE PERFORMANCE.   Nowlin and Siegler, using data from Long II, found that within any age group, people with moderately high blood pressure or moderate atherosclerosis (hardening of the arteries) got somewhat fewer correct answers in the reaction-time test mentioned above than did people without either disease. (The hypertensives, however, had quicker reaction times, the atherosclerotics slower ones, than disease-free panel members.) But encouragingly, neither disease took an increasing toll as time passed; after four years, both healthy and diseased people had slowed down a trifle but the difference between them in numbers of correct answers had not increased.[72]

TERMINAL DROP.   Many cross-sectional studies, correlating intelligence and time of death, had shown a sharp decline in mental performance in the last or last several years before death; some gerontologists called this "terminal drop" and theorized that a decline in intelligence was inevitable when death was not far off. Wilkie and Eisdorfer tested this concept longitudinally, using data gathered over fifteen years of Long I. They found that although nonsurvivors had had lower WAIS scores than survivors of roughly the same age, the differences went back many years; it was not true that mental performance always or usually dropped steeply in the last two and a half years of life. And even in those cases where it did so, treatable acute illnesses were responsible for the impairment of mental function. Their conclusion:

[Although] the majority of acute illnesses among the aged can be detected and respond well to treatment . . . many physicians are overly cautious in their approach to treatment of the elderly [a tactful way of saying that most physicians don't bother with the elderly—M.H.]. . . . The aged might experience less intellectual loss if their acute illnesses [were] vigorously treated.[73]

AGE AND MENTAL PERFORMANCE.   In 1980, Busse, summing up the mental performance of Long II panel members over six years, noted that the WAIS scores of all cohorts had improved on the second and third observations and then leveled off. While most of this gain could be attributed to practice effect, he concluded that "the psychological picture of the older person that emerges from the psychometric data is essentially an optimistic one. The data indicate that the longitudinal changes observed are relatively benign unless some observable disease process is present."[74]

FINDINGS ON SOCIAL ADAPTATION

SES AND AGING.   Higher SES (socioeconomic status) had often been shown to be correlated with higher levels of health, activity, and happiness, though which was cause and which effect remained far from clear. Palmore sought a definitive answer in the longitudinal data. He found that over the six-year span of Long II observations, better-educated and higher-income panel members had retained more of their physical health and mental functioning, and made better emotional and social adjustments to aging, than lower SES panel members had. Since the SES factors came first, one could safely assume that they caused (or at least helped cause) the differences.[75]

DISENGAGEMENT VERSUS ACTIVITY.   Long II enabled various team members to take another and closer look at this issue. Within each age group, they found that men who saw more friends and acquaintances and women who went to more meetings of various kinds remained in better health and were happier than those who did less of each. Thus, again, activity seemed a better adjustment to aging than disengagement.[76]

In addition, Long II panel members were asked the ages of the people they had social contact with, to test the widely accepted hypothesis that, as people grow old, they minimize the stress of generation gap by withdrawing into a "subculture of aging." The data showed the opposite to be true: Over a six-year span, the social network of the panel members in every age group came to include more younger members (most of them, presumably, grandchildren and other relatives). The Durham sample—more typical of older Americans throughout the country than the inhabitants of Sunbelt retirement communities—had adapted by increasing, rather than decreasing, their contact with younger people.[77]

RETIREMENT.   According to both popular belief and cross-sectional data, retirement is often associated with a deterioration in health, mood, and other components of the quality of life. But is this actually a cause-and-effect relationship? Long II offered a before-and-after view of people in each of several cohorts. Although two thirds of those who retired had done so involuntarily, Palmore and research associate Clark Luikart came up with some noteworthy findings:

- There was little decrease in health after retirement.
- Retirees compensated in part for the loss of activities and contacts by increasing their leisure activities and neighborly visiting.
- While the income of most retirees dropped, few complained of a decline in its adequacy.
- Decreases in overall satisfaction, general mood, and feelings of usefulness were either temporary or minor.
- A few people had suffered seriously from retirement, but a few others had benefited greatly.

In sum: "The majority of workers retire because they have to, and yet very few suffer poverty, illness, inactivity, or depression as a result. Most appear to adapt to the 'crisis' of retirement with little or no lasting negative effects."[78]

ADAPTATION TO BEREAVEMENT.   A great deal of research has shown that widowed persons have lower morale, lower income, and higher mortality and suicide rates than persons with spouses; loss of the spouse is widely held to be the most traumatic of all normal life events.[79] But when Dorothy Heyman and Daniel Gianturco, a psychiatrist, reviewed Long I data based on interviews with, and physical examinations of, widows and widowers, they were surprised to find no deterioration in health or social adjustment and only a minor decline in general outlook. Whatever ills the widowed suffered immediately after bereavement, apparently there were no long-term ill effects. Long II, with more detailed data, did show widowed men to be in not quite as good health as men with spouses, but other than this there was no significant evidence of lasting trauma.[80]

These puzzling findings became more comprehensible when analyzed by age. As Palmore summed up the evidence: "The event of widowhood appears to be more stressful in middle age than in old age, [where it] . . . appeared to have no measurable long-term negative effects. In fact, death of spouse in late life appeared to bring relief and improved adjustment for many who had been suffering through the ordeal of their spouse's disability and terminal illness."[81]

STATUS, SENSE OF CONTROL, SATISFACTION, SEXUALITY

- Long II panel members were asked at each observation how "respected" they felt (a measurement of status). When age, period, and cohort were unconfounded, it became clear that the participants had experienced no loss of respect as they aged.[82]
- The answers to a series of eleven special questions asked of Long II panel members showed that aging diminished only slightly the extent to which they felt in control of their lives rather than under the control of external forces.[83]
- Contrary to the stereotype of the increasingly sour, discontented old man or old woman, the Duke studies found that most people maintained relatively high levels of satisfaction as they aged.[84]
- The percentage of married men and women in Long II who continued to have marital intercourse was smaller in each successively older cohort, and declined somewhat within each cohort during the six years of the Long II observations. But these were only averages; more panel members remained as active as they had been than became less so, and about a tenth were actually more active at Round 4 than at Round 1. Even at 64 and beyond, more than four fifths of the married men and nearly four fifths of the married women were still having marital intercourse; their average frequency was three times a month. Palmore used several analytic methods to see whether keeping up sexual activity had any measurable benefits for aging people and concluded, "There are several indications that sexual activity tends to maintain or enhance both health and happiness among both men and women aged 45 to 70."[85]

These and many comparable findings added up to an overall portrait of aging very unlike that of tradition and popular belief. According to Long I and Long II, old people do not become alike but maintain individual differences. Their personalities remain basically stable; they do not, in general, become suspicious, hostile, withdrawn, or pessimistic. Some adapt to age very successfully, and most others fairly well, while only a minority adapt poorly. In most people, normal aging produces relatively little physical, mental, or social decline over long periods of time; aging is not, and should not be equated with, dying.[86]

This is not to say that there is no pain, no sickness, no sorrow, no loss in aging. The team members, especially those who dealt with panel members personally and got to know them well over the years, saw the long-term changes in them, especially in the men and women of Long I, and were saddened when these old friends grew feeble or ill, suffered mental impairments, became bed-bound, and died. Some of the researchers admit that witnessing these events made them keenly aware of their own mortality and weighed heavily on them. Yet the prevailing attitude toward aging among the team members, including those for whom it was not a distant prospect but an immediate reality, was strongly affirmative.

Admittedly, they had been looking at "normal aging" and seeing nothing of the other side—the palsied, helpless, incontinent, witless, terminal existence of so many of the inhabitants of nursing homes. But those people are only a small fraction of the aging population and, for the most part, are in such homes relatively briefly, either during a crisis or in the last stages of life.[87] The Duke portrait of aging is modal in nature: It shows the typical or most common experience of aging.

In recent years, as gerontology has become an established interdisciplinary specialty, many medical and social researchers have been working in the field and collectively transforming our national perception of aging and the value we assign to it. But it has been the long-term longitudinal studies of aging at Duke and elsewhere that have provided the most credible and convincing grounds for thinking that the aging years are well worth living.

The Coming of Age of Longitudinal Research

Longitudinal studies have proven their value only so recently, and are so difficult to conduct and slow to yield results, that they make up no great part of current social research. This is especially true of long-term panel studies, which, despite their unique advantages, are the most problematic and patience-taxing of all. Typically, a leading 1983 textbook on social research devotes only 2 of its nearly 500 pages to longitudinal research, gives panels a single paragraph of this space, and says not one word about long-term studies.[88]

Nonetheless, within the past decade longitudinal studies of all kinds have been growing in number, with the panel type—mostly short-term, but some fairly extended—gaining a good deal of popularity. We are now in an era of social research foreseen nearly a decade ago by Burton Singer and Seymour Spilerman, both experts in longitudinal methodology, as being "comparatively rich in the existence of multi-wave panel data on large population samples."[89]

Some panel studies of fairly recent date, dealing with economic and other policy issues, are massive efforts funded by various federal agencies and using samples of several thousand to 50,000 or more persons, families, or households drawn from the population of the entire nation. Among 101 national data bases listed in a 1982 compendium, 25 were panel studies of this kind, over half of them launched since 1970. They include such major ongoing projects as the Michigan Panel Study of Income Dynamics, the National Longitudinal Surveys of Labor Market Experience, and the National Crime Survey. A more current list would, of course, include SIPP.[90]

Other longitudinal studies—some of which began many years ago, some recently—are currently exploring areas of behavioral and social science ranging from child development to aging, giftedness to delinquency, fertility to the effects of atom-bomb radiation, and the use of time to suicide. Some are vast in size (one German study has a third of a million respondents) but longitudinal only insofar as they recreate the past through current interviews. Many others are far smaller, with samples ranging from several thousand down to a few dozen, but among them are the most ambitious of all—the kind that doggedly observe the same people for much or most of their lives, seeking to unravel the intricate tangles of causes and effects behind complex aspects of their behavior.[91] Some of the most notable are:

- The Berkeley Guidance Study. Begun in 1928 with a random sample of 248 newborns in Berkeley, California, and still going on, it deals with biological and environmental factors associated with personality development and behavior.
- The Terman Gifted Children Study. Begun in 1921 with a statewide (California) sample of 1,470 high-IQ boys and girls, and continued until 1977, it dealt with the mental abilities, marital and occupational histories, and life satisfaction of the gifted.

- The Framingham Heart Study. Begun in 1949 with a probability sample of 5,200 Framingham, Massachusetts, men and women between 30 and 59, plus, in the early 1970s, 5,135 of their adult children, and still going on, it focuses on biomedical risk factors for heart disease, with some attention to behavioral and social risk factors.
- The Baltimore Longitudinal Study of Aging. Begun in 1958 with a volunteer sample of 964 men between 25 and 84, plus, in 1978, a cohort of 250 women, and still going on, it deals with physiological, psychological, and pathological changes of aging.
- And, of course, the Duke Studies of Aging, especially Long I.

The kind of evidence produced by longitudinal studies, both short term and long term, is highly persuasive: The method not only deals far less tentatively with causal relationships than cross-sectional analyses but is the scientific analog of Everyman's real-world acquisition of knowledge through before-and-after experiences.

Already, longitudinally acquired insights are having an important influence—and surely will have more in the future—on government policies concerning employment, training, transfer programs, and many other major social issues. According to the National Commission on Employment Statistics, longitudinal analysis has already clarified such matters as the effect of training on earnings at various social levels, the relationship between the work experiences of teenagers and their success in the labor market in later years, and the effect of income transfer payments on the decision to seek or not to seek work. Such information enables legislators and agency administrators to make better assessments of alternative ways of dealing with these problems.[92]

Beyond its impact on policy, longitudinal research seems sure to modify some of our deeply ingrained ways of thinking and behaving. Indeed, it has already done so in a number of ways:

- Major longitudinal studies of aging have played a major part in changing American attitudes and actions toward the elderly and in moderating the fear of aging.
- The Framingham study is one of the most-often cited sources of information about the connections between smoking and heart disease, and between high-fat diet and heart disease; it is rea-

sonable to suppose that this information played a significant part in bringing about the recent beneficial changes in American eating habits and tobacco use.

- Long-term panel studies of human development have helped shift scientific and public thinking about what influences psychosocial development away from simplistic explanations and toward multi-causal and more realistic ones. The Berkeley study, for instance, has shown that parents are far less accountable for the way their children turn out than pop psychology has held; much more of the variance in personality and social adjustment in adults is explained by interacting genetic, environmental, and social factors than by the caliber of parenting.[93] This information is already widely known among professionals and, through the media, has begun to filter down into the public consciousness.

- Panel studies have been an important factor in the appearance, within the past decade, of a distinctive new view of human development and behavior known as the "life-span perspective." As characterized by the sociologist David Featherman in a 1981 report to the National Science Foundation:

> The essence of this approach is that developmental changes in human behavior . . . occur from conception to death, and . . . arise from a matrix of biological, psychological, social, historical, and evolutionary influences and from their timing across people's lives. Scholarly and popular interest in the themes of this perspective have been intense since 1970.[94]

He cites the media interest in the life-cycle view, popularized in terms of "stages" or "passages," and the growth in the academic community of life-cycle studies and multidisciplinary conferences looking at development and aging as lifelong processes.

Among the aspects of this view that seem bound to affect both public policies and private lives in constructive ways are such ideas as these:[95]

- Behavior and personality are far more malleable throughout life than has commonly been supposed.
- Chronological age is less important in understanding any individual's behavior than the stage of development he or she has reached.
- Among the many interacting forces affecting the course of the life cycle are social and historical conditions; each birth

cohort thus experiences a potentially different set of life events, and many of the generalizations that apply to one cohort may not apply to another. (This may be why for every wise proverb there is an equally wise one saying the opposite.)

— Although individuals develop as a result of the interplay of multiple forces, they themselves interact with and are one of those forces; in Featherman's words, "Individuals are agents in their own development." We are not plankton; we swim within the current.

Yet despite the advantages of the long-term longitudinal method of research and the power of its findings to influence thought and behavior, it is hardly likely to displace other methods of social research. It is not essential in the study of a great many subjects, and it is altogether too slow a way of gathering the kinds of information urgently needed to make or alter policies during times of economic crisis, urban disorder, and major population movement.

Above all, it attracts only those researchers who have the patience to wait years for the payoff of their labors or even the willingness to labor without any certainty that the rewards will arrive in their time. As Richard Rockwell of the Social Science Research Council comments:

Lengthy longitudinal studies represent one class of investments in which the original investigator may not recoup his investment. In a sense, this is our equivalent of the astronomer's space probe: It is launched with the sure knowledge that we will be dead before its signal returns. Our major studies (Terman, Berkeley, etc.) have also outlived their creators. That sort of determination and consistency of purpose is not true of much else in social science.[96]

Returns

Happily, the three originators of Long I have lived to see the signals return, though Barnes and Silverman have not been at Duke for many years. Busse, however, remained the chief investigator of Long I and Long II until they ended and as recently as 1984 was revising papers for the third volume of reports on both studies, *Normal Aging III*.

Maddox, Palmore, and Nowlin, who joined the team after Long I was well under way but helped launch Long II in 1968, are still associated with the Duke Center for the Study of Aging and Human Development and are still working on reports based on Long I and Long II data. So are other people at Duke and elsewhere.

By the time the studies ended in 1980, they had cost more than $3 million, a respectable sum in the nickel-and-dime world of social research, and in return had yielded a crop of papers so large (a thousand items, as already noted) that their average cost was only about $3,000. Since then, other papers reanalyzing the raw material have been appearing regularly and no doubt will long continue to do so because, as Ilene Siegler recently noted, "[The] tremendous recent advances in the development of methods appropriate to the analysis of longitudinal data . . . have not yet been applied to the Duke data."[97]

The end of the studies came about only because, as the grants ran out, the team decided not to apply for others to continue observing the Long I and Long II panelists. Maddox:

The temptation was to go on forever, but I argued that we had reached the point of diminishing returns. By 1976, only forty-one Long I panel members were left and we were having to see more and more of them at home. As for Long II, it had completed its scheduled series of four rounds. So we decided that the project *would* come to an end. We continued analyzing the data until the end of the grant period in 1980, and then one Monday night—August 25th, 1980—we had our last official Monday Night Meeting.

The mood at that meeting, however, was neither solemn nor sorrowful, since the people present knew they'd still be working together at the Center and, on other grants, would be using and reusing the Long I and Long II data for years to come.

Most of them have also gone on to other kinds of research in human aging. But in 1980, Nowlin, Palmore, and Wang, assisted by a group of technicians, began a third longitudinal study of aging on a grant from the National Institute of Mental Health. Unlike either of its predecessors, this one was designed to run for only five years—a prudent decision, since its panel of 300 men and women were in their 80s and 90s and, in the euphemism researchers use, would rapidly be "lost to the study." The aim of Long III, as some people call it, is to see why certain people remain mentally healthy into very old age and why others become mentally ill. The panelists are part of a sample of over-65 Durham residents who took part in a special community survey in 1972; the team began with a ten-year follow-up, has continued to see them each year, and will do so until 1985.[98]

But already Nowlin, for one, is thinking about a proposal for yet another panel study of aging. This one, going back to survivors of Long II, would investigate how stresses of various kinds have affected their health as they have aged and why some of them have been able to deal better than others with those stresses. If Nowlin did undertake such a study, he would be in his mid-50s or older before it got under way—twenty years older than Busse was when Long I got started. And if, like that project, the new one set out to run for several years but continued on for twenty-five—always a possibility, in longitudinal research—Nowlin himself might well be lost to the study before the final results come in, a matter that does not seem to bother him.

For Rockwell's point is well taken: Long-term panel studies appeal to researchers with a special quality—an interest in both subject and method that drives them to ask questions they realize only others may ever hear answered.

TWENTY THOUSAND VOLUNTEERS

A Massive Real-World Experiment
Tests a Bold Proposal to Combat
Poverty by Means of a Guaranteed
Annual Income

The Bread and Circuses Question

In a Seattle public-housing project in the fall of 1970, a middle-aged black woman standing in her apartment doorway listened to a pitch earnestly delivered by Gary Christophersen, a pony-tailed hippie-ish young white man. As Christophersen (nowadays a conventionally barbered but informally dressed businessman) remembers the incident, her expression gradually changed from the guarded to the cynically amused.

"She began to smile," he recalls, "and said, 'You've got to be kidding. I don't *believe* you! *Nobody* would do that!' "

He was momentarily taken aback, but then rallied and said that the offer was on the level: As part of a study, Urban Opinion Surveys was prepared to guarantee that her family's annual family income never went below $4,800 for the next three years.

"She said, 'And you say I don't have to do *anything* for it?' I said 'Hardly anything,' and she burst out laughing." He explained that all she would have to do is make out an income report once a month and let an interviewer ask her some questions three times a year; in return, her family would get up to $400 every month, depending on how much they were earning.

"Go *on!*" she said scornfully. "*Nobody's* going to give me income that I don't have to do anything for!" And she shut the door firmly in Christophersen's face, plainly regarding him as some kind of con man.

He was not. He was one of several dozen people, mostly young, college-educated, and idealistic, seeking to enroll 2,000 poor or near-poor Seattle families in a massive experimental trial of a daring new antipoverty program. It had been proposed by the Office of Economic Opportunity during the Johnson Administration and now, in Nixon's time, was being field-tested by the OEO in the East and Midwest, and was about to be tested in Seattle by the Department of Health, Education, and Welfare.

During the 1960s, the nation's welfare system had mushroomed into a welter of overlapping programs; the result was inefficient and costly. Worse, the patchwork had great holes: While the system aided millions of single-parent families and unemployable poor people, it excluded other millions of impoverished two-parent families—the so-called working poor.[1] The new proposal, based on the premise that every American family has a right to an income above the poverty level, would replace the entire conglomeration of welfare benefits, including "in-kind transfers" such as food stamps and public housing, with a single, universally applicable cash benefit called "negative income tax" or NIT.

NIT would work something like the graduated income tax, the rates of which start at zero and increase as income rises, but in reverse. The government would guarantee every family a certain minimum income; the farther below that figure the family's income, the larger the NIT payment. If a family earned any money whatever, it would get less than the maximum NIT payment, and the more it earned, the less NIT it would receive. But to preserve the incentive to work, NIT would shrink by only part of a dollar for every dollar of earnings. Thus, a poor family that brought home, say, three quarters of the guaranteed income would receive from the government not just the difference but substantially more.[2]

The test of the proposal in Seattle and, a little later, in Denver would eventually enroll a total of nearly 5,000 families, comprising some 20,000 persons. The Seattle-Denver Income Maintenance Experiment, or SIME/DIME, would be the fourth, and by far the largest and methodologically most sophisticated, test of the new idea. But all four were much more than mere tryouts of the proposed program; they were bona fide "social experiments," a new genre of social research embodying two key principles of the true experiment—scientific sampling and the comparison of an experimental group with a control group—but taking place on a grand scale in the real world rather than in miniature in a laboratory.

The principal question to be explored in Seattle and Denver, as in the three other IMEs, was of great practical concern to policy-makers in Congress and the welfare agencies, and at the same time of great theoretical interest to social researchers. The four IMEs would eventually invest a dozen years of effort and more than $100 million, with SIME/DIME responsible for two thirds of that outlay (roughly a third of which went to the families, the rest for research costs), in an attempt to answer the following question: If the government guaranteed the poor a livable minimum income, would they continue to work as much as they had or would they slack off somewhat? Or even, like Roman proletarians in the era of "'bread and circuses" (free food and shows, given by the Caesars), become indolent drones?

The answer would have major practical significance, since if the millions of poor and near-poor families eligible for guaranteed income payments worked markedly less than they otherwise would have, they would both produce less and cost more;[3] the rest of society might be overwhelmed by the burden. If, on the other hand, they continued to work as much, or nearly as much as they had, the program might prove not only affordable but even economical. The $100 million spent on research, huge by social-science standards, was a minor expense compared with the cost of the social programs—now running to hundreds of billions annually—that might be importantly influenced by the knowledge the research would yield.

On the theoretical side, the data would provide the first experimental confirmation or disconfirmation of the classic theory of labor supply. This holds that the human being, in deciding how much to work, acts as a "rational man"*—one who seeks to maximize "utility," that is, strike a balance between work and leisure that yields him the greatest total reward.[4] Since taking time off for leisure costs him the money he could have earned by working, economists consider that he "buys" his leisure even as he does other goods. If government were to provide him with a guaranteed income, would he, as theory predicts, rationally choose to work less because his leisure cost him less, and if so, how much less would he work? Or would he, for one reason or another, work as much as before, thus showing this important assumption about human economic behavior to be erroneous?

A second question of great interest had to do with the effect of income maintenance on family stability. A mass of statistical evidence gathered over many years showed that desertion and divorce were highest among the poorest families;[5] moreover, the largest federal welfare program, AFDC (Aid to Families with Dependent Children), paid benefits primarily to single-parent families and thereby, it was widely believed, induced many poor men to abandon their wives and children, who could then collect AFDC payments.[6] On both grounds, there was reason to hope that a program guaranteeing an annual income to intact as well as single-parent families might significantly increase family stability among the poor.

Large-scale scientific experiments of this kind that intervene in people's real-world lives are of quite recent origin. The first major social experiment was, in fact, the New Jersey IME, which began operations in four New Jersey cities in 1968. At that time, the concept of the social experiment was all but unknown, even within the social-science community. The man who would begin designing the massive Seattle experiment in 1969 hadn't even known in 1968 that such a thing was possible. He was Dr. Robert Spiegelman, a tall, soft-spoken, 40-year-old economist at SRI International (then known as Stanford Research Institute), a private research firm in Menlo Park, California.

---

*The term "rational man" antedates present-day egalitarian usage; as used here, it means "rational man or woman."

"I had believed," he recalls, "—and it was generally accepted—that you couldn't conduct an experiment in a social milieu because you couldn't control the environment through experimental design. But I went to hear a lecture by Al Rees, who was working on the New Jersey Income Maintenance Experiment, and learned that it was, in fact, possible."

Albert Rees, an eminent labor economist at Princeton University, was working as a consultant to Mathematica Policy Research, a private research firm in Princeton that was conducting the field work on the New Jersey IME. He explained, among other things, that proper sampling and the random assignment of families to experimental and control conditions would permit a scientific test of whether the income guarantee did or did not act as a disincentive to work. For in an experimental design with a sufficiently large sample, the many uncontrollable influences of the real-world setting would exist in equal numbers in both the treatment and the control groups. Any difference in behavior between them could therefore be ascribed to the one factor they did not have in common—the treatment, in this case the guaranteed annual income available to the experimental group.

Spiegelman found the whole idea "quite revolutionary and very intriguing." Hoping to get in on a new and highly significant kind of social research, he asked his superiors at SRI to provide him with funds to study the matter and, as he says, "to see what was possible"— meaning both scientifically and in terms of landing a government contract. SRI gave Spiegelman a modest in-house grant; with it, he was able to spend time studying early reports about the New Jersey IME and traveling to Princeton and Washington to talk to social scientists and OEO officials involved in it.

He learned that the OEO had first recommended a national negative income tax plan to President Johnson in 1965 but gotten no response from him. (The notion of income maintenance through NIT was neither original with OEO nor an exclusively liberal idea; it had been considered by Treasury officials twenty years earlier and advocated some years later by the conservative economist Milton Friedman, among others.)[7]

Heather Ross, a doctoral student working for the OEO, then made a daring and original suggestion: Perhaps a large-scale experiment, testing an actual NIT program, would provide persuasive evidence of its feasibility and cost-effectiveness. OEO officials, impressed, decided in 1967 to invest part of their agency funds in just such an effort and contracted with researchers at the University of Wisconsin's Institute for Research on Poverty and at Mathematica to design the experiment for them.[8]

Spiegelman became familiar with the details of the design of the New Jersey IME and its early results. What he heard of its successes and its shortcomings—some of each were already becoming apparent—made him increasingly eager to try his hand at designing and running such an experiment. He sensed an opportunity to do so when, at the Department of Health, Education, and Welfare, he talked to Jodie Allen, a researcher and planner in ASPE, the Office of the Assistant Secretary for Planning and Evaluation.

"She told me," Spiegelman says, "that HEW was thinking about running a major income maintenance experiment of their own. It would be HEW's job to operate such a program if it were ever enacted, so they wanted to conduct their own experiment and not rely on OEO's. Also, they felt there was much to be learned that wasn't coming out of the New Jersey IME."

That experiment, it was evident, had used too small a sample and had too narrowly defined the population to be sampled and the income guarantee levels to be tested. The sociologist Peter H. Rossi and the political economist Katharine C. Lyall, in a critique of the New Jersey IME, would later characterize it as "one of the more important happenings in empirical social science research," but regretfully conclude that the design was flawed in ways that made it impossible to extrapolate from the findings to the national population of the poor.[9]

Spiegelman returned to SRI but kept in touch with Jodie Allen. When she told him in mid-1969 that HEW had decided to go ahead with its own IME in Seattle, he swiftly worked up and submitted a proposal, and in October learned to his delight that his proposal had won out over three competing others and that HEW was awarding SRI a $300,000 initial contract to design the experiment. Spiegelman, of course, would head the project.

A real challenge, that. "I had never done anything of this magnitude," Spiegelman says, "and of course I had had no experience with social experiments. In fact, almost no one had, so there was nothing useful in the economic and sociological literature." Many familiar bits and pieces of research machinery—survey techniques, interview protocols, multivariate statistical analysis, and the like—would be part of the experimental design, but the design itself had no precedent other than the New Jersey IME. "The pioneering and innovativeness of the New Jersey people," Spiegelman says, "—Harold Watts and Al Rees, among others, on the academic side, and Dave Kershaw of Mathematica—can't be overstated. But some of the mistakes and shortcomings of that first social experiment were already fairly clear, and I hoped to do better."

To work with him on the design, particularly its theoretical aspects, Spiegelman enlisted Professor Mordecai Kurz, an economist on the faculty of Stanford University whom he had worked with before and whose ability he valued. For help in designing the field operation he conferred with Kershaw, and he subcontracted with Mathematica, which was running the field operation of the New Jersey IME, to do the same thing in Seattle.

Designing the experiment took a year of intense effort, beginning in October 1969. The word "designing" may invoke images of drafting boards, sketches, blueprints, and models, but none of those are part of social research. It is a largely cerebral activity involving reasoning and imagination (as is, indeed, the planning stage of experimental design in the physical and life sciences); its raw materials are theories, formulas, flow diagrams, and other intellectual equipment, and its physical paraphernalia consist of little more than chalk, blackboards, pencils, and lined yellow pads.

"Kurz and I," Spiegelman said, reminiscing not long ago,

would get together in my office, where we'd talk for hours and write things all over the blackboard. Then we'd go back to our own desks and draft pieces of the plan. Then we'd exchange them, scribble all over each other's drafts, and argue for hours about all sorts of issues, both large and small, and try to work them out.

One big issue was sample size. The SRI statisticians we consulted claimed we could do the job with a small sample. There would be only one variable— either the NIT payments would reduce the amount worked or they wouldn't —and for that, a small sample was adequate. But we didn't agree. The question we wanted to answer wasn't simply whether people would work the same amount or work less, but how *much* change in working we could expect under each of a number of different conditions. We wanted to measure the impact of a whole range of different support levels and "tax rates"—that is, different rates at which the payments would decline as the family earned money. But to test all those conditions, we needed a large sample. After we expanded to Denver (which wasn't part of our original plan), our sample was twenty per cent larger than the combined totals of the other three IMEs in New Jersey, two rural areas, and Gary, Indiana.

The wider range of our support levels was one way in which we expected to improve on the New Jersey experiment. Their highest support level was quite low, which meant that they included only the poorest families, and that very few of their two-parent families had working wives. So while they were finding very little reduction in work, their results might not be a good indication of what would happen if the program went into effect nationally. [As in the other sciences, learning from the shortcomings of prior experimental work is an important part of the experimental design process in social research.]

We decided to have three guarantee levels—$3,800, $4,800, and $5,600, which represented 95 percent, 120 percent, and 140 percent of the official poverty line, $4,000, at the time we began making payments. Also, the New Jersey experiment had used a fixed "tax rate"—that is, the NIT payments decreased by a constant amount as the family's income increased. But for good theoretical reasons, we felt that a *declining* tax rate might give greater incentive to work. So we decided that as they earned more, the rate at which their NIT payments decreased would get smaller.

We also wanted to try out *different* tax rates, to see whether we could determine how much additional withdrawal from work would be caused by a specific increase in the tax rate. After a lot of discussion and looking up of survey data on the impact of welfare on work, we chose four different tax rates—two of them constant (50 percent and 70 percent), and two declining (80 percent and 70 percent, going down by 5 percent for each thousand of non-NIT income).

So with four possible tax rates and three income guarantee levels, we had a total of twelve possible "treatments" or experimental conditions. We considered one of them expendable, and went ahead with eleven treatments—a complicated design, you might say.

The design was made even more complicated by several other major treatment variables. The view underlying the NIT experiments was that the poor simply need more money, while the older, more liberal view was that the poor are disadvantaged and need job training, education, and other remedial help.[10] Because HEW wanted to test both approaches, Spiegelman and Kurz planned to offer some participants job counseling, or counseling plus education subsidies, to see whether either would enable or encourage them to get better-paying jobs. This would offset the tendency to work less, since a better rate of pay meant they'd be "paying" more for their leisure.[11]

The design became still more complicated shortly after the experiment had gotten under way. "Our original idea," Spiegelman says,

was to have families in the experimental program for three years. But soon after we got started, we heard from the academic community that we should be very concerned about the experimental "time horizon." People in the experiment would know it was to end in three years, so they probably wouldn't change their behavior as much as they would in a permanent program.

The criticisms convinced us we had to do something, and we came up with the idea of having different lengths of experiment—three years, five years, and in Denver we even signed up a small sample for *twenty* years, to see whether the longer terms would result in different behavior from the shorter one. If there was no time horizon bias, fine; if there was one, we'd measure it and correct for it.

But the debate over guaranteed income was going on in Congress, and HEW wanted results in a hurry. So even while the design of the experiment was being worked out, Spiegelman had Mathematica establish a beachhead in Seattle and prepare to start the experiment. Kershaw rented an office in a downtown office building in November 1969 and began hiring a variety of office workers and a couple dozen interviewers.

The latter, in the course of the next half year or so, fanned out, rang doorbells, and, presenting themselves as workers doing a neighborhood survey for Urban Opinion Surveys (a creation of Mathematica), conducted thousands of five-minute screening interviews. Later they returned to interview in far greater detail those families selected for the program. At that point, for the first time, they explained something of its nature and purposes; many of the families were delighted, others were too proud to want any part of it, and still others, like the woman who closed the door in Christophersen's face, were suspicious and disbelieving.

While all this was going on, Spiegelman and Kurz continued to work on the design. The time pressure being what it was, however, Spiegelman submitted a batch of material to Jodie Allen after only a little over half a year, when the task was still far from complete. But such was his enthusiasm for the project that he had no doubt HEW would give SRI the go-ahead—as in fact it did in September 1970, when it awarded the firm a $20 million contract for a three-year income maintenance experiment in Seattle.

The decision to expand to Denver came a little later, when a severe local recession in Seattle made conditions there atypical. As Spiegelman and his staff were to discover again and again, the best-laid schemes of mice and social experimenters gang aft agley, since the real world is untidy and unpredictable. Spiegelman himself grossly misjudged what part the experiment would play in his own life: "I expected it to run three years, plus six months for analysis," he said to an acquaintance last year, then added with a sigh, "—and I spent twelve years of my life on it."

The Concept of the Social Experiment

Social experimentation is a kind of applied social research that tests proposed social programs to see how well they will work and what modifications they may need. But it is more than that; it is true experimental research in the milieu of the real world and therefore is capable of yielding important new knowledge that could not have been obtained by the statistical analysis of data on existing conditions.

Such real-world experimentation in the social sciences was long thought to be impossible. Since social scientists could neither control nor influence social forces and processes, it seemed they had to rely on inferences based on what they could observe. But as Nobel Laureate Herbert Simon pointed out in a recent essay, observation and inference are not an adequate approach to phenomena as complex and subtle as those of social behavior:

Large numbers of facts of human individual and social behavior surround us in our daily lives . . . [but] casual observation [does not] provide a satisfactory empirical foundation for general descriptive laws. Without systematic observation, including experimentation where that is possible, our samples will be badly biased, our observations will be severely filtered by our preconceptions, and the phenomena will be altogether too tangled and complex for satisfactory analysis.[12]

Social scientists have therefore worked for decades at developing more rigorous research methods—scientific sampling, time-series studies, longitudinal research, multivariate statistical analysis, and so on. But while these techniques can yield inferences of the type, "It is highly probable that A and B are causally connected," only experiments can demonstrate quite unambiguously that "A causes B."

Until recently, social researchers attempted only such experiments as could be conducted in the laboratory, where the environment and the stimuli could be fully controlled and the costs were minor. Experiments in real life seemed both unscientific and unfeasible: There would be a multitude of uncontrolled variables—including those introduced by ongoing history and social change—and hence many possible explanations of whatever took place. In any case, social researchers had no access to the major funding needed to draw large scientific samples, observe and gather data on all its members for years, and analyze the resulting millions of pieces of information.

But as the nation's social programs exploded in size and scope, policy-makers became acutely aware that they needed hard experimental evidence of the probable effects of alterations in existing programs and of proposed new ones. It was as impossible, however, to run experiments on programs as vast and complex as AFDC or Model Cities in a laboratory as it would be to study wave mechanics in a teaspoon or tornado development in a retort. In the 1960s, therefore, policy-makers and social scientists turned to a new specialty called "evaluation research," which, in lieu of true social experiments, used what was available, namely, natural experiments and quasi-experiments.

A natural experiment, as we have seen, exists when a historical event such as the advent of a new law or social program alters the lives of a number of people in some way. To judge the impact of such an event, evaluation researchers look at the condition of these people before the event and afterward. But because it is not politically feasible to exclude some eligibles from a new national program, there is no control group to compare with the affected people, and lacking a control group, one can't be sure that any differences in the participants weren't due to other concomitant influences, such as a period of inflation or unemployment, a social change occurring at the same time as the event under scrutiny, or merely the fact that the people being observed have grown older.

Nor does a natural experiment include different versions of the program being studied that would reveal the relative influences of its key variables. Lacking such data, an evaluation study can show that a program has not achieved its goals but cannot identify the components which, if modified, would enable it to do so. Thus, evaluation studies of "manpower training programs" (as they used to be called) show that they have largely failed to reduce poverty—although better education is known to be linked to higher socioeconomic status—but say nothing about what changes in the programs might make them effective.[13]

Similarly, many social innovations that are loosely called "experimental" lack control groups and so are not amenable to scientific analysis of their effects. As the social psychologists Leonard Saxe and Michelle Fine remark in *Social Experiments*, "Some people might view the women's liberation movement as a social experiment in the sense that women (and men) are urged to try different roles. Changes in men's and women's roles have not, however, been implemented on a systematic experimental basis."[14] If liberated men and women are either happier or less happy than traditional men and women, one cannot ascribe the difference to their role changes; those who adopted the new roles may have been psychologically and socially somewhat unlike traditional men and women to begin with, and these factors, rather than the role changes, may be responsible.

Closer to the scientific ideal is the quasi-experiment, in which a group of participants in some program or in a "demonstration" (trial) of a proposed program are compared, after they have been in it for a while, to a group of nonparticipants. The latter—the controls—are "matched" to the experimentals, that is, chosen for their similarity to them in age, income, education, and other influential variables. Any difference between the experimentals and the controls is assumed to be due to the only known remaining difference between them—participation or nonparticipation in the program.

This method is often used when there is insufficient time or money, or interest on the part of policy-makers, to conduct a true experiment, with its random assignment of individuals to experimental and control groups, a procedure requiring far wider sampling and roughly double the observational effort and cost effort of the quasi-experiment.[15] Yet only random assignment can ensure that all unknown contaminating variables will be equally divided between the experimentals and the controls, thus nullifying their potentially biasing effects. Matching, even though carefully done, cannot exclude the possibility—or even the likelihood—that the experimental and the control groups are not wholly comparable and that unsuspected factors are partly or largely responsible for the observed differences.[16]

Head Start is a case in point. Begun in the 1960s, this program, an important component of Johnson's War on Poverty, sought to prepare disadvantaged preschool children to cope successfully with school. Not until Head Start had been running for some time did Congress ask to have it evaluated. At that point, researchers matched a number of 1st-, 2nd-, and 3rd-grade children who had taken part in Head Start with similar children who had not, and found that Head Start students were doing no better in school than non–Head Start students. The finding created a fierce controversy: Defenders of the program claimed that despite matching, the two groups were not really equivalent, that Head Start had attracted those who needed it most, and that even if the Head Start students were doing no better than the others, they would have been doing worse without it.[17]

Whether or not these claims are correct, it is clear that unknown biasing factors may be involved in any comparison of non-randomly assigned experimental and control subjects and that the evidence so obtained is not scientifically compelling. The evaluation study of Head Start did not prove conclusively that it helped, or that it didn't; people could interpret the findings as confirmation of their beliefs. Such studies do little to promote rationality in the making of policy decisions.

The evaluation research studies and quasi-experiments of the 1960s, however, led to true social experiments. To be sure, there had been a few methodologically crude efforts at social experimentation earlier, such as a handful of public health campaigns and community-based clinical trials in the 1950s and one in the 1930s.[18] But true social experiments did not appear in modern form until two developments of the 1960s made them possible. One was the growth of the nation's social programs, which became so costly that it made sense to pay for research to see whether those that existed might be made more efficient and to predict the costs and effects of proposed new ones. The second was the advent of sophisticated statistical methods that could deal with the horde of variables of real-world observations and of computers that could swiftly perform the millions of computations called for by those methods.

In this fertile soil, the concept of social experimentation germinated, grew, and bore fruit. Its essential characteristics were set forth early by the social psychologist Henry W. Riecken and several co-authors in a widely quoted definition:

An experiment is one or more treatments (programs), representing intervention into normal social processes, that are administered to some set of persons (or other units) drawn at random from a specified population; observations or measurements are made to learn how (or how much) some relevant aspects of their behavior differ from those of a group receiving either another treatment or no treatment, also drawn from the same population. [19]

The first modern social experiment embodying these criteria was, of course, the OEO's New Jersey Income Maintenance Experiment, designed in 1967 and conducted from 1968 to 1972. With this exemplar marking the way, policy-makers in other agencies, and researchers in universities and foundations, began suggesting and conducting social experiments to test other proposed policies or policy changes. "From the perspective of the social sciences," write the economists David H. Greenberg and Philip K. Robins in a review of this development, "the 1970s might be called 'the Decade of the Social Experiments.' " By their reckoning, half a billion dollars of federal funds were spent during the decade on controlled experiments exploring the feasibility and effects of proposed policy changes. [20]

According to Greenberg and Robins's compilation, from 1968, when the New Jersey IME got under way, to 1983, the last year for which they had data, thirty-five social experiments were conducted in the United States. Most were federally funded and large in size; the rest were chiefly state- or municipally funded and smaller. A few cost less than $1 million, most cost from $1 million to $2 million, and a few ran to $50 million and even more. (A 1978 compilation by others that includes all randomized experiments in human service fields, even if quite small and restricted in scope, lists several hundred projects.) [21]

The major social experiments performed since 1968 have covered a wide range of programs and social processes. In addition to income maintenance, they have dealt with job training, medical services, career advancement, and housing, among other subjects. Some examples:*

- From 1972 to 1974, the Vera Institute of Justice, with $1.4 million in federal, municipal, and foundation funding, ran the Wildcat Supported Work Program, which offered temporarily subsidized jobs to unemployed ex-addicts in New York who had a record of chronic unemployment.
- From 1973 to 1977, Abt Associates and the Rand Corporation, with $206 million from the Department of Housing and Urban Development, conducted three experiments in a dozen cities to see whether cash housing allowances given to the poor would improve the supply and quality of their housing.
- From 1974 to 1981 (analysis is still going on), the Rand Corporation, with $75 million from the Department of Health, Education, and Welfare, conducted an experiment in two major cities and four counties to see how various health insurance plans, if put into effect nationally, would affect the demand for health services, and whether free care would yield a better level of health than systems in which patients paid some share of costs.
- Beginning in 1982 and running until 1985, two universities and two research corporations will be spending $12 million in HUD grants to run an experiment—in three rural areas, two small cities, and five large cities—testing schemes of long-term care of the elderly outside of institutions.

The political climate existing since 1980 has brought about a sharp cutback in all social research, but social experimentation remains an invaluable tool of policy evaluation. As the social experimenters Rae W. Archibald and Joseph P. Newhouse, director of the Health Insurance Study, write, "social experimentation can provide the strongest evidence that certain programs or policy actions actually cause or, if implemented, would cause certain outcomes."[22]

This rightly identifies social experimentation as applied social sci-

---

*Some major findings of the first three experiments listed here will be mentioned later in the chapter; no findings of the fourth one were available as of this writing.

ence, intended to yield practical answers. But in finding that a particular policy is likely to succeed or fail, a social experiment reveals relationships between the social milieu and human behavior, and thus makes significant contributions to scientific knowledge and theory. The goal of a policy-oriented social experiment, say Saxe and Fine, "is the same type of unequivocal statements of causal processes for which traditional basic research strives."[23]

Hard Start

One might suppose that in a city the size of Seattle it would be easy to gather an appropriate sample of a couple thousand poor families who would gladly accept the gift of a guaranteed income for three or five years. But the enthusiastic young interviewers of the Mathematica field staff found it a difficult task and, for some categories of poor families, a nearly hopeless one.

Their objective, according to a model worked out by Spiegelman and Kurz, was to gather a sample of some 2,500 low-income families. Seemingly, they would have many times that number to draw upon: In the low-income areas of central Seattle alone, 1960 Census records listed 24,168 housing units, in each of which might live a family suitable for the study. But when the several dozen interviewers made their way into those areas and, door by door, sought to do five-minute interviews to identify possibly eligible families, they found the gleanings meager. Almost 10 percent of the units were vacant, and in the occupied units the interviewers found that about half the families either were not eligible, were never at home, or were but wouldn't come to the door. Of the remainder, over a quarter refused to talk to them or broke off the interview after a few questions.[24]

Refusal to come to the door or to be interviewed was hard to explain. It couldn't be due to misgivings about taking part in an experiment, since at this juncture interviewers were saying only that they were making a survey to see if Seattle was a good place to test a family assistance program. Nor was it due to class or ethnic antagonism; most of the interviewers, dressed in T-shirts and jeans, were students, dropouts, or street people, many of them from minority groups, and went to areas where racially and ethnically they'd fit in. But the poor, apparently, were suspicious of and hostile to whatever came from the Establishment, no matter in what guise.

Public relations efforts didn't help; although key staff people talked to community groups, it made the going no easier. Stories about the project placed in local newspapers only "generated noticeable public outrage," according to the *Final Report* of the project.[25]* But this should have been expected; as Michael Linn of the Washington State Department of Public Assistance (which was technically in charge of SIME) told a reporter, "We are dealing with the political belief that if you give people this money, they are all going to go home, sit in the living room, drink beer, and do nothing."[26]

(The Department of Public Assistance was involved in SIME because, to make the experiment possible, the state had had to agree to temporarily withdraw welfare benefits from families receiving NIT payments, and wanted to supervise Mathematica's making of those payments. The Internal Revenue Service was involved, too; it had agreed not to tax the income of families getting NIT because NIT payments replaced welfare benefits, which were not taxable, and because only by eliminating all taxes other than the one built into the research design could the researchers measure the incentive or disincentive effects of their experimental tax rates.)

The long lists of occupied dwelling units melted away as interviewers, returning to SIME's dingy offices late each evening from their rounds, told their supervisors of the many families they found ineligible, of hostile remarks and doors closed in their faces, and of families silently lurking in their homes. Occasionally, some interviewer would openly voice the doubt many of them felt as to whether the project was possible. Yet over the months, by dint of persistence and belief in the value of the experiment, they eventually compiled a list of 5,295 families who seemed worth interviewing again in greater detail.

But when the interviewers returned months later to offer these families five dollars for a one-hour interview, they found that one out of every ten no longer lived there (many of the poor move often), while

---

*Spiegelman vigorously disagrees with this comment, but he was not on the scene, as was Christophersen, who wrote this part of the *Final Report*.

of those who still did, one out of every six, though previously cooperative, now either avoided them, refused to be interviewed, or broke off the interview partway through. Nearly as many more turned out to be technically ineligible for one reason or another.

In the end, only 3,132 eligible families completed this round of interviews; this was far from enough. For although the SRI research design called for fewer than 2,200 families, it specified that the total be made up of a great many special subsamples, each of a designated size, a number of which could not be filled from the sample of 3,132 families. For analytic purposes, the design required groups of single-parent families and two-parent families at each of five different income levels; each of these groups was to be made up of subgroups of families who would be in the program for three years and others who would be in it for five; each of these sub-subgroups was to be made up of still smaller ones of whites and blacks; and so on.

The exact number of families in every smallest subset or "cell" was prescribed by a statistical model originally worked out for the New Jersey IME and now adapted to SIME by statisticians at SRI. This would ensure that there would be enough representatives of every experimental condition to permit statistical analysis, but its requirements made gathering the sample a Procrustean task. As the SIME/DIME *Final Report* says:

Sample selection . . . [was] driven to a large degree by the need to find enough families to fit the characteristics needed for the sample cells with the fewest potential members (for example, black, two-parent families with normal annual incomes between $1,000 and $3,000). The magnitude of the effort to find such families often seemed to the field staff involved like the proverbial search for a "needle in the haystack."[27]

Nonetheless, the morale and energy of the office staff and the interviewers remained high; they were sustained by dedication to what they regarded as a mission. An idealistic, argumentative, often flamboyant, and rather populist lot, they felt themselves part of a daring and historic social advance. So did their more conservative superiors; the economist Mike Wills, a tie-and-jacket type who was working on the interview to be used during the experiment, says, "It appealed to us because it appeared to be a logical solution to a social problem. By doing something simple in place of all those many welfare programs, you could put out more money for the beneficiaries without any increase in spending. It was hard to believe—but we believed it." Charles Thompson, SRI's Seattle representative, succinctly comments, "In Menlo Park, they were very pro-research; in Seattle we were very pro-people."

The staff researchers went back to Census records and compiled a list of 12,000 more housing units in low-income areas outside central Seattle; from these the interviewers scraped together another 1,683 eligible families. In all, the first and second lists had totaled some 36,000 units and produced a pool of not quite 5,000 families. But when the interviewers went back to enroll 2,542 of them as per the design, there was still further shrinkage, due chiefly to refusals and moves. In the end, they managed to sign up 2,042, thus nearly—but not fully—meeting the goal called for by the statistical model.[28]

Even as they were achieving this, an unforeseen social development—the kind of uncontrollable event that can damage social experiments—bade fair to abort SIME altogether. "Just as we were getting under way in Seattle," Spiegelman says, "the world there came to an end." In 1970, Boeing, Seattle's biggest employer, was in deep trouble and cut its work force from 105,000 to 30,000. The unemployment rate in Seattle soared to 15 percent at a time when nationally it was 5 percent. Some wag posted a message on a billboard on the freeway to Tacoma: "Last person to leave Seattle please turn out the lights."

Spiegelman called a crisis meeting in Menlo Park. Kershaw and other field staff leaders glumly agreed with him and SRI statisticians that the high unemployment rate might contaminate the sample with out-of-work families that normally had a good income and were not part of the real poverty population. Furthermore, with jobs so hard to get, some workers who in normal times would quit work to get NIT payments might not do so now for fear that when the project ended, they'd be unable to go back to work. In either case, the behavior of the poor in Seattle might not be representative of behavior of the poor under normal circumstances.

"We were so concerned," Spiegelman says, "that we even talked about giving up Seattle and going somewhere else. But Senator Warren Magnuson of Washington was Chairman of the HEW Appropriations Committee, and there was no way HEW was going to offend him by canceling Seattle. So we decided to make a plus of this problem by running the experiment in two cities and seeing what difference unemployment made." After considering a number of cities generally similar to Seattle but with normal unemployment rates, they settled on Denver and made the necessary arrangements with Colorado's welfare department.

In early 1971, HEW authorized Spiegelman to clone SIME in Denver; at once, a Mathematica representative, Mary Scowcroft, opened a field office in a shabby old building, began to hire staff, and set things in motion. The Denver group drew up Census lists of nearly 58,000 addresses and set about ringing bells and knocking on doors. They encountered more or less the same difficulties their counterparts in Seattle had met, plus another complication—the presence of many Chicanos, which made for yet another set of cells in the experimental design. Eventually, they located 3,361 suitable families, 2,758 of whom they were able to sign up. As in Seattle, this sample was somewhat smaller, particularly in some cells, than the theoretical ideal.[29]

SIME/DIME had by now expanded into an experiment with $50 million to spend (and more to come when the field phase gave way to the analytic one) and affecting the lives of 4,800 families in the two cities; it was social research on an unprecedented scale. A visitor asked Spiegelman a few months ago how he had felt as head of a project of this scope, directly affecting so many people. "I had never done anything of this magnitude," Spiegelman replied, "but at that point, working at SRI in Menlo Park, I was far from all those thousands of persons in Seattle and Denver. I was preoccupied by the mechanisms and techniques of the experiment, by the tremendous number of details to be worked out, and by the intellectual challenge of the whole thing. It was only later that I became aware of the effects on people's lives."

Those effects would be measured by means of two data-gathering instruments. One was an income report several pages long that each family receiving NIT payments would fill out every month and send to the "Council for Grants to Families." (The Council was an office set up by Mathematica to review the income reports, calculate how large an NIT payment each family was entitled to each month, and send out the checks.)

The second and far more important one was the "periodic interview." Three times a year, an interviewer from Urban Opinion Surveys (also a Mathematica creation) would visit the family with a questionnaire as thick as a suburban telephone book and go through the main part of it with as many as three family members, one at a time—and then top this off by asking one of them scores of extra questions contained in "modules" (addenda on special subjects) tacked on from time to time. Interviews took anywhere from forty-five minutes to more than two hours, and interviewers had to use all the skills they had been trained in by Mathematica staffers to keep family members from lapsing into a grumpy series of "don't knows."

The questionnaire's length and content had caused a certain amount of shouting and table-pounding at meetings of SRI and Mathematica personnel. From time to time, Spiegelman would call Kershaw in Seattle or, later, J. Alan Brewster, who replaced him as director of the field office, and say, "Come on down. We have some ideas we want to talk to you about." This often meant new items the SRI staff wanted to include in the questionnaire. But the social researchers on the Seattle field staff were sensitive to the problems of their interviewers and strongly objected to some of the questions that the SRI theoreticians said were essential if they were to perform the analyses they had in mind. Mike Wills remembers these meetings vividly:

We'd get several of our brightest, most articulate interviewers in a room with Mordecai Kurz and a few other SRI people, and in no time the two sides would be shouting at each other. Kurz was the most forceful of all. He'd say, "You've *got* to collect this or that data and ask these questions," and we'd say, "It's *trash*. You *can't* ask those questions!" Then Kurz—he was an erect, wiry little man who had recently been on active duty in the Israeli army and always wore a leather jacket and sunglasses—he'd bark, "I'm not an *idiot*! You *can* ask that question and you *have* to ask it because we *must* have the data."

One time he was telling us why he wanted us to ask questions testing the time-horizon effect, which he and other economists regarded as very important. He said to one of our field people, "Look, if Mathematica owes you a thousand dollars and it's due a year from now, how much would you be willing to take to get it right now?" The guy said, "If they owe me a thousand dollars, that's what I'd take and no less." Kurz started screaming, "That's *stupid*! You would *discount* a debt in order to get paid sooner. That's the rational way to act." The guy wouldn't agree; he saw it as a moral question. But Kurz wouldn't give up. An hour later, when we came back from lunch,

he was still carrying on. He couldn't accept irrationality. In the end he won—
he always won—and we did things his way.

(Kurz, looking back, says, "My attitude was, 'Mathematica isn't capable of it.' We had to put the input in there or we would not get the
work done. We had to get the interview staff in gear, and well-oiled.")

The field staff had no objection to the greater part of the basic
questionnaire except its length; the bulk of the items in it consisted of
solid, nuts-and-bolts economic questions about the rate of pay on the
current or last job, number of hours worked, and the like, that would
present no great problem to the interviewers. The hotly debated items
were another matter. In many of the modules, the SRI researchers
hoped to explore far subtler and more sensitive issues—the social and
emotional concomitants of poverty and the countervailing effects that
a guaranteed income might have, and with considerable effort they
had devised questions that they thought would be valid indicators of
these matters. Yet understandably, the field staff balked at the thought
of ordering their interviewers to ask people in a decaying apartment,
with a mattress on the floor, a packing crate for a table, and several
children under foot, such questions as these:[30]

—How satisfied are you with the affection and understanding you receive
    from your wife?
—When you go out for the evening together, who usually decides where to
    go?
—How many hours a week do you usually spend doing family bookkeeping,
    paying bills, balancing the checkbook, etc.?
—[How important, in your work, is] self-fulfillment—a job which provides a
    sense of accomplishment?
—About how many hours a week would you say you spend reading?
—Say the word you think makes the best, truest, most sensible complete
    sentence: "The vanquished never yet spoke ——— of the conqueror."
    1. Ill   2. Well   3. Little   4. Nastily   5. Often

In October 1970, when interviewers finally began enrolling families
in the experiment, they ran into yet other problems. As Christophersen, who was then an interviewer (he later became the field director of
SIME), recalls:

We had to spend a lot of time convincing people who simply didn't believe
the offer was on the level, and others who were old-fashioned, independent

working-class people who wanted nothing to do with "welfare"—even though we explained again and again that this wasn't welfare. One old, disabled woman wouldn't sign up because she didn't want a "government handout." Amazing!

And we had to keep our stories straight. With the "experimentals"—the ones who would be getting money—we'd say, "Hey, here it is!—guaranteed income for the next three (or five) years, and all you have to do is send in a monthly income report and let us interview you three times a year." But with the controls, whom we didn't want to tell anything about the experiment because knowing might bias their behavior, we'd say, "We're doing an income study and all you have to do to get eight dollars a month is send back a post card each month giving any change of address or membership in the family, and let us interview you three times a year." We had a set of canned answers for the questions they might have—but they often came up with some that put us on the spot.

Explaining the rules to an experimental family took at least an hour; among other things, interviewers had to spell out which of the welfare benefits they might be receiving would be withdrawn (cash benefits were withheld but service benefits, such as free medical treatment, were continued). These details, and the tables showing how much NIT money they'd get and how it would change according to their other income, were hard going and sometimes jeopardized the enrollment process. So did the somewhat intimidating enrollment agreement the family had to sign.

So, too, did a document unpleasantly labeled "Affidavit of cohabitation." Many of the poor live in informal alliances, but Spiegelman and Kurz had decided that it would be a mistake to limit NIT benefits to the legally married or to exclude from benefits a male living with a female head of a family. Spiegelman explains:

We felt that in SIME/DIME marriage should not be based on legal documents but on an observed system of support. The AFDC program encourages cohabitation by not counting the income of a man living with a woman if he isn't the natural father or legal guardian of the children in the household. We didn't want to encourage cohabitation by rewarding such arrangements. We *did* want to know what effect NIT had on family stability whether or not people were legally married. So we accepted couples as married if they called themselves "husband" and "wife," signed an affidavit that they were living together, and stayed together at least three months after signing it.

Somehow, despite all these start-up difficulties, by the end of November 1970 the first contingent of thirty-five families had been signed up. One day, a month or so later, the office staff and a handful of interviewers looked on, smiling, as a secretary started making out the initial small batch of checks by hand. Thompson remembers it well: "When we saw those first checks going out in the mail, we looked at each other and said, 'Hey, people are really on the project! It's starting to happen!' "

Spiegelman, many hundreds of miles from the scene and functioning on a very different level, was deeply gratified for his own reasons: At long last, he could stop worrying—he had had good grounds for doing so—that, despite all his and other people's best efforts the project might die prematurely.

"In 1969," he recalls, "without waiting to see what SIME/DIME would find, Nixon submitted an income maintenance proposal to Congress, and it actually passed the House just as we were getting our experiment started. All I could think was, 'It's going to be all over. They'll enact the program and we'll have to pack up and go home.' But it failed in the Senate—and we kept on going." Even now, fifteen years later, he smiles broadly, recapturing the relief he felt as his vast experiment, freed by the defeat of the Nixon plan, began to gather research evidence as to what the effect of such a program would have been.

Sundry Problems of Social Experimentation

The early problems of SIME/DIME were in no way unusual; similar problems during startup, plus equally vexing ones in later phases, seem inherent in this most ambitious form of social research. Some of the chief difficulties follow.

SAMPLE SELECTION.   This problem tends to be particularly vexing. In a cross-sectional or even a longitudinal survey it is feasible to use a national sample, but in a social experiment the close and continuous contact required with subjects, especially if they are to be provided with various services, makes the use of a dispersed sample prohibitively costly.[31] Social experimenters therefore usually have to do their sampling in one or a very few sites.

This creates a problem of external validity: Only if the population of the chosen site or sites is similar in composition to that of the nation as a whole can the findings be extrapolated nationally. But only if the experiment also possesses internal validity, that is, measures what it is supposed to measure. It may not, however, if in the chosen site or sites there are too few people of the kinds the experiment is concerned with to yield a sample including all the subgroups that need to be examined.

This may be the case if researchers draw a probability sample from too small a population. If, for instance, one randomly draws a probability sample of 1,000 people from a population of 100,000, there is only 1 chance in 100 that any particular person will be selected. If some subgroup of that population has only 100 members, the sampling process may well fail to select any of them, even as bridge hands sometimes contain few or no high cards. The usual remedy is to use stratified random sampling, in which one chooses randomly from a number of groups—but according to varying ratios, so as to get enough members of even the smallest groups. (It's a little like dividing a deck of cards into the high cards and the others, and dealing some from each stack to make up a hand.) After analyzing the data from each stratum, researchers can reweight the results to get a normal distribution, from which they can then make national projections.

Social experimenters also arbitrarily weight the segments of their samples in the interests of efficiency. Early in the brief history of social experimentation, the econometricians John Conlisk and Harold Watts, and later others, worked out statistical formulas by which to "optimize" sample design, that is, to assign either more or fewer cases to specific cells than probability would dictate in order to get the greatest amount of useful information for the available money.[32] Their reasoning was that it is cost-effective to keep uninteresting cells smaller than they would be on a probability basis, and to make interesting ones unduly large to allow them to be subjected to especially fine-grained statistical analysis.

Such optimization, however, can muddy the research waters. In SIME/DIME, the Conlisk-Watts formulas called for filling the treatment cells of the most generous guarantee level chiefly with higher-income families, since they would get much smaller payments under those plans than lower-income families and thus save the project considerable money. But for the findings to be valid, one would need to assume that higher-income and lower-income families would react in the same way to the generous guarantees. This assumption, Archibald and Newhouse point out, may or may not be correct—and the unbalanced allocation makes it difficult to test.[33] Some methodologists now argue that the classic approach of random assignment, though considerably more costly than sample optimization, is best after all, since it permits evaluation of the data by simple analysis-of-variance methods.[34]

Sample design thus remains a chronically vexing methodological problem in social experimentation.

CONSTRUCT VALIDITY. The theoretical construct (hypothesis) offered as an explanation of the observed effects may not name the only or even the real cause even though it clearly appears to. Other factors—unintended and unrecognized correlates of the treatment—may be partly or wholly responsible. Such extraneous aspects are known as biases.

The Hawthorne effect is one such: As we saw in chapter 1, workers in that experiment increased their productivity with every change in lighting—even when it was reduced—not because every change made their work easier but because their awareness that they were taking part in an experiment heightened morale. Such effects are a constant hazard in social experiments: Whenever subjects have some idea what researchers are looking for, they may to some degree respond accordingly. Even controls, nominally ignorant of the purpose of the experiment, are likely to hear about it, since social experiments are often conducted within localized neighborhoods, and to react in some biased way. Only sophisticated design and analysis can sort out such biases from the treatment effect proper.

This is only one of many biases that may affect social experiments. Some others:[35]

- The "dowry effect": This exists when eligible persons can extend their eligibility to others by marrying them (as in the case of SIME/DIME), thereby adding persons to the sample who were not chosen by the sampling process.
- The "time horizon effect": People may react differently to a short-term experiment than to a long-term one. To offset this bias,

researchers schedule treatments of different lengths and compare their effects.

- Misreporting: If subjects stand to gain greater benefits by understating their income or misrepresenting other facts, they will tend to do so. Unless the researchers can verify the figures or allow for the errors, their conclusions will be distorted.

- "Community effects": Local mores, according to economists Robert Ferber and Werner Z. Hirsch, may affect the response to an experimental program in a way that might not prevail if the program became national policy. In some parts of the country, as mentioned earlier, the "work ethic" could offset the tendency to work less when given a guarantee of annual income, but that ethic might lose force if such a program were part of the American way of life.

- The "learning effect" (or "panel bias"): In social experiments, as in other longitudinal studies, two principal methods of gathering data are testing and retesting participants, and interviewing them at regular intervals; participants, however, learn from these experiences and often perform better on later tests or, in later interviews, answer questions knowingly rather than naively.

CHOICE OF THE RIGHT INDICATORS.   In social experiments, choosing the indicators by which to measure the impact of the treatment is especially difficult since they are so apt to be influenced by unknown extraneous variables.

An experiment in Kansas City in the early 1970s tested the crime-prevention effect of increased police patrolling as compared with "reactive patrolling," in which police would enter a test area only when called. The best indicator of effectiveness, it seemed obvious, would be the reported crime rate. But the results were distinctly counterintuitive; there was just as much reported crime under increased patrolling as under reactive patrolling.

The anomaly was explained, post hoc, by data from other studies showing that the reporting of crimes to the police is strongly influenced by the public's trust in them. The decreased visibility of police in the reactive patrolling plan probably decreased public trust and reduced the number of crimes reported, but not the number committed.

For such reasons, say Saxe and Fine, in almost all social experiments there is no one best indicator of the effects; multiple indicators are needed to measure the program's effects and to account for the multiple variables involved.[36]

CONFLICT BETWEEN RESEARCH STAFF AND WORKING STAFF.   In all research that gathers data by means of a series of interviews with subjects, problems such as interviewees' hedging or withholding of certain data, missing interviews, and so on, are chronic. In social experiments these are compounded by yet another: Because such research involves a vast amount of field work, it is usually necessary to have a bipartite staff—a theory-oriented and analytical research team and a pragmatic, hands-on team of interviewers and treatment providers. But the two have very different perspectives on their work; according to Archibald and Newhouse, "The most frequent source of dissonance cited by those who have analyzed social experiments [is] a conflict between the *Weltanschauung* of the designer-researchers and of those who must carry out the day-to-day activities."[37]

As in SIME's case, the conflict often centers on the content of the interviews. The field staff is apt to resist asking questions they consider insensitive, annoying, or absurd and likely to cause participants to drop out of the program; the research team may passionately defend their belief that without the data these questions should yield, the scientific value of the experiment will be seriously diminished.

ATTRITION.   The sample studied in a social experiment, as in all longitudinal studies, undergoes attrition—the loss, over time, of some panel members due to moving, death, disappearance, or refusal to continue—resulting in possible distortion of the results. This problem can be more severe in a social experiment than in other kinds of longitudinal studies, since members of the control group or of groups receiving minimal benefits are less likely to remain in the active sample than those receiving high benefits. This is particularly true of experiments like the IMEs, which drew their samples from circumscribed communities within which word could easily get around.[38]

Even when controls are unaware that others are getting benefits they themselves are not, they are far less motivated to stay in the program than the experimentals. "In most experiments," Riecken and Robert F. Boruch say, "membership in a control group is an unrewarding experience, usually accompanied by boring requests for informa-tion."[39] In the New Jersey IME, they note, controls had a much higher dropout rate than even the most minimally benefited experi-mental group, and the Health Insurance Study actually abandoned its control sample because of their lack of cooperation.

ETHICAL PROBLEMS. Even though the purposes of any social experi-ment may be admirable and its subjects may knowingly agree to its terms, such research often involves serious ethical issues.

One is the matter of privacy. Those who participate in an experi-ment lay themselves open to questions they may find disturbing or intrusive ("Have you ever had an abortion?" "Have you ever been convicted of a crime?"). If they answer affirmatively, a second issue is created, namely, the matter of confidentiality: Unless researchers use costly and time-consuming techniques (codes, aliases, "linking files," and so on), any damaging information elicited may be subpoenaed or used in other ways that violate the rights of the participants.[40]

Another ethical problem is related to the inequitable treatment of participants. In most social experiments, the benefit-nonbenefit dichotomy does not create the agonizing dilemma it does in clinical medical trials, where it may be equated with life and death. Nonethe-less, field workers and certain others may find it morally repugnant that rent subsidies, free medical treatment, or similar highly desirable benefits are given to certain poor or ailing people in the experiment but withheld from others who are equally poor or ailing. Court cases have even been brought challenging the right of social researchers to ran-domly assign participants in a social experiment to treatment and to control status; more often than not, however, that right has been upheld.[41]

The key to ethical experimentation with human beings is generally held to be informed consent, but in social experimentation this solves some problems and creates others. Experimentals, when fully in-formed, may, as we know, respond in a biased way; controls, if they were fully informed, might well resent not receiving program benefits, and in their interviews consciously or unconsciously exaggerate the difficulties of life without them. Thus, some information has to be withheld from all subjects in order for the experiment to remain inter-nally valid.

For another, the experimentals, even if they were to be fully informed, could not foresee all the ways in which the treatment they
agree to undergo might affect their feelings and behavior. Nor could
researchers tell them, since the very purpose of the experiment is to
discover both the expected and unexpected effects of the policies being
tested. Certain of these outcomes may be harmful; for instance, Ferber
and Hirsch say that families who receive housing subsidies

[are] placed in an exposed position as a result of the experiment and, regard-
less of what they are told, may be misled into taking actions detrimental to
their welfare. For example, although they may be told that the supplemental
payments they receive would be continued only for five years, they may begin
to think after two or three years that these payments are likely to be permanent
and act accordingly. . . . The family may move into more expensive housing
which it is unable to afford when the supplemental payments cease. The
resulting readjustment could be far more painful than if the more expensive
housing had not been obtained in the first place.[42]

UNCONTROLLABLE CHANGES IN THE MILIEU.   Researchers conducting a
social experiment can control sample selection and the treatment variables but not unforeseen changes in social conditions that may drastic-
ally affect their experiment. These may range from droughts and crop
failures to recessions, the outbreak of hostilities, and the enactment of
laws or programs related to the experiment. In 1969 the state of New
Jersey instituted a generous welfare program that overlapped and com-
peted with the income offered by the New Jersey IME, thus radically
altering in mid-experiment the premises on which it had been based
and weakening the validity of its findings.[43]

At least, that change affected experimental and control groups alike;
the damage is worse when an event affects the two differently. Suppose, for instance, a new educational program were experimentally
offered in one consolidated school in a town but not in another, which
was to serve as the control. Suppose, too, word spread through the
school system that the new program was raising achievement scores,
and teachers in the control school, feeling challenged, worked out
innovations of their own to improve their students' scores. These
changes would make the control school also an experimental one but
of a different kind. The result: There would now be two dissimilar
experimental groups, each without controls, and hence there no
longer would be a true experiment.[44]

DATA HANDLING. Social experiments operate complex benefit programs and collect information on their effects; they therefore generate vast quantities of data, especially if there are many variations in the experimental treatment. "Managing these huge amounts of data," say Ferber and Hirsch, "is a major task in itself, a task whose complexity was substantially underestimated in the New Jersey and some of the other experiments."[45]

Not only must data be gathered and entered into the files, but since participants may receive varying amounts month by month, move in and out of the program, enter or leave families, and so on, the organization of the files is exceedingly complex; the flood of new data must, however, be continuously and rapidly entered. "If it is ignored for very long," Archibald and Newhouse warn, "it can get out of control and chaos may result."[46]

The above list of difficulties in starting up and operating a social experiment is far from all-inclusive; many others—perhaps as many as those named here—exist. And yet researchers who have attempted social experimentation remain enthusiastic about it. Archibald and Newhouse, after reviewing the complexities and difficulties of this form of social research, conclude with these hopeful words to the would-be experimenter:

Do not be easily discouraged. We believe social experimentation, if properly used, can be an extraordinarily valuable tool. To be sure, it is time-consuming, sometimes frustrating, expensive by usual standards of social science research, and risky—a mistake in the design or its application may vitiate the entire endeavor. But new knowledge is seldom easily achieved.[47]

The Long Haul

The complete record of SIME/DIME's field operations and research studies fills several thousand pages of reports, papers, and memoranda. Even greatly condensed in the two-volume Final Report, *it runs to 638 pages; the following notes, in 1 percent of that space, can offer only a few glimpses of the complex story as it unfolded during the 1970s.*

THE PAYOUT. Every month, clattering machines in the grubby SIME/DIME field offices churn out many hundreds (and in some years thousands) of NIT payment checks averaging $150 to $160. In Seattle, the flow of money will last from 1971 to 1977; in Denver, from 1972 to 1979. During the decade, over $20 million will be distributed to the experimental families and $1.5 million to the control families;[48] most of this, however, is saved in the form of the withheld welfare benefits it replaces.

THE STAFF.   At times, the field staff in each city numbers well over a hundred. About a third are interviewers; the rest are quality-control personnel, who review the questionnaires; payment analysts, who use the data in each family's monthly report to calculate how large its next check should be; computer specialists, clerks, and others. In Seattle, they occupy several floors of drab offices and three storefronts, in Denver a warren of little rooms partitioned out of what used to be an auditorium, plus several storefronts.

VERIFICATION.   The payment analysts carefully compare each family's monthly income report with its paycheck stubs and a copy of its income-tax report. These procedures inhibit the tendency (documented by research) of welfare families to sharply underreport their income in order to increase their benefits. Many SIME/DIME families, aware that their income statements are closely scrutinized, report even such income as cash for housecleaning. One woman calls up to ask how to report money received for a TV set that her husband stole; the staff mulls this over, then straightfacedly tells her to list it, under self-employment, as "TV pickup service."[49]

The staff does, however, uncover some cases of cheating and fraud. One intriguing instance: A Seattle man, eligible for NIT payments, deserts his "wife" for a succession of other women, each of whom he tells (correctly) that by living with him they will qualify for NIT benefits, and will continue to do so even if he leaves them. By the time the staff is on to him, he has added five women to the program.[50]

INTERVIEWING.   Every four months, each family is visited by an interviewer. In addition to asking as many as three family members some 200 questions about their jobs and income, the interviewer often makes scores of additional queries about leisure activities, family roles, health, the school performance of children, and so on. More than 65,000 interviews will be conducted before the experiment is concluded—the most expensive task in it.[51]

For a while, in Seattle many an interviewer arrives at front doors panting and sweating from the effort of hauling up several flights of stairs a twenty-pound portable computer terminal. Martin Gorfinkle, a computer expert, had persuaded Spiegelman that a great deal of time would be saved if interviewers typed the answers, as they received them, into a terminal that sent the data over the family's telephone directly to a Burroughs 6700 computer at SRI in Menlo Park. But the scheme fails for a curious reason: In the 1970s, many black people in Seattle have Princess telephones—a status symbol—and the computer can be connected only to a standard instrument. "A quarter of a million dollars went down the tube on that one," laments Charles Thompson. Actually, it isn't really a total loss: Out of that effort came SIME/DIME's data entry system, one of the first in the country in which data from field offices were simultaneously transmitted, edited, and entered in the computers in the research center.

In order to keep families from dropping out, interviewers get special training in techniques of persuasion. But persuasive arguments can't prevent attrition due to migration, and if the families that leave Seattle and Denver are dropped, the sample may be skewed in some unknown way. So the field staffs do considerable sleuthing by mail and phone to keep track of movers, continue paying them NIT benefits, and send interviewers to wherever they are. Nonetheless, some 20 percent of husbands, 15 percent of wives, and 15 percent of female heads of families are lost over the first two and a half years of the experiment, a sizable number but not enough to invalidate the findings.[52]

COUNSELING AND EDUCATION.   In cubicles and conference rooms at Seattle Central Community College and Denver Community College, about half of the poor and often ill-educated people in the SIME/DIME sample take part in private and group counseling sessions. They spend an average of half a dozen sessions with the counselors, thoughtfully exploring their abilities, accomplishments, and employment goals, a novel experience for most of them. Roughly half of those who get counseling decide to go on, with subsidies from SIME/DIME, to take vocational courses in crafts, trades, and health or social service professions, and some ambitiously enroll in academic programs leading toward bachelors degrees. (Although not part of the NIT experiment as such, the counseling and education effort is a second experiment within SIME/DIME and draws upon the same sample of families.)[53]

DATA PROCESSING.   In the field offices, computer operators convert the information in families' monthly reports and the completed questionnaires into coded data that they send over leased lines to the computer at Menlo Park. There the data are digested and stored in a special data base in various ways, some of which allow the field staff to easily call up information they need for day-by-day dealings with the families, others of which enable SRI researchers to extract either cross-sectional or longitudinal summaries of whatever information they need for the analyses they are performing.

For some time, however, the problem of how to store the data so as to make all this possible seems overwhelming; Spiegelman sometimes fears it may kill the experiment. But before the accumulating undigested information becomes a hopeless mass, Virgil Davis, a systems programmer at SRI, writes a program that compiles it into a workable and researchable data base. From then on, the data entry system functions well—except when, at busy periods, failures of the leased lines between the field offices and the Menlo Park computer cause the data processors in the field offices to swear and storm about the offices.[54]

WORKING IN THE DARK.   Day by day, year after year, the field staffs in Seattle and Denver gather and transmit their data to SRI without having any idea what they reveal. Robert Williams, a 26-year-old who heads the field operations in Denver, thought he'd be doing research (he has a doctorate in public affairs), but, as he tells a friend, finds that his job is "running a data factory." Spiegelman and his colleagues at Menlo Park are no better off; analysis of the data—the only part of the work they dignify with the name of "research"—cannot begin in earnest until a considerable number of families have completed their grants and been disenrolled.

The field staffs do, though, hear from a few families who begin leaving the program in 1974 as to what it has meant to them. Most, like these two, are thoroughly positive:

This program as an alternate to Public Assistance is so much better by far. As a participant I didn't feel the embarrassment or shame as I did feel when I was on Public Assistance twice in my life. . . .

*

Your grant has enabled us to sit back and think about our lives and where we wanted to go. We both started to enjoy our children more and I have started back to school.[55]

There are, though, a few sour notes such as this:

[The program] gives me the impression of it being a Big Brother/C.I.A. watchdog for [the poor]. Every time I am interviewed the Bureaucracy's attitudes come through. . . . The Big Man is watching.[56]

These are only straws in the wind; no one knows what trends the accumulating data will reveal when subjected to statistical analysis. Every three months, Spiegelman writes a 30- or 40-page report to the Office of Income Maintenance Research at HEW and to state welfare officials in Washington and Colorado, but these communiqués deal only with operational matters, giving no hint of findings—since, for half a dozen years, there are none.

RESEARCH.   In 1974 Spiegelman's researchers at SRI are able to begin analyzing data on the first families completing their experimental terms and by 1977 are in high gear; between then and 1980 they turn out a hundred research and technical papers and scores of journal articles.

At their work, the researchers seem to be doing what other social scientists do during this phase of social research: pore over data print-outs, write equations on note pads and blackboards, punch in orders to the computer on desk-top terminals, and the like. But behind this façade, the thinking of the SIME/DIME researchers is quite special. In other social-science disciplines, researchers often use "theory-free" analyses of variance to look for differences between their experimental and control groups; if they do find a strong covariance between two factors (if one changes markedly whenever another does), they assume there must be a causal connection between them and suggest a theory to account for it. But Spiegelman, like most economists, scornfully calls this approach "data-mining" and says it can tell you nothing—or almost anything. He and his researchers, most of whom are economists, work the other way around: They begin with theory, and then use data to prove or disprove it.[57]

First they "build a model"—an equation or set of equations applying some piece of economic theory to the specific conditions of their experiment. In the case of SIME/DIME, they start with a very simple equation expressing labor supply theory (the rational man's tendency to strike a balance between work for pay and leisure). From this, they construct various complicated equations—the basic one is four lines long and contains thirty different terms—showing the relationship of the many variables in the experiment to each other and to the number of hours worked.[58]

They then retrieve from the computer the data that have been pouring in from the field. After making innumerable fussy adjustments to them for underreporting, attrition, and other biases, they "plug the numbers in"—that is, put the corrected figures in the equations where unknown constants have been represented by algebraic symbols. When the equations are then run through the computer, the results will confirm or disconfirm the theory—they do, in this case, confirm it—and show the magnitude of the relationships, specifying the amount by which work decreases for each dollar increase in NIT payments or each increase in the so-called tax rate.

LABOR SUPPLY RESPONSE.   As three-year families and then five-year families disenroll, Robins and fellow economist Richard West, working and reworking their computations, spell out the details of the "labor supply response" to the guaranteed annual income, the central issue of the whole experiment. Their major findings:

- In general, variations in the tax rate made little difference in the amount of work reduction. Higher income guarantees, however, reduced work far more than lower ones.[59]
- Overall, husbands in three-year families worked 7 percent less by the second year, then began to resume their more usual work level as the end of their NIT benefits neared. Husbands in five-

year families slacked off 13 percent in their third year and eased back thereafter.[60]

- Black and Chicano men decreased their work effort more than white men. Perhaps not working was more attractive to them, because they have poorer job opportunities, than it is to white men.[61]
- Wives in both the three-year and five-year families cut back on work about twice as much as husbands. Single female heads of families did so even more—up to 22 percent on a three-year grant, and up to 32 percent on a five-year grant.[62]

The startlingly large figures for single female heads of families worry the research staff, most of whom hope that income maintenance will prove economically possible. But the data on work reduction are based on the actual results with the experimental families—a stratified (and thus distorted) sample; when the economists construct a complex mathematical model to compensate for these distortions, they get somewhat more reassuring numbers:

- Overall, by the second year husbands worked 8 percent less, wives 20 percent less, and single female heads of families 14 percent less.[63] These are higher figures than in the other IMEs, which was to be expected, since SIME/DIME includes more generous payment plans. Allowing for the fact that many wives and single female heads of families work relatively little anyway, there is no evidence in SIME/DIME or any of the IMEs of a massive withdrawal from the labor force such as to indicate that a national NIT program would be economically unworkable.[64]

But it would be costly unless there were work requirements of some sort to reduce the tendency of the poor to take the money and work less: Without a work requirement feature a national NIT program would run anywhere from several billion to thirty billion more than the current welfare system, depending on how generous it was, chiefly because it would benefit millions of working-poor couples not currently covered by welfare.[65] Too late, the research team realize that they should have included work requirement as one of the variables in the experimental design. The word from Washington now is that without such a feature, Congress will never enact an income mainte-

nance proposal; the researchers believe such a requirement could substantially reduce costs but have no data to show by how much.

COUNSELING AND EDUCATION.   The researchers can scarcely believe
the results of their analyses of the effects of job counseling and education. They had expected that those who took part in these programs
would move up to better jobs and increase their income, but their
findings, though rechecked using various approaches, indicate that
this did not happen. To the dismay and puzzlement of the researchers
it appears that those who received counseling actually wound up holding worse jobs and earning less money than those who did not. Just as
puzzling, education had no appreciable effect on job level or income.[66]

In characteristically low-keyed terms, Spiegelman tells his staff that
he finds these results "bothersome" and "hard to interpret." Years
later, in the *Final Report*, two of his researchers, Katherine Dickinson
and West, more outspokenly admit that the staff found the results
"startling" and with the wisdom of hindsight ruefully suggest that "the
nondirective nature of the counseling and training programs may have
induced participants to set unrealistic goals."[67]

MARITAL STABILITY.   In late 1974 Christophersen, by then the director
of field operations in Seattle, gets a phone call from Spiegelman, who
says something like, "What are you people doing up there? There's
something very wrong with your data on marital stability." Christophersen asks what's wrong. Spiegelman says he's been hearing from
three Stanford University sociologists on his research staff, Michael
Hannan, Nancy Tuma, and Steven Beaver, that marital breakup
seems to be far more common among the families on a guaranteed
income than among the controls. But this runs counter to a quarter
century of research data showing marital breakup to be most common
among the poorest and less so among those with more money. Income
maintenance should increase marital stability, not decrease it.

It becomes clear as time passes that nothing is wrong either with the
raw figures or the analyses made at SRI. Year after year the data from
both Seattle and Denver yield the same findings: For blacks and whites
(but not Chicanos), marital breakup is 40 to 60 percent higher among
experimentals than controls. Yet inconsistently, low and medium in-

come guarantees increase marital dissolution but the highest one does not.[68]

Eventually, Hannan, Tuma, and Lyle Groeneveld (who replaces Beaver after he dies in an auto accident) hypothesize that income maintenance has two contrary effects: It increases family stability but also makes nonworking women less dependent on the men in their lives. (This is a good example of what Spiegelman considers data-mining; since, however, the results were unexpected, they were not the test of a hypothesis but an anomaly for which a hypothesis had to be offered.) Among the poorest families and at low NIT support levels, the net result is largely to enable women in bad alliances to escape from them; among better-off families and at the highest NIT support levels, the two effects balance out.[69] This explanation is tentative; the facts, however, are unarguable. And unsettling: Many of the SRI researchers fear that these findings may be useful to the opponents of income maintenance. But Spiegelman, the very model of an impartial scientist, is unflapped. "This is scientific information that people have to know about and understand," he says. "If they don't like what's going to happen with an income maintenance program, it's much cheaper to find out now."

HEALTH AND SPENDING HABITS. A number of different researchers, pursuing special interests, dig into the data base to look for other interesting effects of the experiment. Some of what they report at SRI round-table seminars:

- Among the experimentals, white families decreased their fertility, Chicanos increased theirs, and blacks remained unchanged—all of which, the researchers candidly admit, is "somewhat bewildering."[70]
- Against all reasonable expectations, people whose incomes were increased by SIME/DIME showed no reduction of psychological distress, to judge by symptoms they cited in interviews; in fact, some actually showed more psychological distress than before. The sociologists Peggy Thoits and Michael Hannan offer an explanation of the paradox: Additional income can help bring about desired but stressful changes, such as divorce.[71]
- Families getting NIT benefits increased their purchases of clothing more than other consumables. While many of them lived in

substandard housing, they spent relatively little of the extra money for better accommodations; apparently, this had lower priority for them than other things they could buy with the money.[72]

As the experiment slowly pursues its course, the time when its findings might help shape policy runs out and the political base of the income maintenance concept erodes.

President Nixon's entry in the field, the Family Assistance Plan, passes in the House in 1969 but is defeated in the Senate. Thereafter, other bills with income maintenance provisions are offered by Nixon, then Ford, then Carter, but with waning support; none is passed. By 1978 (as we will shortly see), Senator Daniel Moynihan, who has long espoused income maintenance—and whose support, as chairman of the Subcommittee on Public Assistance of the Committee on Finance, is crucial to its passage—publicly changes his mind. With this, the decade-long effort to enact income maintenance legislation is effectively ended—long before the research findings are all in or have been carefully considered.

The Politics of Social Experimentation

Unlike most other kinds of scientific research, social experimentation is intimately joined to politics. The union, while symbiotic, is marred by inherent incompatibilities that often prevent the government from making the best (or, sometimes, any) use of the findings it has paid for and that severely frustrate the researchers who have devoted many years to the work. These are the chief areas of disharmony:

TIMING.   The most serious and intractable problem has to do with the timeliness of the knowledge provided by social experimentation. "Research and policy are often uncomfortable as bedfellows," writes James Coleman. "Policy decisions have a time schedule of their own and research has time schedules as well. These schedules are often in serious conflict."[73]

The government generally funds a social experiment only when it is ready to enact a new policy intended to deal with a serious problem. But planning the experiment may take one or more years; obtaining contractors' proposals and getting the money from Congress may take that much time again; and it may then require several years of field work to collect the data and as many more to analyze them.[74] Agency heads, Congress, and the President cannot wait that long; problems that are pressing enough to have come to their attention must be dealt with before they get out of hand, and certainly before the next election. The President is therefore likely to propose and Congress to consider the policy being tested long before researchers can say whether or not it seems likely to achieve its goals.[75]

During the debate, moreover, impatient policy-makers may demand that researchers divulge their early, tentative results. Congressional committees press researchers into giving premature findings that are often misleading but that leave a stronger impression than the final results. The publicity given the early revelations may, furthermore, seriously contaminate the ultimate findings by making the participants aware of what is being said about their behavior and thus affecting it.[76]

If, on the other hand, the program is not prematurely enacted, the political tide may turn before the research is completed and the advocates of the program may no longer command a majority or the mood of the public may have changed. If the findings show that the policy would have failed to achieve its goal, the experiment will appear to have been a waste of money and effort; if they show that the policy would succeed either as tested or with certain modifications, they will go unheard and unused.[77]

INTERPRETATION.   Policy-makers and the public find social experiments confusing and hard to follow; the methodology is complex and difficult, and the findings, which often vary from one segment of the tested sample to another, may seem self-contradictory. Social experimenters themselves should explain and interpret all this to the laity, but most of them are not good at the task or are uninterested in it. According to Greenberg and Robins:

In many instances . . . researchers have been unable or unwilling to provide simplified discussions of the experimental design and the evaluation methodology, consequently causing general confusion as to what was tested and what was found. Indeed, sometimes the researchers appear to have been more concerned with methodological issues than with policy issues. This is partly a reflection of the fact that scientific journals place more emphasis on articles having innovative methodological content than on articles merely reporting results using standard evaluation techniques. . . . [This] not only creates problems in communicating results, but also in convincing policymakers of the usefulness of the results.[78]

The agencies that commission and oversee social experiments could act as interpreters of the work, but the agency personnel who are closest to it and understand it best are usually professionally trained and, like the researchers, tend to speak in academic rather than lay terms. A 1981 report by the General Accounting Office attributes the early failure of President Carter's 1977 welfare reform proposal partly to the confusing presentation of the findings of the IMEs to Congress by HHS spokespersons.[79]

When legislators hear complicated and seemingly inconsistent answers to their questions, they are apt not to grasp the overall import of the findings but to seize upon those scraps of evidence, often peripheral, that support their own values.[80] Opponents of a proposed policy may, for instance, concentrate on marginal findings that have moral implications and that permit them to ignore major findings favorable to the policy. (Advocates of a proposal may, of course, do much the same thing in reverse.) The most devastating attack on income maintenance was the side issue that the NIT benefits of SIME/DIME had increased the rate of marital breakup, a result a policy-maker could state simply and in tones of outrage.

UNWELCOME DISCOVERIES.   Policy-makers and social researchers usually expect a social experiment to show that the policy being tested will work either as tested or with certain modifications. As in other sciences, those who back or conduct a social experiment hope to prove a theory they believe in rather than to disprove one they do not; the preference for confirmatory evidence—"confirmation bias"—is a fundamental human tendency.[81]

Social experiments, however, because of the complexity of their raw material, often produce findings that unexpectedly cast doubt on the theory being tested or at least suggest that it is simplistic and incomplete. Three social experiments mentioned earlier exemplify this kind of outcome:

- The Wildcat Supported Work Program tested the hypothesis that if chronically unemployed ex-addicts were supplied with subsidized jobs, they would work, earn money, and consequently become better adjusted and less likely to return to the use of drugs and to criminality. The experimental group of ex-addicts did indeed work more and earn more than the control group, become less dependent on welfare, and develop more stable family relationships. But although at first they also were less likely to use drugs or resort to criminality, these gains were temporary; at the end of several years, they were no better in either respect than the controls.[82]
- The Housing Allowance Program tested the notion that the inadequately housed poor, if given direct cash subsidies for housing, would find better accommodations or would significantly improve those they already had. The experiment yielded valuable information as to how subsidies affect the supply and price of housing, but its major finding was negative: The cash allowances did little to improve recipients' housing for the unexpected reason that, like the NIT experimentals, by and large they chose to spend the extra money on other things.[83]
- The Health Insurance Study tested the belief of advocates of national health insurance that free medical care would raise the average level of health of participants without causing an inordinate increase in demands made on the medical care system. The evidence showed, however, that people given free care did make far greater demands on the system (thus considerably increasing overall costs) than those who had to pay some part of their own bills, but that the extra care did little to improve their health.[84]

These and similar disagreeable discoveries may and sometimes do mean that the theories underlying the programs are incorrect and that the experiment will save the nation a great deal of wasted money and effort by scuttling the program. But such negative findings more often mean that the theories need to be refined, or that the programs based on them must be modified in order to deal with counteracting influences. Legislators and the public, however, are more likely to take the first and simpler view: that the negative findings prove that the proposed program cannot work and the theory behind it is wrong. Thus, the very findings that could lead to successful program design may bring about the death of the proposal.[85]

Exacerbating this tendency, the complexity of social experiments permits researchers to use differing methods of analysis of the same raw data to arrive at different conclusions for their own purposes. Greenberg and Robins explain: "Once the first set of findings are published, other researchers eager to make a name for themselves must come up with different methodologies and results to get their studies published."[86] Most analysts, for instance, found the work reduction in the New Jersey IME trifling, but at least one proved to his own satisfaction that it was large and statistically significant.[87] While scientists are used to such professional competition and can shut their ears to self-promotional noise, policy-makers and the public often take the brouhaha to mean that the experiments have been failures.

In view of these inherent incompatibilities, what is the social utility of social experimentation, and is it ever worth what it costs?

Some commentators say that despite all the difficulties, it is valuable, but chiefly for practical reasons: It either helps policy-makers construct a program that will succeed or prevents them from enacting one that will fail or have undesirable side effects. In either case, they say, the experimentation is well worth what it costs; large experiments may run to many millions of dollars but the programs they either improve or forestall cost billions of dollars, year after year.[88]

Other commentators, in contrast, suggest that social experiments are of more value to social scientists than to policy-makers. The sociologists Howard Freeman and Peter Rossi, for instance, say, "Large-scale true experiments are jewels, especially to researchers. . . . As instruments of policy formation, however, their utility has been limited."[89]

The majority opinion among both policy-makers and researchers seems to be that social experimentation serves both purposes. Saxe and Fine conclude their examination of the field by finding that social experiments "help us understand the effects of social interventions and social problems . . . generate knowledge for improving social conditions . . . highlight the inadequacy of present interventions and suggest alternative approaches."[90] And a 1981 report by the General Accounting Office says of the income maintenance experiments and, by implication, social experiments in general:

> In our opinion . . . [they] represent an important contribution to the social research field. The experiments demonstrated the feasibility of the experimental approach for assessing many social and economic consequences of proposed programs, gathered voluminous data about human behavior, identified better ways to administer existing programs, and developed valuable experience about the conduct (planning, monitoring, and results dissemination) of social experiments.[91]

For such reasons, despite all the impediments we have looked at and the distaste of the Reagan Administration for social research, social experimentation is continuing. To be sure, experiments are fewer in number than they were during the 1970s, and in general they are smaller. But even now, the largest social experiment ever undertaken is just getting under way: It will use a sample of 31,000 people, take at least ten years to complete, and test a major modification of a program currently costing the government over $19 billion per year. The experiment, sponsored by the Social Security Administration, will appraise the effects of proposed changes of the disability insurance program that are designed to give recipients an incentive to return to work and get off the benefit rolls. The payoff in money saved and human lives enriched could be huge—to say nothing of what social scientists will learn about the desires of the disabled, the psychosocial value of work, and other related aspects of human behavior.[92]

Results and Second Thoughts

The highlights of the concluding phase of the Seattle-Denver Income Maintenance Experiment:

1977

The Carter Administration, using preliminary SIME/DIME data as a guide, proposes the Program for Better Jobs and Income. The income guarantee in this package requires those who can work to do so; the administration believes this will eliminate the work reduction manifested in SIME/DIME and thus keep costs moderate. Congress is cool to the proposal; since the effect of the job requirement is unknown, many legislators think the administration's cost estimates far too low.[93]

In November, a correspondent in the Washington, D.C., bureau of the Los Angeles *Times* reads two obscure SRI research papers on file at HEW and writes an article in the November 4 editions headlined, "Divorce Linked to Income Gains in Welfare Study." It is picked up by other papers, and a few days later the AP does its own syndicated story; from then on marital dissolution is the most publicized effect of income maintenance and the one most often cited by its opponents.

In Seattle, the final postexperimental interviews with five-year families are completed (the last of these families had been disenrolled by the end of 1976), and the field office closes down.

1978

On May 1, at a hearing of the Senate Finance Committee's Subcommittee on Public Assistance, the chairman, Senator Moynihan, asks Spiegelman and other SRI people to testify about the SIME/DIME findings to date on work reduction and marital dissolution. The former effect has been the major concern of the experiment, but the latter makes the headlines the next day in the Washington *Post* ("Welfare Plan Linked to Family Splits") and many papers across the country.

Later that month, at a conference on Orcas Island near Seattle, SRI researchers present their results to an audience of social scientists and state and federal officials. Most of their findings deal with work response but again the media pay attention chiefly to the simple, unexpected, and headline-worthy findings on marital dissolution.

By September, Senator Moynihan, who for a decade has backed a guaranteed annual income, has second thoughts about it and does a public about-face. In a letter to William F. Buckley, published in Buckley's conservative *National Review*, he writes, "Were we wrong about a guaranteed income! Seemingly, it is calamitous. It increases family dissolution by some 70 percent, decreases work, etc. . . . As chairman of the Subcommittee on Public Assistance of the Committee on Finance, I propose to hold hearings after the election, confronting one and all with the evidence."[94]*

On November 15, Senator Moynihan opens the hearings with a verdict delivered in advance of the testimony:

What have we learned? What are the implications of this research for future public policy? This round of hearings is addressed to those questions. It does not seem likely that the answers will be comforting to those of us who had hoped to replace existing programs with some form of national income maintenance or negative income tax program.[96]

He cites the weakening of family ties and substantial reductions in work effort—in that order—as evidence that these hopes were wrong.

For three days, the subcommittee hears testimony from Spiegelman, Robert Williams, Jodie Allen (Spiegelman's original contact at HEW), three economists from Mathematica, and over a dozen other experts. The SIME/DIME researchers present a generally positive interpretation of their results but are no match for Senator Moynihan, whose "vorpal blade goes snickersnack," deftly beheading the points they made. A few examples:

- "Do you *know* what I am going to have to explain to this Senate?"
- "We march into those communities and break up those families. That is a big thing to happen to a three-year-old kid, you know."
- "I am sort of sorry about these hearings. I am certainly sorry about your findings. . . . But that is what intellectual work is about. It comes up with things you do not want to hear, once in a while. But we need to know them."
- "What are the limits of experiments with communities? You write it all up and say, 'Gee it was very interesting. Everything went to hell.' What about those people you leave behind?"
- "I am not enjoying this hearing one damn bit."
- "The results are clearly a disappointment to us and to many researchers in the sense that we would have hoped for a more

---

*The 70 percent figure was unrelated to the facts. The correct figures: at the $5,600 support level, 20 percent for blacks, 14 percent for whites; at the $3,800 support level, 58 percent and 51 percent, respectively.[95]

resounding confirmation of the fact that there are large social benefits to be derived."

And, despite all the above:

- "I have been at great pains not to be criticizing anything in these hearings."[97]

The mass media widely report the Senate Subcommittee hearings and run commentaries saying that the evidence shows the guaranteed income concept to be a failure. A few typical headlines:

Washington *Star:* "Study Raises Questions On Welfare Reforms"[98]
Washington *Post:* "A Failed Experiment in Guaranteed Income"[99]
New York *Times:* "Welfare Reform on 'the Same Old Rock' "[100]
Fortune: "Some Negative Evidence about the Negative Income Tax"[101]

In December, the final postexperimental interviews of five-year families in Denver are concluded and the field office prepares to shut down.

1979

At Menlo Park, analysis reaches a peak; this year the research staff turns out dozens of research papers, technical memos, and journal articles.

In Washington, HEW isn't much interested and does nothing to publicize them. Agency officials dislike the marital dissolution findings, are smarting from widely publicized charges that they concealed them (the General Accounting Office later finds no grounds for these accusations),[102] and can read the handwriting on the wall, which says that guaranteed annual income is a losing issue.

1980

The final SRI research papers are written, including a series of projections made by SRI economists, using a simulation model developed by

Mathematica, of the costs and benefits of different NIT programs, if put into effect nationally.

Aside from the scientific community, no one cares; guaranteed income is no longer a popular topic in Washington. At HEW (or HHS—the Department of Health and Human Services—as it is called from May on), discussion of the subject is largely limited to the question of what to do with the 200-odd Denver families who had been signed up in 1974 for 20 years. Agency officials say they've learned as much as they can from SIME/DIME and don't want to continue with the long-term study. They decide to exercise a contract clause letting HEW escape from its commitment to the families, who are bought out for lump sums of a few thousand dollars or given a two-year phasing-out. [103]

On October 8, SRI gives a buffet supper party in its main Menlo Park building for all who worked on the Seattle-Denver project; the invitations cheerfully announce that the event is to "celebrate the successful completion of SIME/DIME."

On November 4, Ronald Reagan defeats Jimmy Carter. No more is heard about guaranteed income in Washington; it is apparently an idea whose time has come, and gone.

1981–84

The research staff is disbanded, but under special contracts a number of the researchers and Gary Christophersen write the various sections of the *Final Report*. It is published in May 1983 with no government fanfare. The title pages even suggest that SRI published volume 1 and Mathematica volume 2; the fact that the Government Printing Office published both is acknowledged in a single line of tiny type buried at the back of each volume.

Yet the principal investigators, both those who were on the field staffs and those who were at SRI, look back at their work with pride, and nearly all of them feel that the results did show that a guaranteed income would be both manageable and socially beneficial.

Christophersen, for instance, says, "The experiment showed that such a program could be successfully administered. The overall costs would be more than the present welfare system, but based on what we saw the program do for the families in it, I'm not convinced that that's a bad thing, and I think most people who worked on SIME/DIME feel the same way."

Robert Spiegelman, now director of the Upjohn Institute for Employment Research in Kalamazoo, is even more affirmative: "I do think our experiment showed that income maintenance through NIT was the right direction to go, though our results showed that you'd have to include a work requirement, and you'd have to worry about the marital impact, and you'd have to do something different about job training than we did. But our conclusions came too late for NIT; its time had passed."

He pauses a moment, then adds firmly: "But it will come back. The existing system is not very equitable, it's overly expensive, and we continue to have a lot of poverty in America—in fact, in 1983 it was at its highest level in eighteen years. On the next cycle, when a somewhat more liberal administration comes back in, they're going to look at all that, and want to do something positive—and I think they're going to dredge up income maintenance, because there's no other show in town."

NOTES ON SOURCES

Direct quotations from participants in the social research projects described in the text or commentators on the projects, if not noted here, are from interviews with those persons.

Specific page references are given only where, due to the length of the cited source, it might be difficult to locate the noted material.

CHAPTER 1:
THE WORLD OF SOCIAL RESEARCH

1. Latané and Rodin 1969.
2. Evan Davey, Bureau of the Census, personal communication.
3. Rosenhan 1973.
4. All the details are from Liebow 1967.
5. Malinowski 1927, 1929. The quotation is from Malinowski 1967, p. 259.
6. Catton 1964, pp. 924–25; Douglas 1976, pp. 41–42.
7. Weber 1947, p. 88.
8. Mannon 1982.
9. Campbell and Fiske 1959; Campbell 1961.
10. LeVine 1981.
11. Personal communication, c. 1950 (at which time I was writing an article about him).
12. Freeman 1983, pp. 289–90.
13. Nearly all the details are from Festinger, Riecken, and Schachter 1964; two minor details are via personal communication from Schachter.
14. Melville Dalton, *Men Who Manage*; cited in Johnson 1975, pp. 54–55.
15. Rosenhan 1973.

16. Johnson 1975, p. 54.
17. Douglas 1976, p. 35.
18. Jules-Rosette and Hayward, cited in Douglas 1976, p. 111.
19. Alfred 1976.
20. Coser and Davis are cited in Friedrichs 1972, pp. 348–49.
21. Goffman 1972, pp. 29–30.
22. Goffman, pp. 23–24.
23. Hall 1966, pp. 109–10.
24. Gans 1976a, 1976b.
25. Weinberg and Williams 1975.
26. H. T. Moore; cited in Webb et al. 1966, p. 129.
27. Zimmerman and West 1975.
28. Whyte 1980.
29. Webb et al. 1976.
30. Rathje's statement and all the following details are taken from various articles by Randall H. McGuire and by Rathje in the *American Behavioral Scientist* 28 (September/October 1984).
31. Weber 1958.
32. Merton, "Puritanism, Pietism, and Science," in Merton 1968.
33. Thomas and Znaniecki 1918.
34. Erikson 1966.
35. Funkhouser 1973.
36. Cited in Krippendorf 1980, p. 77.
37. Banks 1976.
38. Durkheim 1951.
39. Sessions 1974. The estimate for today (November 1984) is by Barbara Settani of Science International Associates.
40. Murdock 1967; Miller 1983, p. 154.
41. Babbie 1979, pp. 239–40, and personal communication.
42. Kasarda 1972.
43. U.S. Congress, Joint Economic Committee 1984.
44. Crano 1981.
45. Hunt and Hunt 1977, p. 17; Arthur Norton, Population Division, Bureau of the Census, personal communication.
46. Saxe and Fine 1981, p. 49.
47. Andrews et al. 1981.
48. Heise 1981, p. 438.
49. Study by the Institute for Economic Analysis reported in *Scientific American*, September 1984, p. 70.
50. *Psychology Today*, October 1984, p. 16.
51. The following details: Dr. Barbara G. Farah, director, the New York *Times* Poll, personal communication.
52. Dr. Thomas Juster, director, Institute for Social Research, University of Michigan, personal communication.
53. The New York *Times*/CBS News Poll, reported in the New York *Times*, November 19, 1984.
54. The study: Roethlisberger and Dickson 1961; the later analyses are mentioned in Williamson et al. 1982, p. 223; and Vroom 1969, p. 224.
55. Franke and Kaul 1978; but see rebuttal in Bloombaum 1983.
56. All the details are from Erikson 1976.
57. Cooper 1980.
58. Greenberg and Robins 1984, Table I-A.

CHAPTER 2:
DILEMMA IN THE CLASSROOM

1. Cohen 1983.
2. Small 1895.
3. Berger and Kellner 1981, pp. 6, 106.
4. Cohen 1983.
5. Drake 1966; see also Myrdal 1962, chap. 31 and p. 1377, n. 5.
6. Myrdal 1962, p. lxxi.
7. Myrdal, p. 1024.
8. Myrdal, pp. 1057–64.
9. Clift 1966.
10. Parsons and Clark 1966, pp. xiii, xxi.
11. Garfinkel 1959.
12. *Brown* v. *Board of Education of Topeka*, 1955.
13. Clift 1966.
14. Coleman et al. 1966, p. 557.
15. Coleman et al., p. 8; Leeson 1965.
16. Coleman et al. 1966, pp. 221–45.
17. Myrdal 1962, pp. 339–40, 946–48.
18. Leeson 1965.
19. Coleman et al. 1966, pp. 10–12.
20. Coleman et al., pp. 571–75.
21. Coleman et al., p. 307.
22. Grant 1973, p. 25.
23. Grant, p. 25.
24. Grant, p. 28.
25. Caldwell 1970.
26. Coleman 1980, p. 12.
27. Coleman et al. 1966, p. 13.
28. Johnson 1975, pp. 15–26; Lindblom and Cohen 1979, pp. 73–74.
29. Quoted in Johnson 1975, p. 83.
30. Goode 1977, pp. 26–29; Johnson 1975, pp. 82–83.
31. Johnson 1975, p. 83.
32. Berger and Kellner 1981, pp. 41–42, 59–61.
33. Berger and Kellner, p. 62.
34. Hunt 1982, pp. 188–89, citing Darwin, Einstein, Peter Medawar, and Karl Popper.
35. Inkeles 1982.
36. Coleman 1970.
37. Grant 1973, pp. 31–32.
38. Grant, p. 32.
39. Grant, pp. 32–33; Jencks 1972, p. v.
40. The two major critical articles: Bowles and Levin 1968; Cain and Watts 1970.
41. Coleman 1968.
42. Grant 1973, p. 51; Caldwell 1970.
43. Grant, pp. 51–53; Caldwell 1970.
44. *Green* v. *New Kent County*, 1968; *Alexander* v. *Holmes County*, 1969.
45. *Swann* v. *Charlotte-Mecklenberg Board of Education*, 1971.
46. Grant 1973, pp. 43–45.
47. Grant, pp. 43–45.
48. Frederick Mosteller, personal communication.
49. Coser 1970, p. 137; Berger and Kellner 1981, p. 130.

50. Cited in Gouldner 1971, p. 24.
51. Lindblom and Cohen 1979, p. 37.
52. Singer and Glass 1975.
53. Berger and Kellner 1981, p. 53.
54. New York *Times*, June 11, 1972.
55. Inkeles 1982.
56. Armor 1972, p. 99; St. John 1975, pp. x–xi, 39, 119.
57. St. John, pp. xi, 36–39, 52, 58–60, 119, 121.
58. Coleman 1975; Coleman, Kelly, and Moore 1975, pp. 11–13, 37–39.
59. Coleman; Coleman, Kelly, and Moore, pp. 11–13, 37–39.
60. Coleman; Coleman, Kelly, and Moore, pp. 56–72, 78–79.
61. Coleman.
62. Pettigrew and Green 1976; Goodman 1975.
63. Ravitch 1976.
64. Pettigrew and Green 1976.
65. Orfield 1978, p. 107.
66. Orfield, p. 100; for confirmations of Coleman's thesis, see Coleman 1978.
67. Merton 1936.
68. Berger and Kellner 1981, p. 75.
69. Tanur 1982, pp. 335–36.
70. Armor 1972, pp. 93, 112–13.
71. Tumin 1970.
72. Ferber and Hirsch 1979.
73. Quoted in Lindblom and Cohen 1979, p. 48.
74. Lindblom and Cohen, p. 48.
75. Coleman, Hoffer, and Kilgore 1982a.
76. Coleman, Hoffer, and Kilgore 1982b.
77. New York *Times*, October 21, 1982, Op-Ed page.

CHAPTER 3:
SAMPLING SOCIAL REALITY

1. Extrapolating data in Turner and Martin 1981, p. 20; also, Herbert Hyman, personal communication.
2. Duncan, personal communication; Orcutt, in U.S. Department of Health, Education, and Welfare 1979a, p. 1.
3. Orcutt, p. 3.
4. Memorandum, U.S. Department of Health, Education, and Welfare, January 13, 1975, to the Secretary, from Assistant Secretary for Planning and Evaluation; Subject: New Income Survey.
5. Chamberlain and Feldman 1961, pp. 8–10, 113, 146.
6. Hauser 1975, pp. 9–10.
7. U.S. Bureau of the Census 1980, p. 12.
8. Hauser 1975, p. 11.
9. Hauser, p. 108.
10. U.S. Bureau of the Census 1980, p. 28, quoting *Congressional Record*, August 4, 1939, pp. 11092–93.
11. Quoted in Hauser 1975, p. 3.
12. Schuman 1982, p. 22.
13. Hauser 1975, pp. 315, 317–20; Norman M. Bradburn, personal communication.

14. U.S. Bureau of the Census 1978a, p. 2.
15. For the three disciplines, see Turner and Martin 1981, p. 20; for sociology alone, Wells and Picou 1981, p. 115.
16. Hauser 1975, pp. 7–9.
17. Dawn Nelson, "Overview of the Site Research Test," in Olson 1980.
18. The quotations have been abridged without ellipses from "Site Research Test Field Evaluation," in Olson 1980.
19. Martynas A. Ycas, "An Introduction of the Income Survey Development Program," in U.S. Department of Health, Education, and Welfare 1979a, p. 63.
20. Details in this paragraph: Evan Davey, personal communication; and Kasprzyk 1982, pp. 7–8, 11–12.
21. Ycas 1979.
22. Ycas, "An Introduction of the Income Survey Development Program," in U.S. Department of Health, Education, and Welfare 1979a, p. 53.
23. Evan Davey, personal communication.
24. "The Quality of Supplemental Security Income Recipiency Reporting," in Olson 1980, ch. 10, pp. 13, 27.
25. "The Mathematica Analysis: A Summary," in Olson 1980, pp. 4–7.
26. Ycas 1979, p. 11.
27. Gallup and Rae 1940, pp. 34–38, 50.
28. Gallup and Rae, pp. 38–43.
29. Gallup and Rae, pp. 64, 69; Blankenship 1943, p. 113.
30. Kruskal 1982.
31. See note 13 above.
32. Details in this and the next three paragraphs: Ferber et al. 1980, p. 12; Kish 1965, pp. 20–21; Blankenship 1943, pp. 98, 101–2.
33. Schuman 1982.
34. Cantril 1944, pp. 108–9.
35. Singer and Kohnke-Aguirre 1979.
36. Cantril 1944, pp. 78–80; Roman, n.d.; American Statistical Association 1981, pp. 3, 10, and Table 6.
37. Rockwell 1982, pp. 41–42.
38. Terman et al. 1938, p. 269; Kinsey et al. 1953, pp. 349, 353–54; Clark and Wallin 1964; Levinger 1966.
39. Schuman and Presser 1977.
40. Presser and Schuman 1980.
41. Marsh 1979.
42. Schuman and Presser 1977.
43. Marsh 1979; Cicourel 1982.
44. National Research Council 1979, p. 5.
45. Steeh 1981.
46. Schuman 1982.
47. National Center for Health Statistics 1982, pp. 2, 4–5.
48. Herzog and Sudea 1971, p. 61.
49. Rockwell 1982, pp. 8–9.
50. Rockwell, p. 7.
51. Tanur 1982, p. 329.
52. Details in this and the next three paragraphs: Tanur, pp. 332–36.
53. Nova #1002, p. 15.
54. The following description of the main features draws upon Bergsten 1982; Bergsten and Kulka 1982; Kulka 1982a and 1982b; Moore 1982; and Ycas and Lininger 1981.
55. David 1979.
56. Piper 1982, ch. 6, pp. 32, 35; Ycas 1982.

57. The following description of the main points draws upon Kulka 1982a; Whiteman, n.d.; Czaika 1982; David 1982; Pearl [1982]; and John Coder, personal communication.
58. The following data are drawn from David 1982 and Ycas and Lininger 1981.
59. U.S. Department of Health, Education, and Welfare 1979a, p. iii; Kasprzyk 1978, p. I-1; Lininger 1982.
60. Quoted in Heisenberg 1971, p. 63.
61. Lindblom and Cohen 1979, p. 83.
62. Deutsch, Platt, and Senghaas 1971.
63. National Committee for Research on the 1980 Census, n.d.
64. National Committee.
65. National Committee.
66. Fienberg 1983, p. 3.
67. Parke 1982.
68. Fienberg, personal communication.
69. Hunt and Smith 1982.
70. Social Science Research Council, *Items* 37 (March 1983):26.
71. Herriot and Kasprzyk 1984; Chet Bowie, Bureau of the Census, personal communication.
72. U.S. Bureau of the Census 1984.

CHAPTER 4:
ONE THING AT A TIME

1. Latané, Harkins, and Williams 1980, p. 4.
2. Latané, Harkins, and Williams, p. 18.
3. 1898, according to Jones, in press, p. 1 and bibliog.; 1897, according to Allport 1968, pp. 64–65.
4. Allport 1968, p. 64.
5. Hendrick 1977.
6. Latané, Williams, and Harkins 1979.
7. The series is summarized in Latané and Nida 1981.
8. Latané and Darley 1970, p. 125.
9. Hendrick 1977; Jones, in press.
10. Jones, in press; Allport 1968, p. 3; Freedman, Sears, and Carlsmith 1978, p. 4.
11. Myers 1983, p. 14; Freedman, Sears, and Carlsmith, pp. 11–12.
12. Hendrick 1977; Freedman, Sears, and Carlsmith, pp. 18–19.
13. Aronson and Carlsmith 1968, p. 10.
14. Lewin 1937.
15. Hendrick 1977.
16. Cottrell et al. 1968.
17. Deutsch 1982.
18. Details and the dialogue in the following paragraphs are from Latané, Williams, and Harkins 1979, with additions from interviews with these authors.
19. Latané, Williams, and Harkins, p. 825.
20. Allport 1968, p. 3.
21. Same as note 18.
22. Latané, Williams, and Harkins 1979, p. 827.
23. Latané, Williams, and Harkins, pp. 831–32.
24. Cooper 1976; Freedman, Sears, and Carlsmith 1978, p. 104.
25. Hendrick 1977.
26. Asch 1951.

27. Aronson and Carlsmith 1968, pp. 22, 30; Berkowitz [c. 1976]; Rosenthal and Jacobson 1968; Zajonc 1968, pp. 361–64.
28. Murray 1980; Baumrind 1978; Gross 1982.
29. Murray 1980.
30. Holden 1979.
31. *Schloendorff* v. *The Society of the New York Hospital,* 1914.
32. Katz 1972, p. 313.
33. Bower and de Gasparis 1978, pp. 4–6.
34. Kimble 1978.
35. Milgram 1963, p. 371.
36. Baumrind 1978; Kelman 1977.
37. Bower and de Gasparis 1978, pp. 7–8.
38. U.S. Department of Health, Education, and Welfare 1978, pp. 56186, 56191.
39. Cooper 1976.
40. Latané and Darley 1970, pp. 124–25.
41. "Code of Federal Regulations," in *Federal Register* 46:16 (January 26, 1981), p. 8389.
42. "Code of Federal Regulations," p. 8390.
43. Baumrind 1978.
44. Festinger 1980, p. 250.
45. Schachter 1971; Piliavin and Piliavin 1972; Latané and Darley 1968.
46. Latané, Harkins, and Williams 1980, pp. 15–17.
47. Kipling Williams, personal communication.
48. Williams, Harkins, and Latané 1981.
49. Williams, Harkins, and Latané.
50. Harkins, Latané, and Williams 1980.
51. Harkins, Latané, and Williams.
52. Latané, Harkins, and Williams 1980, pp. 33–37.
53. Latané, Harkins, and Williams, passim.
54. Hendrick 1977.
55. Hendrick.
56. Quoted in Hendrick 1977.
57. Study by David Wilson reported in *Psychology Today,* December 1981, p. 19.
58. Smith 1983.
59. Aronson and Carlsmith 1968, pp. 24–25.
60. Zimbardo and Kabat 1981.
61. Aronson and Carlsmith 1968, pp. 25–26.
62. Gergen 1973.
63. Schlenker 1974.
64. Higbee, Millard, and Folkman 1982.
65. Jones, in press.
66. Williams, Harkins, and Latané 1981.
67. Weiner, Pandey, and Latané 1981.

CHAPTER 5:
THE SLOWEST, COSTLIEST, BUT BEST
(AND WORST) OF METHODS

1. Palmore 1981, p. 3.
2. Schaie and Hertzog 1982; de Beauvoir 1972, passim; Maddox and Wiley 1976.
3. Duke University Center 1980a, pp. 3, 6.

    4. Popper 1977.
    5. Duke University Center 1982; Busse 1970a.
    6. Maddox, 1970.
    7. See discussions of correlation and causality elsewhere in this book, especially chapter 4.
    8. National Commission on Employment and Unemployment Statistics 1979, pp. 209–10.
    9. Nesselroade and Baltes 1979, p. 35.
   10. Schaie and Hertzog 1982; Nesselroade and Baltes 1979, pp. 4, 7; Goldstein 1979, pp. 1–2, 40–42.
   11. Tanur 1982, p. 331.
   12. Hammer 1977.
   13. Tanur 1982, p. 330.
   14. Maddox, in press.
   15. Hamburg, Elliott, and Parron 1982, p. 201.
   16. Hamburg, Elliott, and Parron, p. 201.
   17. Palmore 1981, p. 15.
   18. Cunningham and Owens 1983.
   19. Schaie 1983a.
   20. Baltes and Nesselroade 1979.
   21. Sontag 1969; Goldfarb 1960, pp. 186, 190–91.
   22. Goldfarb 1960, pp. 181–82, 186, 190–91.
   23. Sontag 1969, pp. 17–18.
   24. Sontag, pp. 17–18.
   25. Sontag, pp. 17–18; Featherman 1982.
   26. Sontag 1969.
   27. Busse 1970a.
   28. Siegler, in press.
   29. Dovenmuehle, Busse, and Newman 1970.
   30. Eisdorfer 1970.
   31. Busse 1970b.
   32. Busse 1970a; Maddox 1970.
   33. Maddox 1970.
   34. Busse 1970a; Duke University Center 1980a, p. 9.
   35. Palmore 1974a.
   36. Dovenmuehle 1970.
   37. Heyman and Jeffers 1970.
   38. Palmore and Jeffers 1974.
   39. Anderson and Palmore 1974.
   40. Thompson, Eisdorfer, and Estes 1970.
   41. Palmore, 1970a.
   42. Wilkie and Eisdorfer 1974a.
   43. Eisdorfer and Wilkie 1974.
   44. Duke University Center 1980a, p. 29.
   45. Palmore 1970a.
   46. Verwoerdt, Pfeiffer, and Wang 1970.
   47. Busse and Obrist 1970; Obrist et al. 1970.
   48. Davis 1978.
   49. Schaie 1983b.
   50. Schaie; Tanur 1982, pp. 335–36.
   51. Goldstein 1979, p. 46.
   52. Schaie 1983b; Buss 1979.
   53. Schaie.
   54. Tanur 1982, pp. 336–37; Botwinnick 1977.
   55. Tanur, pp. 336–37; Botwinnick 1977.

56. Goldstein 1979, p. 44.
57. Goldstein, pp. 97–98; Tanur 1982, p. 337.
58. Hamburg, Elliott, and Parron 1982, p. 201; Schaie 1983b; Maddox and Wiley 1976.
59. Quoted in Maddox and Wiley 1976.
60. Schaie 1965.
61. Schaie and Hertzog 1982.
62. Glenn 1976.
63. Glenn.
64. Schaie and Hertzog 1982.
65. Duke University Center 1980a, pp. 7, 10; Palmore 1974b.
66. Palmore 1981, pp. 8, 10.
67. Harkins et al. 1974.
68. Wang and Busse 1974.
69. Busse, in press.
70. Maddox and Douglass 1974.
71. Palmore 1974c.
72. Nowlin and Siegler, in press.
73. Wilkie and Eisdorfer 1974b.
74. Duke University Center 1980a, pp. 35–37.
75. Palmore 1981, pp. 30–31.
76. Palmore, pp. 63–64.
77. Palmore, pp. 70–73.
78. Palmore, pp. 43–46. (Palmore is the author of record, but he credits Luikart's contribution to data analysis of the material; see p. 42, note.)
79. Holmes and Rahe 1967; Palmore 1981, p. 79.
80. Heyman and Gianturco 1974; Palmore 1981, pp. 79–80.
81. Palmore 1981, pp. 111–12.
82. Palmore, pp. 21–22.
83. Siegler and Gatz, in press.
84. Maddox, in press.
85. Palmore 1981, pp. 87–90, 93.
86. Maddox, in press; Siegler, George, and Okun 1979; Palmore 1974d.
87. U.S. Bureau of the Census 1978b, p. 49; U.S. Department of Health and Human Services, 1981 p. 49.
88. Babbie 1983, pp. 83–84.
89. Singer and Spilerman 1976.
90. Taeuber and Rockwell 1982, p. 29 and passim.
91. Data in this and the next four paragraphs: Migdal, Abeles, and Sherrod 1981.
92. National Commission on Employment and Unemployment Statistics 1979, p. 210.
93. Arlene Skolnick of the Berkeley Guidance Study, personal communication; Kagan 1984.
94. Featherman 1982, p. 237.
95. The following four items: Featherman 1982, p. 238; Baltes and Nesselroade 1979.
96. Rockwell, personal communication.
97. Siegler 1983, p. 184.
98. Duke University Center 1980b, p. 9.

CHAPTER 6:
TWENTY THOUSAND VOLUNTEERS

1. Spiegelman and Yeager 1980.
2. *Final Report*, SIME/DIME, vol. 1, pp. 14–15.

3. Masters and Garfinkel 1977, p. 2.
4. Fisk and Roth 1980, pp. 1–5.
5. *Final Report*, SIME/DIME, vol. 1, pp. 264–66; Hunt and Hunt 1977, pp. 15–16.
6. *Final Report*, SIME/DIME, vol 1, pp. 264–66.
7. Kershaw and Fair 1976, pp. xii–xiii.
8. Kershaw and Fair, pp. xiii–xvi; Hauser 1975, pp. 146–47; Neubeck and Roach 1981; U.S. General Accounting Office 1981, App. IV, p. 37.
9. Rossi and Lyall 1976, pp. ix, 189.
10. Kershaw and Fair 1976, pp. xii–xiii.
11. *Final Report*, SIME/DIME, vol. 1, p. 16; Spiegelman, personal communication.
12. Simon 1980.
13. AuClaire 1977.
14. Saxe and Fine 1981, p. 64.
15. Freeman and Rossi 1981.
16. Saxe and Fine 1981, pp. 59–60.
17. Saxe and Fine, p. 14.
18. Ferber and Hirsch 1979, pp. 78–79; Freeman and Rossi 1981; Saxe and Fine 1981, p. 58.
19. Riecken et al. 1974; quoted in Archibald and Newhouse 1980.
20. Greenberg and Robins 1984.
21. Boruch, McSweeney, and Soderstrom 1978.
22. Archibald and Newhouse 1980.
23. Saxe and Fine 1981, p. 24.
24. *Final Report*, SIME/DIME, vol. 2, p. 20; Christophersen, personal communication.
25. *Final Report*, SIME/DIME, vol. 2, p. 11.
26. Associated Press story, March 9, 1970, datelined Olympia, Washington, in *Skagit Valley Herald* (Mt. Vernon, Wash.) and elsewhere.
27. *Final Report*, SIME/DIME, vol. 2, pp. 13–14.
28. *Final Report*, pp. 16–26, 32.
29. *Final Report*, p. 33.
30. The following questions are from various modules in "SIME Thirteenth Periodic [questionnaire]" and "DIME Twelfth Periodic [questionnaire]," on file at Mathematica Policy Research library, Princeton, N.J.
31. Freeman and Rossi 1981.
32. Conlisk and Watts 1969, 1979; Archibald and Newhouse 1980.
33. Archibald and Newhouse 1980.
34. Greenberg and Robins 1984.
35. Ferber and Hirsch 1979, p. 85; Saxe and Fine 1981, pp. 16, 69–79.
36. Saxe and Fine 1981, pp. 30–32, 91.
37. Archibald and Newhouse 1980.
38. Tanur 1982, p. 341.
39. Riecken and Boruch 1978.
40. Riecken and Boruch.
41. Riecken and Boruch.
42. Ferber and Hirsch 1979, p. 89.
43. Kershaw and Fair 1976, p. 4.
44. Saxe and Fine 1981, pp. 52–54.
45. Ferber and Hirsch 1979, p. 89.
46. Archibald and Newhouse 1980.
47. Archibald and Newhouse.
48. *Final Report*, SIME/DIME, vol. 1, pp. 117–18; vol. 2, pp. 66, 91–96.
49. Halsey et al. 1977; Greenberg, Moffitt, and Friedmann 1981; *Final Report*, SIME/DIME, vol. 2, pp. 140–41.
50. Charles Thompson, personal communication.
51. *Final Report*, SIME/DIME, vol. 2, pp. 123, 129.

52. *Final Report*, vol. 1, pp. 31–32; vol. 2, pp. 65, 134–35.
53. *Final Report*, vol. 1, pp. 205–6, 211–13; West 1980.
54. *Final Report*, vol. 2, p. 133.
55. *Final Report*, vol. 2, p. 103; letter of May 4, 1976, reproduced in a press clipping collection lent me by Philip Robins.
56. *Final Report*, vol. 2, pp. 102–3.
57. Personal communications from Spiegelman, Kehrer, Robins, and West.
58. *Final Report, SIME/DIME*, vol. 1, p. 136.
59. *Final Report*, pp. 128, 138.
60. *Final Report*, pp. 122–23.
61. *Final Report*, p. 123.
62. *Final Report*, p. 124.
63. *Final Report*, pp. 129–31, 150.
64. *Final Report*, p. 169.
65. *Final Report*, pp. 190–91.
66. *Final Report*, p. 202.
67. *Final Report*, pp. 202, 248.
68. *Final Report*, pp. 357–65.
69. *Final Report*, p. 325.
70. *Final Report*, p. 395.
71. *Final Report*, pp. 391–92.
72. *Final Report*, pp. 398–400.
73. Quoted in U.S. General Accounting Office, 1981, App. I, p. 23.
74. U.S. Department of Health, Education, and Welfare 1979b, p. 99; Freeman and Rossi 1981.
75. Ferber and Hirsch 1979, p. 81; Freeman and Rossi 1981.
76. Saxe and Fine 1981, p. 78.
77. Greenberg and Robins 1984.
78. Greenberg and Robins.
79. U.S. General Accounting Office 1981, App. I, pp. 16–18.
80. Boeckmann 1976.
81. Hunt 1982, pp. 191–94.
82. Friedman 1978.
83. Bendick and Zais 1978; Ferber and Hirsch 1979, pp. 101–3, 106–7.
84. Brook et al. 1983; Newhouse et al. 1982.
85. Greenberg and Robins 1984.
86. Greenberg and Robins.
87. Cogan 1978, p. v.
88. Ferber and Hirsch 1979, pp. 112–13; Riecken and Boruch 1978.
89. Freeman and Rossi 1981.
90. Saxe and Fine 1981, p. 204.
91. U.S. General Accounting Office 1981, p. 4.
92. U.S. Department of Health and Human Services 1983, pp. 3–4, and Attachment A, pp. 1, 10, 12.
93. Neubeck and Roach 1981.
94. *National Review*, September 29, 1978.
95. *Final Report, SIME/DIME*, vol. 1, p. 357.
96. U.S. Senate 1978, p. 9.
97. The series of quotations: U.S. Senate 1978, pp. 20, 59, 79, 81, 82, 119, and again 119.
98. November 16, 1978.
99. November 20, 1978.
100. November 27, 1978.
101. December 4, 1978.
102. U.S. General Accounting Office 1981, App. I, pp. 14–15.
103. *Denver Post*, February 14, 1980, and September 15, 1980.

WORKS CITED

This list is limited to works cited in the Notes or referred to in the text.

Where a work is included in another, the larger work is named there by short-title reference and cited in full under its own author's name.

Adams, Robert McC.; Smelser, Neil J.; and Treiman, Donald J., eds. 1982. *Behavioral and Social Science Research: A National Resource*. Parts 1 and 2. Washington, DC: National Academy Press.

Alfred, Randall. 1976. "The Church of Satan." In Glock and Bellah, eds.

Allport, Gordon. 1968. "The Historical Background of Modern Social Psychology." In Lindzey and Aronson, eds., vol. 1.

American Behavioral Scientist. 1984. Vol. 28 (September/October). Special issue on refuse analysis.

American Statistical Association. 1981. "Agenda Topic C. Results of Methodological Research in the Current Population Survey." Paper presented at the meeting of the Census Advisory Committee, March 5–6.

Anderson, Banks, Jr., and Palmore, Erdman. 1974. "Longitudinal Evaluation of Ocular Function." In Palmore, ed.

Andrews, Frank M., et al. 1981. *A Guide for Selecting Statistical Techniques for Analyzing Social Science Data*. 2nd ed. Ann Arbor, MI: Institute for Social Research, University of Michigan.

Archibald, Rae W., and Newhouse, Joseph P. 1980. "Social Experimentation: Some Whys and Hows." Pamphlet. Santa Monica, CA: Rand Corporation.

Armor, David J. 1972. "The Evidence on Busing." *Public Interest*, Summer, pp. 90–126.

Aronson, Elliot, and Carlsmith, J. Merrill. 1968. "Experimentation in Social Psychology." In Lindzey and Aronson, eds., vol. 2.

Asch, S. 1951. "Effects of Group Pressure upon the Modification and Distortion of Judgment." In Guetzkow, ed.

AuClaire, Philip A. 1977. "Informing Social Policy: The Limits of Social Experimentation." *Sociological Practice* 2(Spring):24–37.

Babbie, Earl R. 1983. *The Practice of Social Research.* 2nd ed. Belmont, CA: Wadsworth.

Baltes, Paul B., and Nesselroade, John R. 1979. "History and Rationale of Longitudinal Research." In Nesselroade and Baltes, eds.

Baltes, Paul B., and Schaie, K. Warner, eds. 1973. *Life-Span Developmental Psychology.* New York: Academic Press.

Banks, James A. 1976. "A Content Analysis of the Black American in Textbooks." In Golden, ed.

Baumrind, Diana. 1978. "Nature and Definition of Informed Consent in Research Involving Deception." In National Commission for the Protection of Human Subjects, App., vol. 2.

Bendick, Marc, and Zais, James P. 1978. "Incomes and Housing: Lessons from Experiments with Housing Allowances." Pamphlet. Washington, DC: Urban Institute.

Berger, Peter L., and Kellner, Hansfried. 1981. *Sociology Reinterpreted: An Essay on Method and Vocation.* Garden City, NY: Anchor Press/Doubleday.

Bergsten, Jane W. 1982. "Sample Design." See Research Triangle Institute.

———, and Kulka, Richard A. 1982. "Survey Design." See Research Triangle Institute.

Berkowitz, Leonard. [c. 1976]. "Some Further Complications Resulting from the Regulation of Deception in Behavioral Experiments." Mimeographed. Madison, WI: University of Wisconsin.

Binstock, Robert, and Shanas, Ethel, eds., 1976. *Handbook of Aging and the Social Sciences.* New York: Van Nostrand Reinhold.

Birren, James, and Schaie, K. Warner, eds. 1977. *Handbook of the Psychology of Aging.* New York: Van Nostrand Reinhold.

Blankenship, Albert B. 1943. *Consumer and Opinion Research.* New York: Harper and Brothers.

Bloombaum, Milton. 1983. "The Hawthorne Experiments: A Critique and Reanalysis of the First Statistical Interpretation by Franke and Kaul." *Sociological Perspectives* 26(January):71–88.

Boeckmann, Margaret E. 1976. "Policy Impacts of the New Jersey Income Maintenance Experiment." *Policy Sciences* 7:53–76.

Boruch, R. F.; McSweeney, A. J.; and Soderstrom, E. J. 1978. "Randomized Field Experiments for Program Planning, Development, and Evaluation: An Illustrative Bibliography." *Evaluation Quarterly* 2:655–95.

Botwinick, Jack. 1977. "Intellectual Abilities." In Birren and Schaie, eds.

———, and Siegler, Ilene C. 1980. "Intellectual Ability among the Elderly: Simultaneous Cross-Sectional and Longitudinal Comparisons." *Developmental Psychology* 16:1.

Bower, Robert T., and de Gasparis, Priscilla. 1978. *Ethics in Social Research: Protecting the Interests of Human Subjects.* New York: Praeger, 1978.

Bowles, Samuel, and Levin, Henry M. 1968. "The Determinants of Scholastic Achievement—An Appraisal of Some Recent Evidence." *Journal of Human Resources* 3(Winter):3–24.

Brewer, Marilynn B., and Collins, Barry E., eds. 1981. *Scientific Inquiry and the Social Sciences.* San Francisco: Jossey-Bass.

Brook, Robert, et al. 1983. "Does Free Care Improve Adults' Health? Results from a Randomized Controlled Trial." *New England Journal of Medicine* 309(December 8):1426–34.

Buss, Allan R. 1979. "Toward a Unified Framework for Psychometric Concepts in the Multivariate Developmental Situation." In Nesselroade and Baltes, eds.

Busse, Ewald W. 1970a. "A Physiological, Psychological, and Sociological Study of Aging." In Palmore, ed.

———. 1970b. "Psychoneurotic Reactions and Defense Mechanisms in the Aged." In Palmore, ed.

———. In press. Introduction to Section B. In Palmore, ed.

———, and Obrist, Walter D. 1970. "Significance of Focal Electroencephalographic Changes in the Elderly." In Palmore, ed.

Cain, Glen G., and Watts, Harold W. 1970. "Problems in Making Policy Inferences from the Coleman Report." *American Sociological Review* 35(April):228–42.

Caldwell, Catherine. 1970. "Social Science Ammunition." *Psychology Today*, September, pp. 38–40, 72–73.

Campbell, Donald T. 1961. "The Mutual Methodological Relevance of Anthropology and Psychology." In Hsu, ed.

———, and Fiske, D. W. 1959. "Convergent and Discriminant Validation by the Multitrait-Multimethod Matrix." *Psychological Bulletin* 56:81–105.

Cantril, Hadley. 1944. *Gauging Public Opinion*. Princeton, NJ: Princeton University Press.

Catton, William R., Jr. 1964. "The Development of Sociological Thought." In Faris, ed.

Chamberlain, Roy B., and Feldman, Herman, eds. 1961. *The Dartmouth Bible*. 2nd ed. Boston: Houghton Mifflin.

Christophersen, Gary. See *Final Report of the Seattle-Denver Income Maintenance Experiment*, 1983b, vol. 2.

Cicourel, Aaron. 1982. "Interviews, Surveys, and the Problem of Ecological Validity." *American Sociologist* 17:11–20.

Clark, Alexander, and Wallin, Paul. 1964. "The Accuracy of Husbands' and Wives' Reports of the Frequency of Marital Coitus." *Population Studies* 18:165–73.

Clift, Virgil A. 1966. "Educating the American Negro." In Davis, ed.

Cogan, John F. 1978. *Negative Income Taxation and Labor Supply: New Evidence from the New Jersey–Pennsylvania Experiment*, R-2155-HEW. Santa Monica, CA: Rand Corporation.

Cohen, Steven R. 1983. "From Industrial Democracy to Professional Adjustment: The Development of Industrial Sociology in the United States, 1900–1955." *Theory and Society* 2(12):47–67.

Coleman, James S. 1968. "Equality of Educational Opportunity: Reply to Bowles and Levin." *Journal of Human Resources* 3(Spring):237–46.

———. 1970. "Reply to Cain and Watts." *American Sociological Review* 35:243–49.

———. 1975. "Recent Trends in School Integration." *Educational Research* 4(July–August):3–12.

———. 1978. "Beneficial Desegregation v. Destructive Desegregation." *Washington Post*, December 8.

———. 1980. Untitled; miscellaneous introductions to a planned collection of Coleman's papers on equality of educational opportunity and school desegregation; in Coleman's files.

———; Hoffer, Thomas; and Kilgore, Sally. 1982a. "Cognitive Outcomes in Public and Private Schools." *Sociology of Education* 55(April/July):65–76.

———. 1982b. "Achievement and Segregation in Secondary Schools: A Further Look at Public and Private School Differences." *Sociology of Education* 55(April/July):162–82.

Coleman, James S.; Kelly, Sara D.; and Moore, John A. 1975. *Trends in School Segregation*, 1968–1973. Washington, DC: Urban Institute.

Coleman, James S., et al. 1966. *Equality of Educational Opportunity*. U.S. Department of Health, Education, and Welfare, Office of Education, OE-38001. Washington, DC: U.S. Government Printing Office.

Conlisk, John, and Watts, Harold. 1969. "A Model for Optimizing Experimental Designs for Estimating Response Surfaces." *Proceedings of the Social Statistics Section*, American Statistical Association.

———. 1979. "A Model for Optimizing Experimental Designs for Estimating Response Surfaces." *Journal of Econometrics* 11(September):27–42.

Cooper, Joel. 1976. "Deception and Role Playing: On Telling the Good Guys from the Bad Guys." *American Psychologist* 31(August):605–10.

———. 1980. "Reducing Fears and Increasing Assertiveness: The Role of Dissonance Reduction." *Journal of Experimental Social Psychology* 3(May):199–213.

Coser, Lewis A. 1970. *Men of Ideas: A Sociologist's View*. New York: Free Press.

Cottrell, N. B., et al. 1968. "Social Facilitation of Dominant Responses by the Presence of an Audience and the Mere Presence of Others." *Journal of Personality & Social Psychology* 9:245–50.

Crano, William D. 1981. "Triangulation and Cross-Cultural Research." In Brewer and Collins, eds.

Cunningham, Walter R., and Owens, William A., Jr. 1983. "The Iowa State Study of the Adult Development of Intellectual Abilities." In Schaie, ed.

Czaika, John L. 1982. "Subannual Income Estimation." Mimeographed. Princeton, NJ: Mathematica Policy Research.

David, Martin. "Income, Net Worth, and Human Capital." In U.S. Department of Health, Education, and Welfare, 1979a.

———. 1982. "Measuring Income and Program Participation." Mimeographed. Madison, WI: University of Wisconsin.

Davis, James A. 1978. "Studying Categorical Data over Time." *Social Science Research* 7:151–79.

Davis, John P., ed. 1966. *The American Negro Reference Book.* Englewood Cliffs, NJ: Prentice-Hall.

de Beauvoir, Simone. 1972. *The Coming of Age.* New York: Putnam.

Deutsch, Karl W.; Platt, John; and Senghaas, Dieter. 1971. "Conditions Favoring Major Advances in Social Science." *Science,* February 5, pp. 450–59.

Deutsch, Morton. 1982. "Conflict Resolution: Theory and Practice." Mimeographed. Inaugural lecture as Edward Lee Thorndike Professor of Psychology and Education, Teachers College, Columbia University, April 22.

———, and Hornstein, Harvey A., eds. 1975. *Applying Social Psychology: Implications for Research, Practice, and Training.* Hillsdale, NJ: Lawrence Erlbaum.

Douglas, Jack D. 1976. *Investigative Social Research: Individual and Team Field Research.* Beverly Hills, CA: Sage.

———; with Rasmussen, Paul K.; and Flanagan, Carol Ann. 1977. *The Nude Beach.* Beverly Hills, CA: Sage.

Douglas, Jack, ed. 1970. *The Impact of Sociology: Readings in the Social Sciences.* New York: Appleton-Century-Crofts.

Dovenmuehle, Robert H. 1970. "Aging versus Illness." In Palmore, ed.

———; Busse, Ewald H.; and Newman, Gustave. 1970. "Physical Problems of Older People." In Palmore, ed.

Drake, St. Clair. 1966. "The Social and Economic Status of the Negro in the United States." In Parsons and Clark, eds.

Duke University Center for the Study of Aging and Human Development. 1980a. *Final Report. The Duke Longitudinal Studies. An Integrated Investigation of Aging and the Aged, Ancillary Studies, and Research Support Services, 1955–1980.* Mimeographed. Durham, NC: Duke University Medical Center.

———. 1980b. *Center Report* 8(November).

———. 1982. "The Duke Multidisciplinary Longitudinal Studies of Normal Aging." *Center Reports on Advances in Research* 6(July).

Duke University Council on Aging and Human Development. 1969. *Proceedings of Seminars, 1965–69.* Frances C. Jeffers, ed. Durham, NC: Center for the Study of Aging and Human Development.

Duke University Council on Gerontology. 1965. *Proceedings of Seminars, 1961–65.* Frances C. Jeffers, ed. Durham, NC: Regional Center for the Study of Aging.

Durkheim, Émile. 1951 [1897]. *Suicide: A Study of Sociology.* Glencoe, IL: Free Press.

Eisdorfer, Carl. 1970. "Developmental Level and Sensory Impairment in the Aged." In Palmore, ed.

———, and Wilkie, Frances. 1974. "Intellectual Changes." In Palmore, ed.

Erikson, Kai T. 1966. *Wayward Puritans: A Study in the Sociology of Deviance.* New York: Wiley.

———. 1976. *Everything in Its Path: Destruction of Community in the Buffalo Creek Flood.* New York: Simon and Schuster.

Faris, Robert E. L., ed. 1964. *Handbook of Modern Sociology*. Chicago: Rand McNally.

Featherman, David L. 1982. "The Life-Span Perspective in Social Science Research." In Adams, Smelser, and Treiman, eds., pt. 2.

Ferber, Robert, and Hirsch, Werner Z. 1979. "Social Experiments in Economics." *Journal of Econometrics* 11:77–115.

Ferber, Robert, et al. 1980. "What Is a Survey?" Pamphlet. Washington, DC: American Statistical Association.

Festinger, Leon. 1980. *Retrospections on Social Psychology*. New York: Oxford University Press.

———; Riecken, Henry W.; and Schachter, Stanley. 1964 [1956]. *When Prophecy Fails*. New York: Harper & Row.

Fienberg, Stephen E. 1983. "Comment on J. T. Bonnen's 'Federal Statistical Coordination Today: A Disaster or a Disgrace?' " Technical Report no. 268. Department of Statistics, Carnegie-Mellon University, Pittsburgh, Pa.

Final Report of the Seattle-Denver Income Maintenance Experiment. 1983a. Vol. 1: Design and Results. SRI International. Washington, DC: U.S. Government Printing Office.

———. 1983b. Vol. 2: Administration. Gary Christophersen, Mathematica Policy Research. Washington, DC: U.S. Government Printing Office.

Fisk, John D., and Roth, Dennis M. 1980. "Work Disincentives and Income Maintenance Programs: A Review of the Empirical Literature." Report No. 80-119E, Congressional Research Service, Library of Congress.

Franke, Richard Herbert, and Kaul, James D. 1978. "The Hawthorne Experiments: First Statistical Interpretation." *American Sociological Review* 43(October):623–43.

Freedman, Jonathan; Sears, David O.; and Carlsmith, J. Merrill. 1978. *Social Psychology*. 3rd ed. Englewood Cliffs, NJ: Prentice-Hall.

Freeman, Derek. 1983. *Margaret Mead and Samoa: The Making and the Unmaking of an Anthropological Myth*. Cambridge, MA: Harvard University Press.

Freeman, Howard E., and Rossi, Peter H. 1981. "Social Experiments." Milbank Memorial Fund Quarterly/*Health & Society* 59:340–73.

Friedman, Lucy N. 1978. *The Wildcat Experiment: An Early Test of Supported Work in Drug Abuse Rehabilitation*. National Institute on Drug Abuse. Washington, DC: U.S. Government Printing Office.

Friedrichs, Robert W. 1972. *A Sociology of Sociology*. New York: Free Press.

Funkhouser, G. Ray. 1973. "The Issues of the Sixties: An Exploratory Study." *Public Opinion Quarterly* 37:62–75.

Gallup, George, and Rae, Saul Forbes. 1940. *The Pulse of Democracy: The Public-Opinion Poll and How It Works*. New York: Simon and Schuster.

Gans, Herbert. 1976a. "The West End: An Urban Village." In Golden, ed.

———. 1976b. "On the Methods Used in This Study." In Golden, ed.

Garfinkel, Herbert. 1959. "Social Science Evidence and the School Segregation Cases." *Journal of Politics* 21(February):93–115.

Gergen, Kenneth J. 1973. "Social Psychology as History." *Journal of Personality & Social Psychology* 26:309–20.

Glenn, Norval D. 1976. "Cohort Analysts' Futile Quest: Statistical Attempts to Separate Age, Period, and Cohort Effects." *American Sociological Review* 41:900–4.

Glock, Charles, and Bellah, Robert, eds. 1976. *The New Religious Consciousness*. Berkeley, CA: University of California Press.

Goffman, Erving. 1972. *Relations in Public: Microstudies of the Public Order*. New York: Harper & Row.

Golden, M. Patricia, ed. 1976. *The Research Experience*. Itasca, IL: Peacock.

Goldfarb, Nathan. 1960. *An Introduction to Longitudinal Statistical Analysis*. Glencoe, IL: Free Press.

Goldstein, Harvey. 1979. *The Design and Analysis of Longitudinal Studies*. London: Academic Press.

Goode, William J. 1977. *Principles of Sociology*. New York: McGraw-Hill.

Goodman, Walter. 1975. "Integration, Yes; Busing, No." *New York Times Magazine*, August 24.

Gouldner, Alvin W. 1971. *The Coming Crisis of Western Sociology*. New York: Equinox/Avon.

Grant, Gerald. 1973. "Shaping Social Policy: The Politics of the Coleman Report." *Teachers College Record* 75(September):17–54.

Greenberg, David H., and Robins, Philip K. 1984. "Trends in Social Experimentation." Paper presented at the December 1983 meeting of the American Economic Association; revised 1984.

Greenberg, David [H.]; Moffitt, Robert; and Friedmann, John. 1981. "Underreporting and Experimental Effects on Work Effort: Evidence from the Gary Income Maintenance Experiment." *Review of Economics & Statistics* 63(November):581–89.

Gross, Alan E. 1982. "Twenty Years of Deception in Social Psychology." *Personality & Social Psychology Bulletin* 8(September):402–8.

Guetzkow, H., ed. 1951. *Groups, Leadership, and Men*. Pittsburgh: Carnegie Press.

Hall, Edward T. 1966. *The Hidden Dimension*. Garden City, NY: Doubleday.

Halsey, Harlan, et al. 1977. "The Reporting of Income to Welfare: A Study in the Accuracy of Income Reporting." Research Memorandum 42, Center for the Study of Welfare Policy. Menlo Park, CA: SRI International.

Hamburg, David A.; Elliott, Glen R.; and Parron, Delores L., eds. 1982. *Health and Behavior: Frontiers of Research in the Biobehavioral Sciences*. Washington, DC: National Academy Press.

Hammer, Eliot R. 1977. "Validity in Longitudinal Research." *Social Science* 52:158–68.

Harkins, Stephen G.; Latané, Bibb; and Williams, Kipling. 1980. "Social Loafing: Allocating Effort or Taking It Easy?" *Journal of Experimental Social Psychology* 16:457–65.

Harkins, Stephen W., et al. 1974. "Effects of Age, Sex, and Time-on-Watch on a Brief Continuous Performance Task." In Palmore, ed.

Hauser, Philip M. 1975. *Social Statistics in Use*. New York: Russell Sage Foundation.

Heise, David, ed. 1981. *Microcomputers in Social Research*. Beverly Hills, CA: Sage. A special issue of *Sociological Methods and Research*.

Heisenberg, Werner. 1971. *Physics and Beyond*. New York: Harper & Row.

Hendrick, Clyde. 1977. "Social Psychology as an Experimental Science." In Hendrick, ed.

———, ed. 1977. *Perspectives on Social Psychology*. Hillsdale, NJ: Lawrence Erlbaum.

Herriot, Roger A., and Kasprzyk, Daniel. 1984. "The Survey of Income and Program Participation." SIPP Working Paper Series No. 8405. Washington, DC: U.S. Bureau of the Census.

Herzog, Elizabeth, and Sudia, Cecelia E. 1971. *Boys in Fatherless Families*. U.S. Department of Health, Education, and Welfare, DHEW Publication No. (OCD) 72–33. Washington, DC: U.S. Government Printing Office.

Heyman, Dorothy K., and Gianturco, Daniel T. 1974. "Long-Term Adaptation by the Elderly to Bereavement." In Palmore, ed.

Heyman, Dorothy K., and Jeffers, Frances C. 1970. "Effect of Time Lapse on Consistency of Self-Health and Medical Evaluations of Elderly Persons." In Palmore, ed.

Higbee, K. L.; Millard, R. J.; and Folkman, J. R. 1982. "Social Psychological Research During the 1970s." *Personality & Social Psychology Bulletin* 8:180–83.

Holden, Constance. 1979. "Ethics in Social Science Research." *Science*, November 2, pp. 537–40.

Holmes, T., and Rahe, R. 1967. "The Social Readjustment Scale." *Journal of Psychosomatic Research* 11:213–18.

Hsu, F. L. K., ed. 1961. *Psychological Anthropology: Approaches to Culture and Personality*. Homewood, IL: Dorsey Press.

Hunt, Morton. 1982. *The Universe Within: A New Science Explores the Human Mind*. New York: Simon and Schuster.

———, and Hunt, Bernice. 1977. *The Divorce Experience*. New York: McGraw-Hill.

Hunt, P. Nileen, and Smith, Patricia C. 1982. "Data Processing." See Research Triangle Institute.

Inkeles, Alex. 1982. "The Sociological Contribution to Advances in the Social Sciences." Paper presented at Berlin Conference on Conditions Favoring Major Advances in the Social Sciences.

International Encyclopedia of the Social Sciences. 1968. David L. Sills, ed. New York: Macmillan and Free Press.

Jencks, Christopher. 1972. *Inequality: A Reassessment of the Effect of Family and Schooling in America.* New York: Basic Books.

Johnson, John M. 1975. *Doing Field Research.* New York: Free Press.

Johnson-Laird, P. N., and Wason, P. C., eds. 1977. *Thinking: Readings in Cognitive Science.* Cambridge: Cambridge University Press.

Jones, Edward E. In press. "Major Developments in Social Psychology Since 1930." In Gardner Lindzey and Elliot Aronson, eds.

Kagan, Jerome. 1984. *The Nature of the Child.* New York: Basic Books.

Kasarda, John D. 1972. "The Impact of Suburban Population Growth on Central City Service Functions." *American Journal of Sociology* 77:1111–24.

Kasprzyk, Daniel. 1982. "Social Security Number Reporting, The Use of Administrative Records, and the Multiple Frame Design in the Income Survey Development Program." Paper presented at the Social Science Research Council Conference on the Income Survey Development Program.

———, ed. 1978. *Survey of Income and Program Participation. Proceedings of the Workshop on Data Processing, February 23–24, 1978.* Washington, DC: U.S. Department of Health, Education, and Welfare.

Katz, Jay. 1972. *Experimentation with Human Beings.* New York: Russell Sage Foundation.

Kelman, Herbert. 1977. "Privacy and Research with Human Beings." *Journal of Social Issues* 33:169–95.

Kershaw, David, and Fair, Jerilyn. 1976. *The New Jersey Income-Maintenance Experiment.* Vol. 1. New York: Academic Press.

Kimble, Gregory. 1978. "The Role of Risk/Benefit Analysis in the Conduct of Psychological Research." In National Commission for the Protection of Human Subjects, App., vol. 2.

Kinsey, Alfred, et al. 1953. *Sexual Behavior in the Human Female.* Philadelphia: Saunders.

Kish, Leslie. 1965. *Survey Sampling.* New York: Wiley.

Krippendorf, Klaus. 1980. *Content Analysis.* Beverly Hills, CA: Sage.

Kruskal, William. 1982. "Evaluating Social Science Research." Paper presented at Berlin Conference on Conditions Favoring Major Advances in the Social Sciences.

Kulka, Richard A. 1982a. "Survey Content." See Research Triangle Institute.

———. 1982b. "Tests and Experiments." See Research Triangle Institute.

Latané, Bibb. 1981. "The Psychology of Social Impact." *American Psychologist* 36:343–56.

———, and Darley, John M. 1968. "Group Inhibition of Bystander Intervention in Emergencies." *Journal of Personality & Social Psychology* 10:215–21.

———. 1970. *The Unresponsive Bystander: Why Doesn't He Help?* Englewood Cliffs, NJ: Prentice-Hall.

Latané, Bibb; Harkins, Stephen G.; and Williams, Kipling. 1980. "Many Hands Make Light the Work: Social Loafing as a Social Disease." Paper awarded the 1980 Socio-Psychological Prize at the American Association for the Advancement of Science meeting.

Latané, Bibb, and Nida, Steve. 1981. "Ten Years of Research on Group Size and Helping." *Psychological Bulletin* 89:308–24.

Latané, Bibb, and Rodin, Judith. 1969. "A Lady in Distress: Inhibiting Effects of Friends and Strangers on Bystander Intervention." *Journal of Experimental Social Psychology* 5:189–202.

Latané, Bibb; Williams, Kipling; and Harkins, Stephen [G.]. 1979. "Many Hands Make Light the Work: The Causes and Consequences of Social Loafing." *Journal of Personality & Social Psychology* 37:822–32.

Leeson, Jim. 1965. "Questions, Controversies, and Opportunities." *Southern Educational Report*, November-December, pp. 2–7.

LeVine, Robert A. 1981. "Knowledge and Fallibility in Anthropological Field Research." In Brewer and Collins, eds.

Levinger, George. 1966. "Systematic Distortion in Spouses' Reports of Preferred and Actual Sexual Behavior." *Sociometry* 29:291–99.

Lewin, Kurt. 1937. "Psychoanalysis and Topological Psychology." *Bulletin of the Menninger Clinic* 1:202–11.

Liebow, Elliot. 1967. *Tally's Corner: A Study of Negro Street-corner Men.* Boston: Little, Brown.

Lindblom, Charles E., and Cohen, David K. 1979. *Usable Knowledge: Social Science and Social Problem Solving.* New Haven: Yale University Press.

Lindzey, Gardner, and Aronson, Elliot, eds. 1968–69. *The Handbook of Social Psychology.* 2nd ed. 5 vols. Reading, MA: Addison-Wesley.

———. In press. *The Handbook of Social Psychology.* 3rd ed. Reading, MA: Addison-Wesley.

Lininger, Charles A. 1982. "Coordination and Program Management." Unpublished draft version. Washington, DC: U.S. Department of Health, Education, and Welfare, Income Survey Development Program.

Maddox, George L. 1970. "Selected Methodological Issues." In Palmore, ed.

———. In press. "Introduction to Social Aspects of Aging." In Palmore, ed.

———, and Douglass, Elizabeth B. 1974. "Self-Assessment of Health: A Longitudinal Study of Elderly Subjects." In Palmore, ed.

Maddox, George L., and Wiley, James. 1976. "Scope, Concepts and Methods in the Study of Aging." In Binstock and Shanas, eds.

Malinowski, Bronislaw. 1927. *Sex and Repression in Savage Society.* London: Routledge & Kegan Paul.

———. 1929. *The Sexual Life of Savages in North-Western Melanesia.* New York: Halcyon House.

———. 1967. *A Diary in the Strict Sense of the Term.* London: Routledge & Kegan Paul.

Mannon, James M. 1982. "Participant Observer Roles in Emergency Medicine: Problems and Prospects." Paper presented at the annual meeting of the North Central Sociological Association.

Marsh, Catherine. 1979. "Problems with Surveys: Method or Epistemology?" *Sociology* 13:293–305.

Masters, Stanley, and Garfinkel, Irwin. 1977. *Estimating the Labor Supply Effects of Income-Maintenance Alternatives.* New York: Academic Press.

Merton, Robert K. 1939. "The Unanticipated Consequences of Purposive Social Action." *American Sociological Review* 1:894–904.

———. 1968. *Social Theory and Social Structure.* New York: Free Press.

Migdal, Susan; Abeles, Ronald P.; and Sherrod, Lennie R. 1981. *An Inventory of Longitudinal Studies of Middle and Old Age.* New York: Social Science Research Council.

Milgram, Stanley. 1963. "Behavioral Study of Obedience." *Journal of Abnormal & Social Psychology* 67:371–78.

Miller, Delbert. 1983. *Handbook of Research Design and Social Measurement.* 4th ed. New York: Longman.

Moore, R. Paul. 1982. "Introduction." See Research Triangle Institute.

Murdock, George P. 1967. "Ethnographic Atlas: A Summary." *Ethnology* 6:109–236.

Murray, Thomas. 1980. "Learning to Deceive." *Hastings Center Report*, April.

Myers, David G. 1983. *Social Psychology.* New York: McGraw-Hill.

Myrdal, Gunnar. 1962 [1944]. *An American Dilemma: The Negro Problem and Modern Democracy.* New York: Harper & Row.

National Center for Health Statistics. 1982. "A Statistical Methodology for Analyzing Data from a Complex Survey, the First National Health and Nutrition Examination Survey," by J.

Landis et al. *Vital & Health Statistics.* Series 2-No.92. Washington, DC: U.S. Government Printing Office.

National Commission for the Protection of Human Subjects of Biomedical and Behavioral Research. 1978. *The Belmont Report: Ethical Principles and Guidelines for the Protection of Human Subjects of Research.* 2 vols. Washington, DC: U.S. Government Printing Office.

National Commission on Employment and Unemployment Statistics. 1979. [Final Report of the Commission:] *Counting the Labor Force.* Washington, DC: U.S. Government Printing Office.

National Committee for Research on the 1980 Census. n.d. "Summary of Research Program and Funding Proposal." Mimeographed. New York: National Committee for Research on the 1980 Census.

National Research Council. 1979. *Privacy and Confidentiality as Factors in Survey Response.* Washington, DC: National Academy of Sciences.

Nesselroade, John R., and Baltes, Paul B., eds., 1979. *Longitudinal Research in the Study of Behavior and Development.* New York: Academic Press.

Neubeck, Kenneth J., and Roach, Jack L. 1981. "Income Maintenance Experiments, Politics, and the Perpetuation of Poverty." *Social Problems* 28:308–20.

Newhouse, Joseph, et al. 1982. "Some Interim Results from a Controlled Trial of Cost Sharing in Health Insurance." Report R-2847-HHS. Santa Monica, CA: Rand Corporation.

Nova #1002: "The Pleasure of Finding Things Out." A PBS television documentary aired in the New York area in January 1983. WGBH Transcripts, 125 Western Ave., Boston, MA.

Nowlin, John B., and Siegler, Ilene C. In press. "Psychomotor Performance and Cardiovascular Disease." In Palmore, ed.

Obrist, Walter D., et al. 1970. "Relation of the Electroencephalogram to Intellectual Function in Senescence." In Palmore, ed.

Olson, Janice, ed. 1980. *Reports from the Site Research Test.* U.S. Department of Health, Education, and Welfare, Income Survey Development Program. Washington, DC: U.S. Government Printing Office.

Orfield, Gary. 1978. *Must We Bus? Segregated Schools and National Policy.* Washington, DC: Brookings Institution.

Palmore, Erdman. 1970a. "The Effects of Aging on Activities and Attitudes." In Palmore, ed.

———. 1970b. "Summary and the Future." In Palmore, ed.

———. 1974a. "Health Practices and Illness." In Palmore, ed.

———. 1974b. "Design of the Adaptation Study." In Palmore, ed., App. A.

———. 1974c. "Predicting Longevity: A New Method." In Palmore, ed.

———. 1974d. "Summary." In Palmore, ed.

———. 1981. *Social Patterns in Normal Aging: Findings from the Duke Longitudinal Study.* Durham, NC: Duke University Press.

———, and Jeffers, Frances C. 1974. "Health Care Before and After Medicare." In Palmore, ed.

Palmore, Erdman, ed., 1970. *Normal Aging: Reports from the Duke Longitudinal Study, 1955–1969.* Durham, NC: Duke University Press.

———. 1974. *Normal Aging II: Reports from the Duke Longitudinal Studies, 1970–1973.* Durham, NC: Duke University Press.

———. In press. *Normal Aging III: Reports from the Duke Longitudinal Studies, 1974–1983.* Durham, NC: Duke University Press.

Parke, Robert. 1982. "Responses to Recent Cuts in Federal Budgets for Statistics." *Items* 36 (June):12–13. New York: Social Science Research Council.

Parsons, Talcott, and Clark, Kenneth B., eds. 1966. *The Negro American.* Boston: Houghton Mifflin.

Pearl, Robert P. [1982]. "Measuring Wealth Data in the Income Survey Development Program." Mimeographed. Survey Research Laboratory, University of Illinois.

Pettigrew, Thomas F., and Green, Robert L. 1976. "School Desegregation in Large Cities: A Critique of the Coleman 'White Flight' Thesis." *Harvard Educational Review*, February, pp. 1–53.

Piliavin, Jane A., and Piliavin, Irving M. 1972. "Effect of Blood on Reactions to a Victim." *Journal of Personality & Social Psychology* 23(September):353–61.

Piper, Lanny L. 1982. "Data Collection." See Research Triangle Institute.

Popper, Karl. 1959. *The Logic of Scientific Discovery*. London: Hutchinson.

———. 1972. *Objective Knowledge*. Oxford: Clarendon.

———. 1977. "On Hypotheses." In Johnson-Laird and Wason, eds.

Presser, Stanley, and Schuman, Howard. 1980. "The Measurement of a Middle Position in Attitude Surveys." *Public Opinion Quarterly* 44(Spring):70–85.

Ravitch, Diane. 1978. "The 'White Flight' Controversy." *Public Interest* 51(Spring):135–49.

Research Triangle Institute. 1982. *ISDP 1979 Research Panel Documentation*. Series of separately bound chapters. Research Triangle Park, NC: Research Triangle Institute.

Riecken, Henry W., and Boruch, Robert F. 1978. "Social Experiments." *Annual Review of Sociology* 4:511–32.

Riecken, Henry, et al. 1974. *Social Experimentation: A Method for Planning and Evaluating Social Intervention*. New York: Academic Press.

Rockwell, Richard C. 1982. "An Agenda for Statistical Research on Social Conditions." Mimeographed. Washington, DC: Social Science Research Council.

Roethlisberger, F. J., and Dickson, William J. 1961 [1939]. *Management and the Worker*. Cambridge, MA: Harvard University Press.

Roman, Anthony M. n.d. "Results from the Methods Development Survey (Phase I)." Mimeographed. Washington, DC: U.S. Bureau of the Census.

Rosenhan, D.L. 1973. "On Being Sane in Insane Places." *Science*, January 19, pp. 250–58.

Rosenthal, Robert, and Jacobson, Lenore. 1968. *Pygmalion in the Classroom*. New York: Holt, Rinehart & Winston.

Rossi, Peter H., and Lyall, Katharine C. 1976. *Reforming Public Welfare: A Critique of the Negative Income Tax Experiment*. New York: Russell Sage Foundation.

Russell, Bertrand. 1945. *A History of Western Philosophy*. New York: Simon and Schuster.

St. John, Nancy H. 1975. *School Desegregation: Outcomes for Children*. New York: Wiley.

Saxe, Leonard, and Fine, Michelle. 1981. *Social Experiments: Methods for Design and Evaluation*. Beverly Hills, CA: Sage.

Schachter, Stanley. 1971. "Some Extraordinary Facts About Obese Human Beings and Rats." *American Psychologist* 26(February):129–43.

Schaie, K. Warner. 1965 "A General Model for the Study of Developmental Problems." *Psychological Bulletin* 64:92–107.

———. 1983a. "The Seattle Longitudinal Study: A 21-Year Exploration of Psychometric Intelligence in Adulthood." In Schaie, ed.

———. 1983b. "What Can We Learn from the Longitudinal Study of Adult Psychological Development?" In Schaie, ed.

———, and Hertzog, Christopher. 1982. "Longitudinal Methods." In Wolman, ed.

Schaie, K. Warner, ed. 1983. *Longitudinal Studies of Adult Psychological Development*. New York: Guilford Press.

Schlenker, Barry R. 1974. "Social Psychology and Science." *Journal of Personality & Social Psychology* 29:1–15.

Schuman, Howard. 1982. "Artifacts Are in the Mind of the Beholder." *American Sociologist* 17:21–28.

———, and Presser, Stanley. 1977. "Question Wording as an Independent Variable in Survey Analysis." *Sociological Methods & Research* 6:151–70.

Seattle-Denver Income Maintenance Experiment. See: *Final Report of the Seattle-Denver Income Maintenance Experiment*.

Sessions, Vivian, ed. 1974. *Directory of Data Bases in the Social and Behavioral Sciences.* New York: Science Associates International.

Siegler, Ilene C. 1983. "Psychological Aspects of the Duke Longitudinal Studies." In Schaie, ed.

————. In press. "Psychological and Social Findings, 1973–1983." In Palmore, ed.

————, and Gatz, Margaret. In press. "Age Patterns in Locus of Control." In Palmore, ed.

Siegler, Ilene C.; George, Linda K.; and Okun, Morris. 1979. "Cross-Sequential Analysis of Adult Personality." *Developmental Psychology* 15:350–51.

Simon, Herbert. 1980. "The Behavioral and Social Sciences." *Science,* July 4:72–78.

Singer, Burton, and Spilerman, Seymour. 1976. "Some Methodological Issues in the Analysis of Longitudinal Surveys." *Annals of Economic & Social Measurement* 5:447–74.

Singer, E., and Kohnke-Aguirre, L. 1979. "Interviewer Expectation Effects: A Replication and Extension." *Public Opinion Quarterly* 43(Summer):245–60.

Singer, Jerome, and Glass, David C. 1975. "Some Reflections upon Losing Our Social Psychological Purity." In Deutsch and Hornstein, eds.

Small, Albion. 1895. "The Era of Sociology." *American Journal of Sociology* 1, cited in Cohen 1983.

Smith, M. Brewster. 1983. "The Shaping of American Social Psychology: A Personal Perspective from the Periphery." *Personality & Social Psychology Bulletin* 9(June):165–80.

Social Science Research Council. *Items.* Quarterly newsletter.

Sontag, Lester. 1969. "The Longitudinal Method of Research: What It Can and Can't Do." In Duke University Council, 1969.

Spiegelman, Robert G., and Yeager, K.E. 1980. "Overview" [of the income maintenance experiments in Seattle and Denver]. *Journal of Human Resources* 15(Fall):463–79.

Steeh, Charlotte G. 1981. "Trends in Nonresponse Rates, 1952–1979." *Public Opinion Quarterly* 45:40–57.

Taeuber, Richard C., and Rockwell, Richard C. 1982. "National Social Data Series: A Compendium of Brief Descriptions." Washington, DC: Social Science Research Council.

Tanur, Judith M. 1982. "Advances in Methods for Large-Scale Surveys and Experiments." In Adams, Smelser, and Treiman, eds., Pt. 2.

Terman, L. M., et al. 1938. *Psychological Factors in Marital Happiness.* New York: McGraw-Hill.

Thoits, Peggy and Hannan, Michael. 1979. "Income and Psychological Distress: The Impact of an Income-Maintenance Experiment." *Journal of Health & Social Behavior* 20(June):120–38.

Thomas, W. I., and Znaniecki, Florian. 1918. *The Polish Peasant in Europe and America.* Chicago: University of Chicago Press.

Thompson, Larry W.; Eisdorfer, Carl; and Estes, E. Harvey. "Cardiovascular Disease and Behavioral Changes in the Elderly." In Palmore, ed., 1970.

Thorne, Barrie, and Henley, Nancy, eds. 1975. *Language and Sex: Difference and Dominance.* Rowley, MA: Newbury House.

Tumin, Melvin M. 1970. "Some Social Consequences of Research on Race Relations." In Douglas, ed.

Turner, Charles F., and Martin, Elizabeth, eds. 1981. *Surveys of Subjective Phenomena: Summary Report.* Panel on Survey Measurement of Subjective Phenomena, Committee on National Statistics, National Research Council. Washington, DC: National Academy Press.

U.S. Bureau of the Census. 1978a. "Census Surveys. Measuring America." Pamphlet. Washington, DC: Bureau of the Census.

————. 1978b. *Demographic Aspects of Aging and the Older Population in the United States.* 2nd printing (rev.). Current Population Reports, Series P-23, No. 59. Washington, DC: U.S. Government Printing Office.

————. 1980. *Census '80: Continuing the Factfinder Tradition.* By Charles P. Kaplan, Thomas Van Valey, and Associates. Washington, DC: U.S. Government Printing Office.

————. 1984. *Economic Characteristics of Households in the United States: Third Quarter 1983.*

Current Population Reports, Series P-70, No. 1. Washington, DC: U.S. Government Printing Office.

U.S. Congress, Joint Economic Committee. 1984. "Estimating the Effects of Economic Change on National Health and Social Well-Being." Washington, DC: U.S. Government Printing Office.

U.S. Department of Health, Education, and Welfare. 1978. "Protection of Human Subjects. Institutional Review Boards." Report of National Commission for the Protection of Human Subjects of Biomedical and Behavioral Research. *Federal Register* 43(November 30):56174–98.

————. 1979a. Income Survey Development Program. *Survey of Income and Program Participation (SIPP). The Conference on Potential for Analysis.* Charles A. Lininger, ed. Annandale, VA: JWK International.

————. 1979b. *Statistical Uses of Administrative Records with Emphasis on Mortality and Disability Research.* Selected papers given at the 1979 annual meeting of the American Statistical Association. Washington, DC: Social Security Administration Office of Policy.

————. 1981. Code of Federal Regulations, Part 46 of 45CFR; revisions. *Federal Register* 46(January 26):8386–92.

U.S. Department of Health and Human Services. 1981. Federal Council on the Aging. *The Need for Long-Term Care: Information and Issues.* DHHS Publication No. (OHDS) 81–20704. Washington, DC: U.S. Government Printing Office.

————. 1983. Untitled; solicitation for contractor proposals for the Work Incentive Experiment Data Collection and Management project. Ref: SMM-33, SSA-RFP-83-0115. Baltimore, MD: Social Security Administration.

U.S. General Accounting Office. 1981. *Income Maintenance Experiments: Need to Summarize Results and Communicate the Lessons Learned.* HRD-81-46. Gaithersburg, MD: U.S. General Accounting Office.

U.S. Senate. 1978. *Welfare Research and Experimentation.* Hearings before the Subcommittee on Public Assistance of the Committee on Finance, November 15–17. Washington, DC: U.S. Government Printing Office.

Verwoerdt, Adriaan; Pfeiffer, Eric; and Wang, Hsioh-Shan. 1970. "Sexual Behavior in Senescence." In Palmore, ed.

Vroom, Victor H. 1969. "Industrial Social Psychology." In Lindzey and Aronson, eds., vol. 5.

Wang, H. Shan, and Busse, Ewald W. 1974. "Brain Impairment and Longevity." In Palmore, ed.

Webb, Eugene J., et al. 1966. *Unobtrusive Measures: Nonreactive Research in the Social Sciences.* Chicago: Rand McNally.

Weber, Max. 1947. *The Theory of Social and Economic Organization.* Oxford: Oxford University Press.

————. 1958 [1905]. *The Protestant Ethic and the Spirit of Capitalism.* New York: Scribner.

Weinberg, Martin S., and Williams, Colin J. 1975. "Gay Baths and the Social Organization of Impersonal Sex." *Social Problems* 23:124–36.

Weiner, Nan; Pandey, Janak; and Latané, Bibb. 1981. "Individual and Group Productivity in the United States and India." Paper presented at the meeting of the American Psychological Association.

Wells, Richard H., and Picou, J. Steven. 1981. *American Sociology: Theoretical and Methodological Structure.* Washington, DC: University Press of America.

West, Richard W. 1980. "Effects on Wage Rates: An Interim Analysis." *Journal of Human Resources* 15:641–53.

Whiteman, Thomas Cameron. n.d. "The Measurement of Nonfarm Self-Employment Income: The 1979 ISDP Research Panel." Mimeographed. Washington, DC: U.S. Department of Health and Human Services.

Whyte, William H. 1980. *The Social Life of Small Urban Spaces.* Washington, DC: Conservation Foundation.

Wilkie, Frances, and Eisdorfer, Carl. 1974a. "Intelligence and Blood Pressure." In Palmore, ed.

———. 1974b. "Terminal Changes in Intelligence." In Palmore, ed.

Williams, Kipling; Harkins, Stephen; and Latané, Bibb. 1981. "Identifiability as a Deterrent to Social Loafing: Two Cheering Experiments." *Journal of Personality & Social Psychology* 40:303–11.

Williamson, John B., et al. 1982. *The Research Craft: An Introduction to Social Research Methods.* 2nd ed. Boston: Little, Brown.

Wolman, Benjamin B., ed. 1982. *Handbook of Developmental Psychology.* Englewood Cliffs, NJ: Prentice-Hall.

Ycas, Martinas. [c1979]. "ISDP Research Report #1: Evaluation of ISDP Survey Data Quality." Mimeographed. Washington, DC: U.S. Department of Health, Education, and Welfare.

———. [1982]. "Measuring Annual Income: Conceptualization." Washington, DC: U.S. Department of Health and Human Services.

———, and Lininger, Charles A. 1981. "The Income Survey Development Program: Design Features and Initial Findings." *Social Security Bulletin* 44(November):13–19.

Zajonc, Robert B. 1968. "Cognitive Theories in Social Psychology." In Lindzey and Aronson, eds., vol. 1.

Zimbardo, Philip, and Kabat, Loren G. 1981. "Induced Hearing Deficit Generates Experimental Paranoia." *Science,* June 26:1529–31.

Zimmerman, Don H., and West, Candace. 1975. "Sex Roles, Interruptions, and Silences in Conversations." In Thorne and Henley, eds.

ACKNOWLEDGMENTS

I am indebted to many people for various kinds of help with this book.

First and foremost, it pleases me to acknowledge the special contribution of Marshall Robinson, president of the Russell Sage Foundation, who conceived of this book, provided the financial backing that enabled me to write it, and lent his assistance throughout.

He, Robert K. Merton, and David L. Sills acted as my advisory committee; they were an invaluable source of helpful suggestions and tactfully offered expert criticism.

About a hundred people, most of them participants in the social research projects described in chapters 2 through 6, granted me time for interviews, some of which ran to many hours over a period of days. They themselves know how much I owe to them; I thank them all here, though not by name, since they are named throughout the book.

I am obliged to a number of people (some of whom were primary interviewees) for background information and guidance on the broader issues addressed in the book, and for giving or lending me useful reprints, unpublished manuscripts, and original documents. Those whose help was particularly valuable include:

Steven R. Cohen; Morton Deutsch, Teachers College, Columbia University; Barbara Farah, New York *Times* News Poll; Paula Franklin, Social Security Administration; Gerald Grant, Syracuse University; Edward E. Jones, Princeton University; Thomas Juster,

Institute for Social Research, University of Michigan; Bette S. Mahoney, Office of the Assistant Secretary, Department of Defense; Roberta Miller, National Science Foundation; Senator Daniel Patrick Moynihan, U.S. Senate; Arthur J. Norton, Population Division, U.S. Bureau of the Census; Philip K. Robins, University of Miami; Richard C. Rockwell, Social Science Research Council; Pauline Rothstein, Russell Sage Foundation; and Judith Tanur, State University of New York, Stony Brook.

The following people read portions of the manuscript and offered comments and corrections which, collectively, were an invaluable contribution, and for which I am immensely grateful:

Ivar Berg, University of Pennsylvania; Leonard Berkowitz, University of Wisconsin; Norman M. Bradburn, National Opinion Research Center, University of Chicago; Ewald W. Busse, Duke University Medical Center; Gary Christophersen, American Passage Marketing Corporation, Seattle; Philip Converse, Institute for Social Research, University of Michigan; Evan H. Davey, U.S. Bureau of the Census; Peter E. de Janosi, Russell Sage Foundation; Joseph W. Duncan, Dun & Bradstreet Corporation; Kai T. Erikson, Yale University; Stephen E. Fienberg, Carnegie-Mellon University; Edward E. Jones, Princeton University; David A. Kenny, University of Connecticut, Storrs; Priscilla Lewis, Russell Sage Foundation; Bette S. Mahoney, Office of the Assistant Secretary, Department of Defense; Herbert C. Morton, American Council of Learned Societies; Frederick Mosteller, Harvard University; Dawn Nelson, U.S. Bureau of the Census; John Nowlin, Duke University Medical Center; Erdman Palmore, Duke University Medical Center; Albert Rees, Alfred P. Sloan Foundation; Philip K. Robins, University of Miami; Richard C. Rockwell, Social Science Research Council; William Sewell, University of Wisconsin; and Robert G. Spiegelman, W. E. Upjohn Institute for Employment Research.

Bernice Hunt, my wife, gave me the benefit of her expert editorial judgment and offered a great many suggestions that considerably improved the manuscript.

INDEX